T0367421

BORNE

REVOLUTION

Fight for Humanity

JAHI ISSA JABRI ALI-BEY

BORNE REVOLUTION
FIGHT FOR HUMANITY

iUniverse books may be ordered through booksellers or by contacting:

iUniverse
1663 Liberty Drive
Bloomington, IN 47403
www.iuniverse.com
1-800-Authors (1-800-288-4677)

Because of the dynamic nature of the Internet, any web addresses or links contained in this book may have changed since publication and may no longer be valid. The views expressed in this work are solely those of the author and do not necessarily reflect the views of the publisher, and the publisher hereby disclaims any responsibility for them.

Any people depicted in stock imagery provided by Thinkstock are models, and such images are being used for illustrative purposes only. Certain stock imagery © Thinkstock.

ISBN: 978-1-4917-8147-0 (sc)
ISBN: 978-1-4917-8148-7 (hc)
ISBN: 978-1-4917-8146-3 (e)

Library of Congress Control Number: 2015919156

Print information available on the last page.

iUniverse rev. date: 11/23/2015

"THE LIPS OF WISDOM ARE CLOSED EXCEPT
TO THE EARS OF UNDERSTANDING"
Hermetic Philosophy

"OUR LIVES BEGIN TO END THE DAY WE BECOME
SILENT ABOUT THE THINGS THAT MATTER"
Dr. Martin Luther King

ACKNOWLEDGEMENTS

FYI: I need you all to know that the quotes in this book aren't to acquire any extra book sales or notoriety based on someone else's words or phrases. The quotes are relevant to the chapters they are written in due to the nature and content of the chapter. My intent is to bring to light other mindsets of people who vibrate at the same speed as I do. I intend to ignite a spark of acceptance by exploiting like minds. I welcome analysis and/or criticism by the reader. My publisher is concerned about copyright laws as she should be and I appreciate the concern. I acknowledged all the people and pictures in this book I quoted which is the right thing to do. I would be a hypocrite if I didn't. My moral character is ethically sound; my conscience wouldn't allow it to be any other way. There is a strong thematic connection between the quotations and the subject matter. I don't want credit for someone else's work. I want to give credit for their over-standings regarding life and the fact that I am not the only one who knows the truth about politics, word play, overt operations regarding subliminal mind tactics, indoctrinated religious tactics, psychological warfare and the whole gambit. I wish I could list all the quotes you have noted in your songs that reflect the "Keys of Life" because that would be known as the 8th Wonder, much respect to Stevie. ☺ I feel that we are all represented by Common because his lyrics make sense; he's the conscience denominator that shines "The Light" on "The People" just as Talib Kweli is an underground rejuvenator. People like Lauryn Hill, Erykah Badu and Jill set the stage for us to follow through, much respect do. Kanye West expressed

"Everything I am" which made me "Stronger" to be a "Champion" in order to live the "Good Life" because "Like Tupac said, "That's Just the Way It Is." So if anyone has a problem with my quotes in this book, I guarantee you it won't be the conscience artist because we extend far beyond the material aspects of life. Money can't buy what this book is about and the quotes are just a reference regarding my topics in that particular chapter. "You must Learn" from scholars like KRS 1 on how to present truth and in doing so you will essentially become a "Public Enemy Number 1" like Chuck Dee and Flavor Flav. Sit back and enjoy the book and be attentive because "I Got A Story to Tell" Big up to Christopher Wallace. You will come to know "Who is God" because Rakim expressed that to the world when he said, "Holy are you" Thanks Rah! I also acknowledge the drums of "Alkebulan" (Land of Cush) that were re-awakened by Clyde Stubblefield and Jabo Starks I guess that why melanated people love the drums and that 808 sound so much. Much respect for the horns of "Wynton Marsalis and Dizzy Gillespie." Together with drums your horns keeps me at peace and let me express me. So when you read a quote in this book from a particular artist, it's not reflecting malice, it's reflecting the respect for the art on my part to ignite a solution called, "Borne Revolution."

Most important of all, I would like to acknowledge all the people who inspired me to write this book. The experiences I had with these people shaped me to be who I am, good, bad, or indifferent. The list is too big to list you all individually, with that said, if you were a part of my life for over six years this would include you. I greatly thank you all for the experiences I've encountered. I hope you will continue to grow spiritually and mentally, be a leader in life and maintain your health to sustain life long enough to instill your values and spiritual attributes in the people you love so that your spirit may move through them 4eva.

Lastly, there are those to whom I known for shorter periods of time and you are of equal importance to me and you also had an impact in my life and I acknowledge your presence and influence as well. By no means are you to misinterpret the above statements as disrespect or of less importance. I hope I had something positive to offer you as you did me, I profoundly thank you with all sincerity and I hope you feel my heart felt truth.

Respectfully
Jahi Issa Jabri Ali-Bey

SMALL FORWARD

One day while I was in a debate with some friends about certain aspects of life, politics and religion and its impact on people and how it affects life in general. I realized that most people will not admit fault in respect to their interpretations and perceptions regarding certain views about their religious and political belief system. Because of this and other concerns, I realized there is total discontent with humanity and the quality of human life in the world. I realized that the things you were taught as a child, right or wrong are deeply embedded in your brain and most people refuse to think of possibilities outside of childhood perception or popular belief due to social engineering, programming and repetitive reinforcement of ideologies by the "Power Elite" and this creates a disconnect with the human family, whereby keeping the appearance of strength and economic power at the top and the appearance of weakness and economic despair at the bottom/the masses.

For most people it's a known fact that you don't talk about religion and politics in public places or at work because it creates tension and resentment. Those two subjects are "taboo" as they say. Based on my experiences and the different schools of thought I have attended over the years I've acquired a well-rounded unique philosophical understanding of existence. This has molded and shown me other aspects of life that are relevant outside the norms of social traditions. I have the need to share my spiritual revelations with the world/people in hopes to rescue the lost ones. I am imploring they may be found by self-analysis and discover the full overstanding concerning knowledge of self and the "Borne Revolution, Fight for Humanity." Altogether, I truly anticipate and hope the masses will be enlightened by this book and that it may serve to be your final revelation. This should be your awakening, the time is now and you need to save your life before Satan takes it away.

Also when it comes to knowledge, intellect, intelligence and consciousness, you should understand that there are multiple levels of each depending on your level of understanding of the subject matter. With that being said, this book isn't about your facts, opinions or mine. It's not about having an indebt debate regarding a particular topic unless it's for elevation and overstanding, reason being; consciousness is always evolving and what one person doesn't know doesn't mean they will never know. By the same token, what a person knows is always subjected to change based on new experiences and perception. When it comes to positivity, there is no right or wrong, there is only progression in the right direct, the movement for improvement. In regards to being wrong, it's only warranted when you learn what you previously thought to be truth based on your level of consciousness. When that level becomes obsolete because of a higher level of consciousness and you don't take action to express that to the people you talked to prior to your new revelation and make the necessary corrections, that's when you are definitely wrong. In other words; if you mentally destroy a mental program and/or mind-set, it's mandatory to rebuild a new one. Hence the term, "Build and Destroy"

Your opinion is just that, opinion. Opinion is synonymous with perception. This is why most people never accept or respect opinion. Your perception is your reality which is your opinion. Your perception is subject to change. What is real will never change. Facts are related to real and they come mainly from experiences. Experiences give you factual evidence which turn what you once believed into a true reality. So there is no need to correct positivity in a negative way by discounting it because it's still a walk in the right direction. Remember, truth can't die nor pass-away, but consciousness only evolves if you are willing to allow it. So don't be so quick to judge and prove your facts just to discredit someone else when you are both moving in the same direction. One might travel at a different speed, but it's still the same direction. What you should do is **humble yourself;** uplift that person or group to a higher level of consciousness and spirituality. That way you all will be on the same page. How can you call yourself conscious and intentionally belittle someone else's positive progression just because they are not on your level of overstanding? How conscious are you really? Don't become self-centered because you are on a higher vibration than most of your peers, that's the same attitude used by the same people who oppressed you from the start. As a positive conscious person don't advocate argument, generate compliment. Regarding the positive side a debate, the only debate you should engage in is that which will bring light to the subject-matter for all parties involved allowing the vibration to increase to a higher level. That is what spiritual consciousness should manifest.

I hope all of you will exhibit spiritual positive strength and harmony within yourself and project an honorable will towards humankind after reading this book!

BORNE REVOLUTION

Fight for Humanity

INTRODUCTION

Over the years Jahi has witnessed innumerable amounts of displacement and confusion in the hearts and minds of adults that he didn't realize existed as a child. As a child, Jahi thought all adults were intelligent, responsible and wise. As he continued to mature he realized how far from the truth he was. Jahi would see respectable people with good jobs resort to drug use, or make irrational decisions as children would do. With that being said, many adults displayed a total lack of responsibility for their actions. They made excuses for irrational actions, at the same time made more excuses to justify their actions that created a negative end result of those decisions. Jahi would see disrespectful men disrespect women and vice versa, people who argued and fought viciously over their religious and political belief systems. He witnessed people who aspired to be sports icons or doctors that decide to sell drugs and or drop out of college. You name it, he saw it. This type of behavior intrigued him to ask why are these people so confused and why do they act the way they do. As a teen Jahi witnessed some of his peers become totally different from what they were taught as children in respect to family values, morals, and ethics. Jahi was taught if you are a true friend, you have unconditional loyalty to your friend; you depend on your friend and your friend depends on you, you place exceptions on your friend above all others etc. It's also said that you should not place exceptions on anyone because you set yourself up for disappointment, yes this is true. The paradox in relation to a best friend is that, the reason they are your friend, best-friend, etc.; is due to the fact that you can depend on them and they have proven their loyalty to you. They become the exception to the rule because you expect them to continue to be different than the masses regarding you and that's why you place exceptions on them. Jahi was taught to be respectful to women by; taking off his hat in their presence and also when in someone's house he would remove his hat, open the door for women, pull out the seat for them etc. On the contrary, if some men display the gentlemen quality now for some women in the western culture, most of the woman he witness or came across will look at you as weak, soft, and a push-over etc. If you greet people you don't know, they look at you like you are the crazy one. In the same breath, he also acknowledges the women who appreciate a gentleman and men who appreciate and respect a woman. But for all intent and purpose he's referring to the masses and their mind-state, not the small minority of people who display professionalism and good-will towards humanity.

Jahi grow up attending church and went to Sunday school, served as an usher, sung on the Children's and Young Adult choirs, help to serve dinners on father's day. Etc. His understandings of certain religious doctrine didn't agree with his spirit. He started studying Islam and the same thing happened, He started going to the Kingdom Hall with his Uncle Donald Ali and the same thing happened. He studied the Protestant doctrine which was somewhat close to the Baptist philosophy; He went to a Catholic Church for a brief period as well as the Apostolic Church. All of the religions had several things in common: a certain type of prejudice towards other religions, uncanny spiritual separation from all of creation as a whole, unequivocal questionable contradictions or some form of philosophical instability. His spirit was telling him that there are some irrefutable fallacies in all of the teachings and he couldn't ignore the want to investigate. Some of the doctrines were acceptable to his spirit but most were not. Through all the teachings Jahi witnessed bias, separation, segregation, duality, hypocrisy and contradictions by which all these concerns drove him to find out if he was overzealous or simply ignorant about what he was taught. Perhaps the discontent

Jahi was feeling in his spirit was a figment of his imagination. Based on the doctrines he was taught while traveling through various religious dominations, his spirit was telling him something was wrong; Jahi was taught we all came through the same creative process as children of the "Most High," we are all created by the same Creator. For example, one of his questions was, why would Jehovah's Witnesses even consider the process of disfellowship? To disfellowship a child of God could possibly tell him or her, they are not good enough for God. What would be the implications of that if people felt rejected by there father? Isn't that judging that person and they teach not to judge? "Only God can Judge" Talk about confusion and a conflict of interest, sheesh!!! What type of person would they grow-up to be in society if they believed God shunned them away as well as their direct family and church family? Why are Gods children arguing about which religion is the true religion? Some religions say if you don't agree with their doctrines and belief system you will burn in hell! Jahi felt all of this rhetoric was non-sense; it didn't make no-sense. So he started on a quest to find out why.

By the same token, this was yet another issue he had. Why would two religious groups, Israel's Jews and Palestinian's-Arab Muslims continue fighting over 50 plus years in the name of God/Allah regarding land that was rightfully Palestine's from the start? Religion plays a major role in murdering God's children over land that was created before the two religious groups even conceived the idea of religion. Are they using religion to justify dominance and control over a weaker smaller population of people who once were one united human family? Ironically both sides fight in the name of their God but there is only one Creator? Ironically they both advocate Heaven/Paradise. Could it be a Roman Empire conquers the globe type of mindset crap? They both claim to be children of the Most High. Would that mean they are family via the Creator? It's an awful shame what Israel does to the people of Gaza. Any whoo! Situations like this put me on a quest to get answers to all the madness transpiring around the globe. Think about this, most religious people to say, "We are God's most prized possession, that's why he made us the most intelligent of all creates on the planet" Huh? Oh Really? That sounds like intellectual ignorance, if there is such a phrase and if it isn't, it is now. We are the smartest dummies, who takes pride in that?

His other issue and concern is medical technology and modern medicine. Pharmaceutical companies and doctors has conditioned the minds of most people who live in North America and aboard to believe that they can be healed of a chronic dis-ease almost instantly, or that there is no known cure for most dis-eases. It's obvious to Jahi through his experiences in talking with chronically ill people that is simply not the case. Because of allopathic medicine they express a lack of confidence in homeopathic treatment. Most people are conditioned to want instance relief and that's what drugs give them. Relief not cures. The sad disposition about most drugs is they don't cure illness; drugs tend to disguise the condition and might make you feel better by presenting instant gratification. Due to that fact, most people deal with the superficial aspects of illness instead of having the knowledge and patience to cure the root causes through the natural process which in turn causes a lifetime of pain and misery, or they could suffer premature death, or experience permanent chronic disorders. Most allopathic medicine is designed to sustain you long enough to keep the medical industry thriving, insurance companies paid and pharmaceutical companies in business. We need them without question. Jahi's criticism is the intent regarding medical researchers who purposely use millions of dollars to research the best way to mask an illness and instantaneously stunt the process of producing cures. His disparagement is also regarding researchers who are generating diseases and targeting certain cultures and inoculating them with germs and viruses that kill thousands to make a profit. Most likely this is supported by local government and politicians paid off in that Country of choice and enforcement by the so-called "Peace Keepers" Churches, hospitals and missionaries, etc. In a different light, naturopathic medicine is basically just that, nature. Botanical exactions from plants and organic matter in the form of minerals are nature's cure for the opposition in the form of viruses, germs, chronic ailments and unwanted pathogens. Intuitive Intelligence created the sun, water, carbon minerals and Oxygen along with all plants and most of them have medicinal properties with the ability to cure us of everything we contract. The big pharmaceutical companies use these same plants to create drugs instead of extracting the natural chemical processes of the plant for the greater good of humanity. Let me reiterate, they extract the necessary medicinal compounds to make drugs. They are more concerned with making money than making cures. The crazy thing is Jahi can guarantee you that some of these pharmacist, chemists, researchers and doctors belong to some kind of religious organization, fear God and in the same breath, have a blatant disregard for the welfare of humanity. So the question would be where is your moral character? Where are the principles of God when you write a prescription knowing that the drug you prescribed is not going to help that person recover 100 percent? This is another reason Jahi went on a quest to get answers as to why Gods children are so disrespectful to humanity, self and God, in the same vein they worship God, pray to God, fight in the name of God, make statements like, "In God We Trust" and at the same time, act contrary to the laws of God. In a nutshell, Drugs have programmed most people to anticipate a quick fix. Sugar, TV dinners, frozen foods and fast-food has programmed you to be impatient and mentality you lose control of self. Did you know the use of a micro-wave oven alters the biological structure of cells in your food turning it toxic? Non-stick cookware causes cancer but they sell it anyway like cigarettes and you all buy it without conviction. On another note, do you understand that social programming takes the family structure away from the home; most families no longer sit at the table as a family and bond as a family unit. Most people reading this now never sit at the table with their family, that's sad. Some TV shows and some movies along with the local news have programmed certain people to live a fast life or a life of crime because most of the people that are always portrayed in movies, in the news or TV that's living a fast life and or committing crimes is predominately the same nationality as the ones watching it. Some people watch negativity so much they become consumed by it and start to live it, believing the program they are watching is real. If you allow T.V. is a babysitter for your young, their mind is never cultivated in a positive way. Therefore, without proper guidance and proper education these children grow up and emulate what they see. What they also see is nothing, "as far as substance" so they think they will be nothing so they have nothing to live for and it shows in their actions throughout their entire short lived lives. These are also some of the issues that didn't sit well with Jahi's spirit and he wanted to know why God's children are so dysfunctional? Why is most of the world dysfunctional?

The other thing he noticed in relation to experiences about life in general is that, mentally the will power of most people to motivate themselves has depleted. Jahi barely witnesses people motivated enough to help themselves to be better. He doesn't see cohesiveness among cultures to come together to be better as a nation. He also noticed that the human factor of survival and to co-mingle as a family is being stripped from our spirits by technology and most people don't even realize it. The mind state of the world is so sad. We need to be proactive but since the will of the people is gone, far gone, people are only reactive. People counter-punch only when they get hit and the other people say, it didn't happen to me, so why should I care and they lay dormant. We as a people need to be proactive and not reactive. Proactive is a controlling-responsibility and exemplary leadership. Reactive is a procrastinating Influencer and a supportive-benefactor. The reactive mentality will have to change ASAP or damnation is surely imminent. Jahi admits he is not a saint and he doesn't claim to be. But he strives to be a better person day by day. He witnessed his progression, spiritually and mentally over the years. He acknowledges he still has a lot of growing to do but Jahi must say he's proud of himself based on where he came from to where he is now. He loves humanity and life. He has a soft spot for the underdogs on the planet. He can't help it, it's in his bones and he bleeds Love, Truth, Peace, Freedom and Justice. By the same token he also, "speaks softly and carries a big stick." "Theo Roosevelt" His caring mindset doesn't reflect intimidation. He has empathy for truth and the progression of humanity but based on past history he cannot allow his self to be a martyr because human nature hasn't progressed spiritually enough for his death to be worth the sacrifice. Sometimes he dislikes himself for caring because it hurts to witness so much wickedness, but caring is in his blood, he has to care, as they say, "Somebody's got-ta do it."

Experience alone has afforded him the discernment too question certain doctrines and philosophies. Based on that, he decided to put what he has experienced and learned in life in this book in hopes to help people from all walks of life live a better more productive life. He also would hope his book will help people understand who is God and resurrect the birth of a spiritual revolution and fight for humanity. The places he has been and the adepts he learned from are filled with spiritual understandings, a profound sense of universal enlightenment, logic, reason, well-rounded overstanding of life on a spiritual plane, Godly plane and physical plane. All of those elements have molded Jahi into the person he is today. This book is dedicated to all of humanity and the people who ask the questions of why, why not, why we exist and what is life all about? Basically if there was ever a question you ever asked and the answer was never spiritually fulfilling or heart felt. One things for certain, two things for sure, the answers will be revealed in this book.

Jahi Issa Jabri Ali-Bey

Build inner strength to break away from the strong hold of traditional thought. Rip through the wheels of old philosophy and discover your, "Borne Revolution"

Age Old Mentality of Spirituality will hold you
back from true Reality "Jahi Ali-Bey"

Quote: I am **H**elping **I**ndigenous people **D**iscover **D**iscernment
and **EN**lightenment by **C**ultivating **O**thers to **L**earn spiritual
Obedience to **R**estore **S**alvation and the Reclamation of Self.
H.i.d.d.e.n C.o.l.o.r.s
Jahi Issa Jabri Ali-Bey

The documentary by: **Tariq Nasheed**

Contents

Chapter – 1

In The Beginning a Little About Me

My name is Jahi Ali-Bey, and I would like to share the following with you. I'm currently in the military; I have attended college because of financial issues I never finished. Now that I'm back in the military I might go back to school to help advance my military career. I endeavor to stand up and be counted regardless because that's part of my genetic make-up. One of my dreams in life is to break the impoverished and dysfunctional mind state which echoes in the lives of some of my family, the mis-guided and the under privileged people of the world. The Attributes of dysfunction echoes through the actions of some family members, friends and most people of the world as if it's embedded in our dna and seems to resonates throughout our generational trees. I see success as a powerful motivator. Being a success and giving testimony of overcoming adversities whereas expressing my mental strengths and weaknesses in addition to the untiring focus it takes to endure is the primary reason I believe I will help inspire some of my family members, friends and others to strive to new heights. One of my goals in life is to assist people in reaching greater heights and to inspire them to achieve reachable superior goals throughout life by showing them the spiritual powers we possess manifested in us by the Creator. I anticipate "Borne Revolution" can produce a positive outlook on life for most people and aid to create a desire which will maintain a relentless focus on being the very best you can be as a positive life force via the Creator for all who encounter this experience. My book will enlighten you and take your mind on an elevated spiritual tour and shine new light on some of the hardest questions you have regarding why we exist, our purpose in life, what to aspect after death and what actions we can do to make the world we live in a much better place. I will show you how simple the process is to accomplish these objectives. The most challenging facet of all is your will and desire to make it happen via the powers vested in you by the Creator. I will answer the ultimate question of all, "The Who, what and why of God"

We will dive right into the subject but before we do I wanted to share just a little more about me due to the fact that I am anticipating you as the reader can connect with me on a higher level while indulging in the ebbs of the sacred spiritual abyss. I am a writer, editor, personal trainer, artistic manager, inventor, entrepreneur, motivator, consultant of various natural health products; I give lectures on natural health and I'm also a designer of exotic aftermarket wheels and grills, personal Sports equipment (Abcore 720) (Hand Glide 360s), and special weatherized gloves, which you will see in the foreseeable future. I'm writing a book on health called, "Wheelchairs & Canes" and a science fiction book entitled, "The Separatist" I'm resilient and focused on being an achiever before the dirt is thrown over my eyes. In the same light, I want people to know I came from an average house hold with an average education and whether this book does well or not, it will not stop me from reaching my ultimate quest which is to help people from all walks of life to have a better quality of life and help them understand it's more to life than just a struggle.

I guess it's like Dr. Martin King said, "I have a dream" sometime for me it looks like, with each passing moment the dream fades, however; optimism is that bright light that resides in me, I can't make it shine bright by myself but the creative forces of universal law connects with my spirit creating harmony and balance to anticipate a brighter day. With that being said, I would say that humanity can only survive if we honor it and co-existence as 1 unit and advocate co-existence as a daily practice to unify balance of our minds, bodies and souls to help eliminate our self-destructive behavior and exhibit the attributes we possess as children of a higher power who are here to be fruitful and multiply. I am taking initiative to reach out to everyone with a dream of being successful in life. "LIKE MINDS ATTRACT" If you have a dream and it looks like it will never come true, never give up on it, find new avenues of approach, new people to contact, new ways to bring your idea to fruition, just don't quit. Perform your duties as always but take it up a notch! Come out of your comfort zone and do what most people are not willing to do and remember that 3 percent of the world is wealthy and 97 percent are average. That translates to; only 3 percent of people are willing to do what 97 percent of people are not. You must be that 3 percent which consists of being: resilient, have a relentless drive for success, unwavering focus in the most trying times, able to dismiss your deeply rooted non-productive concepts and adopt new ones spontaneously, accept change, and understand that it might not happen in your time frame but your desire to win will happen when preparation, opportunity and chance meet. You will make it happen because you know and believe in yourself. I love this quote you are about to read I don't know who wrote it, but I love it, cherish it and live by this quote for the rest of your life! Its form a movie but I can't remember which one.

Quote: "I never lose either I win or I learn"

Performance: It needs direct results and a building of self-worth that will help develop new concepts and ambition for tomorrow. Live today, conceptualize for tomorrow and respect yesterday because that's what got you were you are now. "Jahi Ali-Bey"

My aim in writing this book is to set the mental framework that will help us fixate on one mind and spirit that will personify the spiritual performance of many through actions and deeds with the intent to uplift fallen humanity and save us from hell-self-destruction

E PLURIBUS UNUM!

God grant me the power to accept the things I cannot change
The courage to change the things I can
And the wisdom to know the difference

IT WAS ONCE SAID IF THE TRUTH WAS
IN A PILL EVERYBODY WOULD WANT IT,
BUT EVERYBODY CAN'T SWALLOW IT!

CHAPTER – 2

SERENITY

Reinhold Niebuhr wrote the Serenity prayer. I see it as a common sense approach to all aspects of life in general. If you were to use this approach in your everyday life you will experience less negativity because understanding the inevitable is mental liberty. It would be conducive to use this as an action of fate instead of a prayer and wait. Do not procrastinate, put this into action now. The Creator already granted you the power to accept the things you cannot change and the courage to change the things you can and the wisdom to know the difference. All you had to do was act on it by bringing the words to life through your actions. You didn't have to pray for this one. This one was free directly after you have read it. If the Creator gave you "will" and we know without question you have it. You also have the power. Put them together and you have the will-power to do whatever you want to do within reason and The Creator gave you that gift.

Most of you act like you are powerless over Satan who strips most of you of your power every day. Obviously it's true, look at how everyone acts. Like my grandmother would say, "look at'um aint nothin but the devil" lol, she wasn't lying! Can someone look at your actions now and say look at'um, that's the divine spirit working through them, that's nothing but god, that's nothing but a positive energy coming from her or him. You have the ability to create peace in your life via the *actions* of those words. Life really can be easier by excising this one little expression called the "Serenity Prayer." The more you exercise, the less pain you have in life, the easier the work load gets and the pay-off starts to become much greater. God! Grant me the serenity to accept the things I cannot change; Courage to change the things I can, and the wisdom to know the difference.

If you have serenity, in a world of chaos
you will manage to find peace!

You always have a few people in the crowd that say, "Easier said than done" If you just do it with the power vested in you from the Creator and stop making weak lame excuses, *"Thine will be done"* but until then, life will always be hard like your head. When you read the chapter on bad habits things should become much clearer for you and by that time excuses should be a thing of the past. Get yourself together and stop making excuses, excuses do nothing but hold you back. Learn to take charge of you through yourself; because the "I" part of you wants to control you, you have to control you all by yourself. I hope you can understand what that means coming from a psychological stand point. We didn't even get deep in the book yet and some of you are showing signs of weakness. By the time you finish this book, Satan will be history. You can look at negativity in a whole new light and understand that your perception can always change based on your knowledge or lack thereof.

With that in mind, the state of affairs that the world is in could possibly be likely because of; Color of Law, Collusion and Greed. Collusion is basically an agreement between two or more parties, most times illegal and therefore secretive, basically to limit open competition by deceiving, misleading, or defrauding others of their legal and lawful rights, also to obtain an objective forbidden by law typically by defrauding or gaining an unfair market advantage. This word shouldn't even be a problem but it's the epitome of local, congressional and contractual law. Reference; "Blacks' Law Dictionary" and or "Wikipedia.org"

I want you to keep the possibility of collusion in your mind while reading this book and allow yourself to rid your mind of all of your preconceived opinions that's not based on actual experience but based on indoctrinated philosophies. So for the sake of learning and fully understating new material that might appear to be controversial to you, please reframe from conjuring up your own conclusions before giving yourself a chance to experience new possibilities and concepts. If you feel uncomfortable, it means that your mind is on the verge of new enlightenment and it's normal to feel that way. Embrace it and elevate your spiritual vibration.

CHAPTER – 3

INITIATION OF THE QUEST

This book is written in what I call passive progressive sequential order to help assist you in getting a full true understand of all subject matter in each chapter via the next chapter, also with the understanding that everyone doesn't travel at the same speed and I want everyone to completely comprehend what I'm conveying without a shadow of a doubt and with the proper perception. Please don't skip a page or chapter, every page and chapter is crucially essential in understanding the information in order to get a clear and concise understanding regarding the message I'm conveying in the next chapter. It's written for all walks of life. People looking for answers, Atheist, Pagans, Muslims, Wicca, Voodoo, Buddhist, Catholics, Christians, Jehovah Witnesses, the Jewish community and other sects or organizations I didn't mention☺. By the way, when you see words that don't correspond to the doctrines of your organization or belief system, don't become narrow-minded and develop "**Chronic Voluntary Mind Block**," replace it with words you can relate to. Do you want to be a religious buff or have a relationship with the Creator? It's all about divinity. Every religion has their own way of receiving who they call the Creator. The truth is in knowing that no "1" religion is the only righteous "1" or the only true way to Paradise or Heaven is in "1"specific doctrine. It's a shame that some religions promote that type of prejudice, separation, segregation, and predisposition and still scream that they are holier than thou. There is only "1" creator for all of humanity and in the same breath Creation is the intelligence that sustains all forms of life on every level. For people that might be new to knowing the Creator, Higher Power, Divine one, etc. religion might be a good place to start your foundation but always remember that there is no "1" doctrine that is the 'tell all be all: of life and there is always more to life than any "1" organization, Always try to expand your knowledge in everything you do, always strive for perfection and if you miss your mark at least you will be the best at that particular subject. Ignorance is bliss as they say. They also say that knowledge is a gift and a curse. I also wrote this book to liberate my family because I love family 1st. I profoundly hope my family and all of you will read this without prejudice in it's entirely. If some material is over your head, meaning too complex to understand, make a foot note and look for it again in another chapter or study that particular phrase or subject before moving forward. That way you will get the full comprehension and leave no room for doubt or confession. If you believe, you leave room for doubt, but if you know, you are sure and secure, confident and ready. This book also helps the people with like minds to advance to the next level of over-standing. Please do not skip any chapters just to read the one you think is most important to you. There is a lot of information that you need to absorb throughout the book. I truly hope you will see life in a different perspective upon completion of this book. I'm thankful for all my supporters, family, friends and people in like spirit to whom I haven't had the honor of meeting that believed in this book enough to read the content. I implore that you will have a sense of enlightenment, gratitude and fulfillment as you read about the aspects of yourself and your relationship with Creative intelligence. Thank you all in advance, I profoundly appreciate you, 1 love, 1 Mind and 1 truth. I tried to make this book an easy read because I know everyone doesn't travel at the same speed.

Before you get caught up in superficial isms before you start to read this book, remember this. All people have their own interpretation of the Creator, so don't focus on the name and lose focus on the content. As a Life-force of the Life-Source, son/child of God-The Great Architect who sits on Most High I am naturally inquisitive and like most of the populous I have questions about certain things in life that never go away due to the fact that no one seems to have answers that moves my spirit in the direction of truth when an answer is offered. Furthermore, I want the challenge of teaching "old dogs' new tricks," because they say it can't be done. I know why people say it can't be done. Older people are set in their ways and refuse to listen to what they believe to be new information or some information appears to be so profound it frightens or intimidates them so they run from it or make excuses not to listen. I wrote this book to show my son and daughter that it's more to life than what you think you know and what it appears to be. You will always learn new things if you allow yourself to be open to new ideology, information and concepts because what you think you know could be wrong. If you learned most of what you know from a public institution like public school, college, Catholic school, public home school, Mosque, Church, Synagogues or Kingdom Halls and other religious sanctuaries and socially excepted learning institutions, then you know very little about whom you really are or about your culture or how to think outside the box, etc. They all give you an education on specific subject matter and they do the job intended but they don't teach you about self or your culture directly. I'm not saying it's a bad thing, that's not their focus and that's perfectly alright, so don't get all bend out of shape thinking I'm pointing the finger. Relax this book is about Creative thinking, mental & spiritual elevation and positive progression. Again, the biggest issue most people don't realize is they live life not knowing who they really are. I will help you understand who you are in this book if you allow yourself to open up and leave prejudice, preconceived bias and any other close-minded notions somewhere else. In doing so, you will have room in your head to learn and grow. Please know there's always room to grow as a person. Anyone, especially Old dogs can learn new tricks through open-mindedness, patience and having an acceptance of change. So open your heart and soul, open your spirit and mind, take a deep breath and, "Woosah." FOR YOUR INFORMATION, Woosah is sorta the sounds you make through your mouth when you take a deep breath so "breathe easy" and enjoy the ride. Younger people get set in their ways and do the same thing but not as much because their minds have not been contaminated and programmed to the point of no return. So they are much more open to new ideas, information and concepts.

If we as a people "the human family" do not wake up from the governmental matrix that's overtly controlling our minds, actions and deeds via collusion and indoctrination we are headed for self-destruction. By acting as if this isn't going to happen because we can't handle or face the truth perpetuates the problems and these problems are handed down, generation after generation and our DNA is getting weaker and weaker making us vulnerable to false teaching and super susceptible to believing and owning his-story as our story. If the overall spirit of the people was content, the people would be content. We are on the dawn of being extinct and most of you are too naive to see it.

Furthermore; It's deeper than not having a job, it's deeper than human and civil rights, it's deeper than public education or the lack there of, it's deeper than negative words like "Kraut, Mof, Dago, Greaser, Wop, Oreo, Wegro, Wigger, Apple, Banana, Nigger, Limey,Cracker, Spick, Mooly, White Trash, Redneck, Trailer Trash, Hick, Paddy aka Paddy-Wagon it's deeper than a March on Washington, DC., it's deeper than passing new legislation, it's deeper than Equal Rights, it's deeper than Religion. Look at all those negative connotations. This is really sad; it's so many you can write a book just on negative connotative words and phrases. With that being said, it's not too profound to fix; all we need is the right tools and this book is a start in the right direction. I never witnessed any of these formulas I just mentioned work in my lifetime, i.e.; marches, protests, occupying areas, public outcry, or demonstrations and I don't see them work in the foreseeable future. Further-more this type of approach is not working now and I haven't ever known any of these things to work consistently for a period of time or at all for that matter. In relationship to "We The People" as a whole, the only thing I witnessed that these topics did was pacify the public long enough to forget about what it was they were fighting for and the vicious cycle happened all over again. I have 16 further-more's but I will only list a few, with that being said, ignorance is a lack of knowledge and if you read certain passages in this book and get offended and refuse to read any further, you are expressing your ignorance of a particular subject you have little knowledge of. Ignorance will keep the appearance of peace because it's irrational bliss. The only other true peace is the death of Satan hence the expression, "Rest in Peace." If you choose to be ignorant, that's stupid and it brands you a dummy. It's ok to be ignorant and gain knowledge, but to live in ignorance because it's easy to do because you don't want to accept the responsibility that comes with knowledge is selfish, non-productive as a person and a waist of life's energy and time.

Furthermore: I have found out that when I personally talk on this level to convey my convictions about the information and experiences I've learned in life, I run into opposing forces and it distracts the focus and point of the conversation. But if I put it in a book, you can't anticipate the book to argue back. This gives the person reading the material adequate time to absorb the knowledge being presented to them. Another reason I wrote this book is to show people if you allow yourself to come out of your element; meaning your comfort zone, "*for the sake of learning*" you can achieve and grow more as an individual. But the old dog mentality is the kind of behavior that's stunts your spiritual and mental growth and potential to become something more in life than just an average person. Take time to understand something new. Take initiative mentally to aspire to be a leader, that means allowing your higher self to lead you, that's what your quest should be in life instead of your lower animalistic devilish god-self "*The Beast666*" controlling and dictating your every move. Learn who you really are as a child of God. Master yourself. You might just learn that you can learn more if you just come out of the house, you can learn more if you leave the block you live in, you can learn even more than that if you leave your neighborhood, leave the city, leave the country, leave your mindset and explore new possibilities. Get it? In actuality it's nothing new under the sun just different ways of looking at the same picture. You will never reach new heights or excel in life if you are not willing to open your mind to new possibilities. You will never see the ocean if your ship never leaves the shore. With that in mind ponder the possibility of this next passage.

"Preconceived notions are the locks on the doors to wisdom." Merry Browne

If we as a people collective in mind and spirit wrote moral and ethical laws reflecting our respect for the Creator, Nature, The Higher Power and the Love for Humanity, there would not be conflict as we see it today. Everybody would live according to that particular philosophy because based on the subject matter there would be corresponding concepts and 1 common goal.

Laws for financial aid and life-support are mainly for big business. If there is a recession, the same government you support, elect and pay taxes to keep them in office, support the business, help financially and aiding the business in staying alive.

Laws that cover racketeering, Rico, drug selling, criminal and civil are focused on the people. You sell drugs its illegal. They sell drugs it's legal. They kill people via drugs, mis-diagnosis, and its medical mal-practice, you do it and go to jail, and their insurance companies pick up the tab while they still work and do the same thing over again. You kill yourself by allowing the media to convince you these items are not dangerous; plastic, Teflon, cigarettes, microwave ovens, processed food, gmo's and alcohol, etc. your government ok's the sale of these carcinogenic infested materials and chemicals to you. If you sell some of these items you go to jail. You use them and you suffer with high blood pressure, diabetes, heart disease, cancer, mesothelioma, lung disease, cirrhosis of the liver, etc. until premature death ends your life. While you are still living, you pass these habits to family and friends generation after generation. I see why the Power

Elite reigned for so long, it's easy, and they don't work hard because ignorance works for them for free. I hope you are picking up what I'm putting down. We have to move on. Wake up!

On other note, some religious organizations teach about how they feel the Creator is conveying the message of life and to say the least, for the purpose of control, creating their own doctrines and imposing those doctrines and ideology on the people and demanding that their philosophies be the Cardinal Rule of the world and fighting all other religious groups who oppose and follow their own cardinal philosophies and false doctrines. Yes I did say, false! If your spirit has the Creators conviction for truth and is not tinted by the dogmas you were taught as a child up until this point, then you should feel the positive vibration in this next statement, absorb and accept it through your spiritual light and common sense that you were born with.. If the doctrines of religion were true, there wouldn't be fights, murders, coerced pledges of commitment and allegiance to their philosophies and doctrines in the name of their God. There would not be a need for the convening of the, Creed of the Council of Constantinople, Nicene Creed, 1st and 2nd Councils of Nicaea, or the Council of Trent, Ecclesiastical Reconfiguration, Structural Reconfiguration of the bible/theological philosophies or the formation of Religious orders. Without and ulterior motive, all people would get along with respect to one common spiritual vibration throughout the world and positive subliminal psychological reinforcement would be conveyed throughout the world because we as a people would all be on the same page, again this understanding would be spiritually perpetuated throughout the land and confusion as to who's right and who's wrong would be minimal due to a unified spiritual connection that we all have with Creation know matter what nationality, culture you are or religious conviction you have. In the end intrinsic intelligence has the last word as you will learn in this book as a student of the light.

"This little light of mine, I'm gonna let it shine, let it shine, let it shine, let it shine."

The beliefs you accepted in your early childhood unquestionably has a strong influence on what you think especially when focusing your attention on social isms, religion and politics. As you surround yourself with people of the same mindset your beliefs start to gain strength to a degree and alter your perception of life, good, bad or indifferent. It will also influence your belief system which in turn dictates most of your thoughts and actions. Sometimes it's good and sometimes it's not. Contrary to that, there is a higher state of mind that takes you to greater heights than just the mind state of beliefs. If you give yourself a chance to mentally grow, your god consciousness will let you know what you believed was just that, belief. To <u>know</u> is 10x's better than to <u>believe</u>. So do you believe in God? Or do you know God? That my friend is the question? Most of you believe in God. If you reevaluate my question and read it again are you inclined to say you know God because maybe your spirit convicted you to feel compelled to say "Oh yeah I know God" or are you plain old confused? You were not taught to know God, you were taught to "believe in God." Honestly you should have a problem with that. By the same token, do you realize to believe in God would imply that you are leaving room for doubt? There's no room for doubt when you know something but there is always room for doubt if you believe something. Do you believe in yourself or do you know yourself? To believe in God also implies that you are prejudice? Prejudice: intolerance of or dislike for people of a specific race, religion (Collins English dictionary). Each religion claims to be the one true religion but we are all created by the same creator. Religions only adhere to their indoctrinated specific beliefs. Some religions believe one race of people to be God's chosen people. How prejudice is that? Is that not the overt practice of separation and segregation? God created all people on this planet but God singled out all of human creation for one culture of people huh? What does that say about God? Most religions condemn the others based on their Godly beliefs, etc. Some religions believe God takes the lives of the ones closest to you to coerce you or the ones who back-slide or sin to worship Him (Him?) Really God would hurt human creation to get human creation to worship the Great Architect? Most religions are gender specific, referring to God as a he, but a spirit has no gender, vocal cords or shape, so to call God a he is prejudice. Everything I just mentioned alludes to prejudice. Do you not see that? Please don't get offended and put the book down. If you don't agree its ok but don't deny yourself the opportunity to learn, extract the cream as they say.

A quote from the song, Same Love, by Macklemore: "The right-wind conservatives think it's a decision and you can be cured with some treatment and religion man-made, rewiring of a predisposition, playing God ahh, nah, here we go. I don't know"

While I'm thinking about it, I ask that you not be so super analytical because you will lose focus of the subject matter in this book. Please give yourself a chance to digest the information. If you have to, take foot notes of what you might question and research it through multiple sources. Most of the time if you ask a question and someone gives you a bogus or truthful answer your gut-feeling-soul-heart or spirit *"whatever you want to call it"* will let you know if that answer is true or not. If you go against the grain and the outcome is negative you or someone you articulated the situation to will say, "you should have went with your gut-feeling" and your spirit tells you, "Yup I should have or shouldn't have done it" coulda, woulda, shoulda, your spirit says, lol. So this is partly why I took a personal stance in this area of life that's so forbidden for most people. Furthermore; I find that more people are truly lost when it comes to having a real relationship with the Creator. *"They don't' know how to have a relationship with God"* Some people are scared when it comes to expressing how they feel about their God; Life-Force; The Creator. Most people always focus on the differences one has based on their religious beliefs. First off! The sad part is; when most people are speaking of the Creator the focus is never on God the Creator, or god conscious, it's about religious convictions, which doctrines are right or wrong, who's the most creditable, Jesus is mentioned 36 times in the Quran, Christianity came before all other religions,

Jesus is black, Jesus is only a Prophet, Jesus is God and the son, Allah is one, Mohammed was the last prophet, Jehovah is God's real name Jehovah's Witnesses are the true religion, Religion started in Egypt, Amen Rah is the original God, Religion started in Judea or no it didn't start in Judea, Jews are the chosen people of God. I can go on and on but what's the point. There is none! These superficial topics have nothing to do with the essence of Creation and god's will power to overthrow adversarial spiritual forces.

When will we come together as one unit and talk about how to fight Satan and make each one of us a better person because, *"I am my brother & my sister's keeper"* We will do it now while reading this book. Satan is history after you read this book people. I definitely anticipate this book will help you grasp a distinct and concise knowledge of who God is. Mentally prepare yourself to be exceedingly spiritually aware of whom you really are. Bear in mind that this book is not intended to disrespect any governmental sect, people or religious belief system. Nothing I say is written in stone. I see a weakness in some religious teachings across the board and I can't help but to give you a helping hand in making your world a better place to live in by expressing my personal experiences and philosophy because helping people is part of my calling as a Child of the Sun which is Most High. Hopefully the freedom of speech still applies and that part of the constitution is still respected. (smh; shaking my head) My intention though, is to get you to free your minds and consider other possibilities and know its ok to **think outside the box** or **throw the box away.** Bottom line is STOP believing everything you were taught as if it's undeniable truth or absolute, because you might be wrong. I say that for the reason that when most people hear something contrary to what they have known to be true, they don't want to listen to no other principle and they close their ears or argue their point without giving the new information a chance to be heard and or absorbed. Based on that stigma most of you are so critically analytical over different information you know nothing about, you somehow formulate a self-righteous justification and choose not to indulge your mind with new concepts that would enhance your spiritual and mental growth. Figuratively speaking; "I'm not a politician, and it's no need for me to communicate propaganda in this book to deceive you into voting for me." I gain nothing in a lie or deception except heart ache, heart break, losing my name, reputation and credibility. That equates to losing my life and I'm not about losing my life over that non-sense. I'm just an ordinary person that would like to be of assistance to people who are desperately looking for answers to the questions they have been asking for years and if the Creator gave me the wisdom to overstand, then it should be my humanitarian duty to share this knowledge. If it's something in life you don't understand, don't turn your back on it, or push it away, and don't criticize it to justify your ignorance. Be responsible and convict yourself to the fact that, "my people are destroyed for lack of knowledge" and what they don't understand. Ignorance can kill; look at the world around you. If most of us knew who we were, we wouldn't do most of the things we do and the rest of God's children wouldn't let you do them neither. Ok back to thinking outside the box.

Note: this has everything to do with ***thinking outside the box*** and showing you things aren't always what they seem contrary to popular belief.

For example: Some people believe the statue of Rocky on the Philadelphia Art Museum steps is that of a real boxer when in fact it commemorates Rocky Balboa the movie.

For example: We are the third planet from the sun in relation to the original nine planets before the discovery of all the other ones. All of the planets are aligned parallel to each other and each planet revolves around the sun which is also parallel the all the planets. So when you look up at the sun it's not really up higher than we are, it gives you the illusion that it is because we are on earth's surface and we are not tall enough to see across the sky so it looks as if the moon and the sun are up there as we say. We are already up there: So when you speak of heaven or pray to God and you say God and heaven is up there, where is up there? I'm just asking. People we are in space with the other eight planets, we are the third rock from the sun.

For example: You are taught that everyone has a birthday. Not true. Only mothers have a birthday. You are born at conception and you are 9 months old before you exit the womb, considering a full term. *"obviously in some cases, that's why some people go to jail for illegally aborting a fetus"* When your mother gives birth to you; symbolically, out of the darkness you come into the light but you were born 9 months prior to that. If a mother gives birth 1, 2, 3 or 4x's that's how many birthdays she has. She should be celebrated for her blood sacrifice for each of her life giving gifts of life. By the same token; you celebrate your anniversary of life each year. Just as you celebrate the anniversary of marriage; not the wedding. As a couple you are the manifestation of the marriage via the wedding. You are the manifestation of life via the conception not the birth. In the same vein, being created in the image and likeness of God, you are the manifestation of God via the Creator who created you. We must understand that the Creator gave us the power to create on a mundane scale in comparison to the Almighty. The Almighty-Creator-Mother Nature, intrinsic intelligence, etc. is the initiator of creation and the Creator give us the gift of duplication on a mundane creative level. We have the power to re-create, duplicate and procreate. We created just about everything physical you see on the planet on a day to day basis. We even have the power to duplicate each other through a process called, fornication for procreation. It was written that God created man and woman, but there is nothing written that says God created children, it's dully noted that we are God's children but the gift of life is ours to uphold. God gave that awesome gift to the little gods, us. We can't truly create what the Creator can create; like, stars, moons, planets, people, animals, oceans, galaxies, black-holes, universes, brains, etc., but we can clone, imitate, duplicate, and recreated on a mundane level to some degree.

Please understand that I elaborated on this topic to help the ones who are blind, stubborn, and the ones who treat new information as taboo, to come out of the darkness into the light just a little. My brightest hope is that you will allow your mind to see beyond your social programming and think for yourself, without prejudice. By the same token, religious arrogance will have you believing you and your religion is better than any other. Religious arrogance will also have you thinking your religion is more important than anything else and block you from growing. Look up the meaning of arrogance and compare your actions and your willingness to receive other information regarding the subject.

Note: for people who have Chronic Voluntary Mind Block. "CVMB" People who know everything have no more room to know nothing else and you people that know you know everything need to know you know nothing at all. Furthermore: I pray that you destroy the wall that's stopping your mental and spiritual growth so you don't continue to spread involuntary ignorance to people in your life and perpetuate a delusional self-centered condescending state of mind that continues to plague the world causing insurmountable damage to our higher god-self rendering your higher god-self useless. **Your thoughts** are **the/your** reality that propels and influences **your actions** and your actions defined **your character** and character defines **your choices** in life and your choices decide **your destiny** so **you have control** of the direction in life that you will go. "I Self Law Am Master" Sheesh!

> **Quote:** I'm starting with the man in the mirror, if you want to make the world a better place, take a look at yourself, and make a change. "Michael Jackson"

For example: now this has nothing to do with the context of this book but it has everything to do with ***thinking outside the box*** and showing you things aren't always what they seem contrary to popular belief. *"We all say the sky is blue"* but the sky is actually black all the time, it appears to be blue due to the color of algae, sea vegetation and the nucleus of plankton that dominates our ocean's surface combining with the fact that water bends light and the planet is ¾'s H_2O 75percent water and the black sky. In essence, synergistically all of these factors allow for the appearance of a blue sky. The sun is not yellow; it appears to be yellow because the surface temperature is cooler than the core. The sun is white on the surface just as the rays are white on the surface of the planet and the surface of the moon is white, not yellow. It's pretty obvious if all the other stars are white, ☺ yes the sun is a star if you didn't know.

I will break it down another way, it's like looking in a mirror, the mirror has a dark backing, scratch off the backing it's just glass. You need light to see your reflection which is an allusion because the real person is looking in the mirror. Break the mirror or turn off the light and your reflection is gone but the real person is still there. The super analytical nah-Sayers might say, but the sky isn't blue when it rains *"u r killin me"* *"It is blue,"* but for all intent and purposes I will say of course not, due to the fact that the sun's rays can't penetrate clouds and the rain clouds are about one or two mile high. *"all clouds are pure water gray or white, light cant penetrate water, pure water cannot freeze"* Above the clouds the blue illusion is still there people. The earth is 75 percent water; the little city you live in does not dictate the vastness of the sky or ocean and the color or appearance of the sky. If you ever flew through a storm you will see that above the storm clouds, there is still the appearance of a sunny blue sky, by the same token if you flew about 40,000 feet you will see the illusion of the blue sky called the horizon because the plane is high enough for you to see the separation of the illusive blue sky and the vast blackness of space. *Think outside the box* or *throw the box away.* If you still have doubt check it out!

If you have a mirror and you scratch off the silver off the back of the mirror you could not see your reflection. But you would be able to see straight through the glass. Without Light and a dark background and the other factors listed, the sky **would not** appear to be blue. The night sky would reveal its true identity. "Black" Keep in mind that the day starts at 12am and 12pm is in the afternoon. Keep in mind what you do in the dark come out in the light.

Example: The world over will say that extraterrestrials are aliens that come from outta-space and you probably do as well. Based on the general consensus and without truly looking at the word itself, that's the conclusion you and everyone has drawn, Right? After looking at these three definitions, tell me what does your spirit tell you now?

Analyze these terms throughout the book and see how the words and meanings mean more than you imagined. **Celestial:** pertaining to the sky or visible heaven, or to the universe beyond the earth's atmosphere, as in celestial body, relating to, celestial beings. Thank you, Dictionary.com. If I was referring to an alien I would think the proper usage and phrase would be extra-celestial. Personally if I used the term extra-terrestrial, it would refer to something on the earth's surface or in the earth's core based on the meaning of terrestrial. Makes perfect sense to me, but who am I to speak of lexical semantics.

Extra: more than is usual or necessary, something extra or additional; (Dictionary.com) what more can you possibly say about extra. Accept, it is what it is.

Terrestrial: Mundane in scope or character, living on or in or growing from land. Thank you for the meaning (Merriam-Webster. Com) as I stated above terrestrial relates to land not sky.

Based on the definitions above, If you were to describe an alien from outer-space, would you say, extra-terrestrial or extra-celestial. Maybe you should start studying **etymology** which is the root & origin of words to get a better understanding of how to cast a spell. Also understand what **abridged** means. If you start taking words and making secondary meanings and then using the secondary meaning as the primary meaning, the substance of the word becomes vague and the **denotative** meaning comes obsolete to the **connotative** meaning. "It's like what the hell did he just say?" "Read it again and again until it sinks in, or study the meanings of the words I **high-lighted**. "For your information" if a phrase or word is high-lighted and or underlined in this book it's for a reason; it would **behoove** you to seek out the meaning and or understanding thereof" So if a group of people did this in; law, health, science and religion how would you know what is truth or falsehood? Etymology will tell you the truth 100percent of the time. I hope you can handle the truth because you've been living a lie for eons.

Whatever **you** think; is **your** reality, so know this to be **true**, "as a man or woman thinks that is what he or she is. **Your thoughts** are **your** reality that propels and influences **your actions** and your actions defined **your character** and character defines **your choices** in life and your choices decide **your destiny** so **you have control** of the direction in life that you will go. "To a degree" outside forces play a role as well but in the end **you have the power**. Please do not let society dictate your mindset. Remember, "A Mind Is a Terrible Thing To Waste."

In America most people would say, "The majority Rules" this statement applies to the courtroom, voting poles, boardroom meetings, congress, you get the gist. In so far as to say, "Society's values are not your personal values so **stop** allowing them to define your life."

My other reason for Initiation of the Quest is that if God created us equal why does government and religion separate, segregate and disassociate us as a people when we all essentially-theoretical are God's children. As a matter of fact, who is the responsible party that started segregation, separation and division, "The same people who introduced certain forms of religion" Wow! In America most Muslims, Christians, Jehovah's Witnesses, Catholics, Seventh day Adventist and other sects as well cannot commune together because of religious differences and some of them are in the same blood-line "family members." If we are all God's children as we profess to be why can't we leave the differences at the door and be one with the Creator for the sake of humanity? I know why now and this is what leads me on my quest for over-standing the mundane issues we have as a potentially dying species. By the time you finish this book you will know why as well. FYI, don't let lexical semantics control your mindset.

Why would Jehovah's Witnesses dis-fellowship members, disassociate and segregate themselves from all other faiths and want to be forgiven and saved, why did Yahweh's Christians kill Muslims, enslave so-called Blacks and so-called Africans and wage wars all over the world? Why did Hitler want to kill all the Jews and conquer the world? Why did Allah's Muslims want to kill the Christians, whom by the way still fight and quarrel? Why out of 72 sects of Muslims the majority of them have differences and neither sect ever settles differences but they all believe in the same God, "Allah" and Allah is 1? Why did the Pope-Vatican change the religious belief system under the Counsel Nicaea? Why did the Catholic Church, during the dark ages killed people who would not follow Catholicism? People were tortured and killed horribly if they didn't conform to the ideology of the Catholic religion. What about the historical countless horrors about the Roman Catholic Inquisition? Also, why would they lock under the highest security; historical artifacts and facts of certain people, places and things in the Vatican City? Why would people who call themselves Christians come to North America and in most cases they've said, "we come in the name of God" and then; rape, pillage, enslave, murder, spread disease, take land that wasn't theirs, then brag about it in their history books, teach his-story about it and everyone accepts it as a justification because they fled their own Country for fear of persecution as criminals and or religious persecution. These same people fought for freedom from Britain, (Did you ever wonder why?) Any-who, they get their independence become free, celebrate about it every year and its ok. So the cat is out the bag, British America fought for their independence, signed the Declaration of Independence July 4' 1776. So the Brits in America are free and they started their own government and dictatorship. Is it wrong for us to desire to be free from British Roman rule and start our own government, build our own economic and governmental infrastructure and reinforce dejure law with respect to the government that's already in place? Do you find this question to be disrespectful, because every group that has tried in the past as well as present day organizations is labeled, extremist and/or radical groups or domestic terrorists? It appears that most laws are written for the survival of one group of people in the grand scheme of things. If you are trying to fit into a society that doesn't want you there and the signs have been posted for over 650 years expressing the want for you to leave and you still try stay, it would seem to me you are delusional and plain old stupid.

As I said, as a child of the Most High I am naturally inquisitive and I want answers to this thing called life just like some of you. Understand this; his-story "history" is like money, it can make you or break you, you can counterfeit it or duplicate it, attempt to make dirty money clean through the appearance and appeal of a legitimate business *"like a college history class"* steal it and say it's yours, twist it and use it for personal gain, use it to gain power over a people or a nation, burn it like it never existed and reprint it as if it's authentic. All money is not good money; it comes in all shapes, colors, sizes and languages. When you look at most his-tory and fiat money-notes-paper-money, there is a comparison in every way. I will talk about how history has taken a toll on indigenous people throughout the diaspora in a chapter called, "Who we are" which is dedicated to the plight of groups of people deteriorating spiritually and mentally. The power within us as god will be the only weapon capable of defeating the adversary. If we come together in spirit as 1 mind and unite the internal powers of god, every weapon formed again you shall not prosper! "Isaiah 54:17" People who are powerless maintain power by building weapons of destruction creating dissension, separation, segregation and in this day and age they have developed the ability to alter DNA, create DNA banks for tailor-made children, stem-cells, sperm banks, fertility pills, and other means of survival for them to have everlasting life and by the same token destroy the lives of the weak-minded and economically deprived. We need to know, we will prevail, if we only believe, we will fail. They say, "United we stand, divided we fall" They have been united and have proven that statement to be true. We have been divided since our DNA was infiltrated by fear, murder, burnings, religious inquisitons, rape, STD's, disease and the forced imposition of foreign religious practices and physiological warfare which slowly blinded our minds eye of who is god and immobilized the implementation of resurrecting the conscience birth of spirituality.

Allow me to give you another example of a stereotypical mindset that is degrading and keeping the majority of humanity stagnate and unfocused especially in North America. Again this has nothing to do with the context of this book but it will have everything to do with **thinking outside the box** and showing you things aren't always what they seem contrary to popular belief. If you focus on the power vested in you by the Creator, these superficial man-made issues wouldn't affect you as a people. Most people in North America-USA use the term black or white *"which are adjectives"* when referring to a particular group of people. In law and in nationality, there are no such people who exist. If you call yourself, "White, Black" you are saying you don't exist in law and you are not pedigree, in reality you are a mutt, a mixed breed of people. If you are content with that so be it, no problem. If you want to legitimize yourself and acknowledge who you are as a people and have true cultural pride and roots, you most definitely need to seek out your strongest bloodline in your family's history, and that without a doubt is your unpretentious nationality and culture you should live by, honor and respect. This will give you true identity and allow you to study what nationality you really are and not what someone else's his-story portrays you to be. I'm only articulating this fact to drive the point home so stay with me. Remember thinking outside the box is the point. If you don't know where you truly came from, you will always be lost and you will never find your way home, never! It's negative forces out here that want that mindset to exist so that they will always be in power so accept ignorance and things will never change, even down to a simple man & woman relationship.

Here's a good way to explain a thoroughbred as opposed to being a mutt. Irish people come from the Country Ireland and speak their native tongue; Italian people come from the Country Italy and speak their native tongue; Germans come from a Country called Germany and speak their native tongue; Moroccans come from Morocco and speak their native tongue; Liberians come from Liberia and speak their native tongue; Koreans come from Korea and speak their native tongue; Chinese come from China and speak their native tongue. Another thing they all have in common is the land from which they came from, cultural philosophies, their own Flag, their own constitution and their own customs. No known nationality is named after a continent, none! So if you come from Black, Colored, Afro-American, African-American, Negro or White where the hell is that Country and what is your native tongue? No people on the planet are named after a continent or an adjective. People are named in relation to the country-land they have nativity too which makes up part of that continent. North America, South America, Africa, Asia, Europe, for your information, "Europe is not a true continent." You will never find Europe on a globe or map, it's a conglomerate of combined Countries. Exactly like the North America Union, the European Union, African Union and the Asian Union. Australia and Antarctica are all continents, not countries. There is no culture of people who are named after the continent they live on, except Australia because they have a Country within the continent named, Australia. So no matter where pedigree people go on Gods great earth they are still connected to their country of origin in relation to purebred nationality and their culture. We are all Children of the most high so why concern your selfish idle minds with adjectives which are superficial in the grand scheme of things, this is partly why we fall because we are misled and misguided instead of leading ourselves. Most of You have a lazy mindset of, I will follow. For most of you to lead is too much responsibility. That's the problem and the reason we fell and can't get up. Your choice to follow denatured yourself and caused you to fall out of tune with creation and the God in you. Which in turn causes a ripple effect with the universe "everything living is connected in one way or another" and you have multiple isms that's hard to reverse because you can't see the forest for the trees. You start to justify your faults by blaming everybody else which is the beginning of your demise. **Take responsibility for your own actions and life will start to change for you and all around you.**

I'm on a quest to find answers; does that make me a bad person in your eyes? If so, so be it and I love you to. Your beliefs do not dictate my actions and my actions are pure and with good intent for all of humanity so Creation and I are one with my decision and that's one helluva good feeling. Questioning my soul purpose in life and the variations in teachings in regards to religious studies that encompass all religions and why people do what they do is my dilemma. The validity of ethics and principals of religious teachings coupled with a thirst for knowledge-light and the understanding whereof. To open the minds and eyes of people who have similar questions and people who gave up on the Creator-God because they never understood or knew the true essence of the Creator or who God is. I do not question the existence of God-Creator, just the fallacious teachings-programming. I will be rhetorical and or repetitive at times and I purposely do it to drive the point home because everyone isn't traveling at the same speed and I respect that. One scripture read: Ask and it shall be given you; seek and ye shall find; knock and it shall be opened unto you: For every one that ask receive and he, she that seek find; and to him-her that knock it shall be opened. I think the correct scripture is **Matthew 7:7–8**

It seems as thou all of these scriptures elude to asking questions, so who would I ask God? I was taught; don't question the word of God, so that's out. But my Creator-Father gave me the ability to be inquisitive and curious just like Adam & Eve was. It's a human trait. So I started asking questions to the people I confided in. The pastor, He said the same thing the Sunday school teacher said. The congregation, the congregation said, "Don't question Gods word because he works in mysterious ways. The Sunday school teacher, she said, once you have the spirit of God the word will be revealed unto you. I thought I was born with the spirit of God because holy breath is spirit and in order for me to live, God breathed the breath of life into me. A deacon, He said, God knows all things and when he feels the time is right, your question will be answered, pray on it son. Huh? None of these answers sat well with me. My spirit wasn't fulfilled, I became spiritually deprived and I was hungry for answers that would fulfil me spiritually & mentally. The only place to go was outside the box. I also wondered why woman were not mentioned much throughout the scriptures. Ok smart ones, I said mentioned much or hardly at all, "like; Ester, Ruth, Miriam, Jael, Lilith and Deborah. Why everything centered on men. Even the beginning was all about men. To this very day, God which is a title and not a name is referred to as a he, but spirits don't have genders only God's children have genders. Some names of God are, Allah, Jehovah, Yahweh, and Lucifer, yes Lucifer, the Angel of Light. I will explain in another chapter for those who don't understand. I always wondered if religion always portrays Lucifer as this dark being of the under-world. How can Lucifer be the Angel of Light but represent darkness at the same time? In the same light, why is Lucifer alluded to as a man? Is it only men in Heaven? I know all the gay men would love that. Any whoo, other questions plagued my mind as well, like Eve who was so-called deceived into eating the fruit. The problem I see with this is, the devil was beautiful, cunning, smarter and on the level of the Creator who created him, not little old Adam & Eve who's eyes-"mind" were close, dumb, deaf & blind. If you believe Eve was the 1st lady on the planet, then think about this. There are People of this era who have been reported to have DNA thousands of years older than the story of Adam and Eve. So how would religious scholars explain that anomaly? Adam and Eve were both dumb, deaf & blind, created that way by Jehovah and knowing that truth, how can ignorance sin? Ignorance doesn't know knowledge and you can only commit sin if you know the difference between right and wrong. Remember, based on his-story the tree contained knowledge and not their minds/brains. Adam and Eve never knew they were naked until after they received knowledge from a tree in the form of fruit. Is it safe to say, they had the psyche of a child. The so-called cave-man and woman existed at a specific time period and they were primitive and intellectually deprived. I wonder what their mind-state was in that era. As far as I know history does not mention any of them sinning and practicing religious, does it? I said that to emphasize the fact that if we can agree that cave people didn't have a clue in their life time and science emphasizes that mankind as well as the brain evolves over time. How many thousands of years did it take for the cave man evolution to evolve to the mental state that they were in, in comparison to that of Adam and Eve? The word Naïve-"**Na-Eve**": actions showing **lack** of worldly **experience and understanding**; a **person or action** showing a **lack of experience, wisdom, or judgment; inexperience,** what experiences can Eve refer too that would show her right from wrong or good from bad, even though her and Adam were told what not to eat from the tree. I will be partially pretentious, if you will, just to drive home my point. Children don't know what not to do until you chastise or discipline them or tell them that their actions are not tolerated. At that point they start to understand what right and wrong could be. They still can't comprehend the full understanding of right and wrong or good vs evil yet because they are in the beginning learning phases of life. Before the infamous apple story, Adam and Eve never did anything bad or sinful to be taught about the differences between right and wrong. By the same token, how could Adam have known he was lonely if he was the only person on the planet? He had no one or nothing to compare loneness too. You must be exposed to other people and have those people taken away from you to experience loneness. How could Adam name all the animals on the planet when he was residing or limited to the Garden of Eden at that time? He was naked and you can only be naked in warm or hot weather. I deal with common sense and as they say, "If it don't make dollars, it don't make cents." I only deal with facts and your protocols don't make sense and we haven't had nothing in common ever since. So since I know what I'm up against, I'll stick to what I know is important because that's a win-win. (*Para-phrased it*) Thanks Jay Z ☺ FYI, there is documented fact scientist and doctors found DNA in modern day living people which carbon dates far beyond the lives of Adam and

Eve? If you don't know, now you know. Do the research for yourself. Maybe that's why someone created these books eons later, "**B**asic **I**nformation **B**efore **L**ife **E**ver-Lasting." "Torah, Shruti, Tipitaka, Bible, Qur'an, Book of Mormon, I Ching and more. So called Adam and Eve were made of flesh just like you and I so how could you say, there was no sin before she eat the apple. She was made of sin via flesh. Flesh was the 1st sin, not Eve eating the primordial apple or committing an act of sin. If God told her what not to do, how could she fully comprehend it? She couldn't even comprehend the fact that she was naked, that's how naive she was, are you kidding me. God made both of them closed minded. Crazy as it may sound; Lucifer opened their minds and allowed them to receive knowledge. That's if you all agree that Lucifer deceived her and since you do, you have to acknowledge that as well. Remember Satan and God told them both the same thing after they ate the apple, "your eyes are open and now you became like one of **us, knowing good and evil**." Just that quick they both knew all aspects of good and evil, right from wrong Houdini huh? That was after your so-called deception. Before that, they knew nothing because they were both dumb as a rock. Don't get upset with me, take out the book and read it again, it's not rocket science. Question, so Jehovah created them dumb and Lucifer made them smart? I'm just asking. Furthermore they were human and the devil was on a much higher level. I will be painfully blunt, a God Level. Here's proof, if the battle of Armageddon-Holy jihad is a war between good and evil, which is Satan and God, Right? Ok then, to have a war, the opposing force has to be closely matched with the opponent; if not there is no need to war. It would be a landslide victory for God. "Unless you are like the Bush's administration and you cheat to win" So with that being said, for the Church to say women are weaker than men because Eve was so-called deceive by Lucifer and he chose her instead of Adam. Is it because she was the opposite sex? Spirits cannot have genders but some of you might think so. I would allude to the fact that it sounds like it's basically a male chauvinistic deception, right? *"Just to keep women quite in the Church, by the way"* That's a crime/sin committed by the Church right? I will break it down further in another chapter. Now back to the devil, Adam & Eve's spiritual and mental state of mind could not compare to Satan's spiritual power. I don't see the deception; I see human nature being inquisitive and curious with a thirst for knowledge by Eve. Eve was a leader, Satan never told her to eat anything. It's her own curiosity that lead her to do so. Its human nature to be that way, Eve was not the weak one, Adam was, she told Adam to eat the fruit and he did what she told him to do, because Eve was "For all of you who believe his- story" deceived by a higher power and Adam & Eve share the same mental plane, so in essence, Adam is the weaker one. Who wouldn't take the chance to be like God? Satan told Eve the same thing God told Adam, read it again and you will see it right here in black and white no translation needed. Furthermore; "you won't surely die," is not a deception. That meant you won't die instantly. Unless I'm brain dead, my level of comprehension tells me that even if you are convinced that the term, "You won't surely die means that Eve was deceived, **being deceived is not a sin** and on the other hand she was still dumb as a lark and **ignorance is not a sin**. It's a crime by human definition; ignorance is 9 tenths of the law☺ Eve was to dumb too commit a crime. She would have died whether she ate the fruit or not. Because the wages of sin is death and she was made of flesh and flesh is the 1st sin. Stop denying the truth, the truth will set you free. Again I remind you that to understand something is to be liberated from it. I went through all of that to show you the fallacies in the Adam and Eve story just to tell you this. I will liberate you twice. Do you know that the untold truth about Adam and Eve is a fable made up by the Catholic Church to justify the religious existence of humanities' plight of good versus evil? Because of their sacred loyalty-oath that propagates collusion they will not talk about it. But if you ask and Bishop or Cardinal this question, I would hope that his conviction for his people/Gods children is stronger than the doctrine he teaches. Did you ever stop to ask why there isn't a female Bishop or Cardinal? The few that have asked that question, are you really content with that answer, are you really"

Genesis 3:4 Satan 1st- For **God** doth know that in the day you eat thereof, your eyes shall be opened and you shall be as **gods** knowing good and evil. Wow! Excerpt from my KJV at home. This is what the talking snake told Eve. Snake meaning; slick or real snake? Or real story?

Genesis 3:22 God– The man has now become like **one of us**, knowing good and evil. This is what the talking spirit with vocal cords called God told Adam. Excerpt from my KJV at home. Knowing that the Creator is the **God "Big G"** of all things and since the Creator created us in his image and likeness along with God's spirit in us to animate our bodies, it would make common sense that we are **gods. "Little g"** I'll tell you why in another chapter

Remember this book isn't to bash or disrespect anyone, person or religious sect. The issues I had with some religious teaching and the contradictions thereof is all I'm expressing and these issues are what lead me to write this bible I mean book, Well laugh out loud because bible means book in the Greek language. **"Basic Information Before Life Everlasting"** Question for you, what's bad about knowing the difference between good and evil? If you had a chance to be like God would you take it? Don't lie! If Adam and Eve didn't know good and evil does that make them robots, puppets or just dumb as hell? Just asking, so what do you think? Would you rather be ignorant or educated? Just asking, Why would the almighty Creator want his creations to be ignorant=eyes closed and once their eyes-mind was opened by Lucifer they were punished forever, forever ever, forever ever, yup longer than a lifetime we are talking for eternity. I have more questions relating to why I wrote this book in the chapter called, "Questions' repetitive huh?

And **God said**; Let **us** make man in **our image**, after **our likeness**: God created man in **his** own **image**, in the **image of God** created **he him**; **male and female** created **he** them.

God never made babies he gave that power of creation to us. We have many godly powers I'm just referring to this one for now.

Think about that. Don't take **god** nonchalantly. Our creative power has to come from a higher source because we can't create spirit, we cannot create a natural light called the sun naturally. Nothing that God, Nature, the Universe or higher power has created naturally can we create on the same level. The Creator did give us the power to duplicate which is a restatement to drive the point home.

In order for the words us, we, or our, to exist there would have to be more than one.

Please tell me how did the Greeks and the Israelites agree on who wrote the old and new testaments and they spoke two entirely different languages and the time frames were so far apart, not to mention the lack of navigational skills to experience life in other parts of the world and to assume their God only spawn one group of people to populate the globe and also decided that one biblios would be the deciding factor for the human family regarding everlasting life? Also if all you people who advocate your doctrine as being authentic, why would you hide books, delete and burn books and put information about religion and certain people under armed guard? Did God tell you to do that? (SMH) shaking my head.

Chapter – 4

Hearing vs Listening

Most people do not believe there is a difference between hearing and listening, but it is a major distinction; for instance, you hear everything you are reading in your head while reading this book. If someone gives you a directive, you hear the instruction, but do you act on what you heard?

When you hear your boss, parents, or anyone else telling you what direction to go in or try to assist you with questions you might have and or give you advance on a specific subject or topic of discussion, do you act on the information you hear or do you let it go out of one ear and through the next?

When you hear what is being conveyed by the person talking, do you really care what they say? Are you really listening to the message or the words? Are you faking a response because you want to show respect to the person talking?

If you are hearing the conversation but you are not listening with the intent to act, then you are wasting your time and the person talking to you. So why do it?

Some things that could result from not listening are; a possible job opportunity you could have had or a chance for advancement. Missed opportunities for other people closely connected to you that could affect you in the future. Opportunities to take other paths that would allow you to avoid possible drama for yourself. Not listening might put your reputation on the line because of misunderstandings that can blow out of proportion. Not listening can issue small issues to get out of hand and a loss of respect for you or the other person can ensue and considering the circumstances you can lose everything you worked hard for and the list goes on.

The crazy thing is, most people blame everyone else for their demise, when in reality most of the time you do it to yourself. When you exercise the higher god in you, the drama listed above will be avoided completely. All you have to do is listen to logic and use your common sense to dictate your actions or tell the person talking to you in a respectful tone, you are not interested in the conversation or subject matter, or don't go to that particular person for answers. If you are the type to draw up preconceived answers when asking someone for an opinion or a question, stop asking questions that you think you know the answers too or be submissive and respect the person giving you the answer to the question you're asking about. I always wondered why people would ask me a question and before I could answer it, they had an answer before I did, that always irritated me. Why ask a question? Absorb the understanding of what is meant by this cliché, "it's better to understand than the want too always be understood" "I hope you can hear me and listen to what that cliché is telling you."

Listening on the other hand is a skill that allows your brain to process the meaning of what's being conveyed. Discerning what you hear in order to better understand what someone is saying will help your communication skills and make you more proficient at whatever you do. Listening is a practice that lets you comprehend, construe and put meaning and action to whatever you hear. Listening builds better relationships with family, friends and people from all walks of life. Motivation and respect for the person speaking plays a spirited role in listening, because if you don't respect a person, you will not be motivated to do anything they say even though you hear everything they are saying.

In the same vein; I always tell people that if someone is talking about a topic or subject you don't wanna hear, extract the cream by taking ownership of what part of the conversation has credibility and focus on the valuable of that information, throw the rest away. You have to realize - vagueness is sometimes unavoidable so don't get discouraged have patience and bear with it instead. Don't be so quick as to pass judgment, it's like reading this book, some people pass judgment before completing the book and lose out on the message. They might have read what was being said, but because of other factors they let distract them, they no longer feel the need to listen to the message. Most likely icebergs, closed-mindedness and impatience attributed to them losing focus and respect for the content of the book. You have to understand that the world doesn't revolve around your ideology alone, there's more than meets the eye, so to listen means to accept different interpretations and concepts and act on them "good or indifferent to show that you received the message.

Question, when you hear your higher-self, your lower-self, the Creator, Allah, the Imam, Priest, Bishop, Pastor, Evangelist, God or whoever you listen to when they speak, do you take action?

Answer, to take action is to listen, not to take action is disrespectful to the messenger and yourself unless you know it will cause detriment to you or others.

This is all about **willing** yourself to exercise your higher power. When it's all said and done, we need the exercise our higher power and unit the power of the Creator with 1 mind. Your mind is the tool you need to learn how to control. Refuse to let your mind control you. If something in your mind tells you to do something, remember it's either your **higher** god-self or your **lower** god-self and in essence it's still you, you have the final say as to what **spirit** you will **listen** to. All things considered, it's you in the physical that will see that jail cell, Heaven, Hell, demise, hardships, depression, a hard knock life or a beautiful wonderful fruitful life. It is said that the choice is yours. My philosophy is you don't have a choice if you want a fruitful life. **Choice is not an option.**

Chapter – 5

Programming and Icebergs

Sigmund Freud's view when referring to Icebergs, are similar to what I use.

1. Conscious Mind: Thoughts & Perceptions are at the tip of the Iceberg.
2. Subconscious Mind: Memories and Stored Knowledge are below the water.
3. Unconscious Mind: Fears, Violent Motives, Irrational Wishes, Immoral Urges, Shame, Selfish Desires are in the deepest part of water and are unseen by all.

If you need further understanding relating to this concept, you can visit; processcoaching.com/unconscious after you finish reading the book, that way you won't lose focus on the point I want to get across.

Before we advance to a new level of acceptance, I would like you to understand a part of your brain that most people never knew existed on this level.

With that in mind, from my personal understandings in life, it seems as though through my personal experiences, if a person exposes their self to endless streams of knowledge or shows an interest in learning new concepts, thought processes and have an overall necessity to learn more than the average person, you acquire the ability become well rounded and diversified culturally and it gives you the mental and possible spiritual capacity to acquire discernment in all your actions. It might also effort you the ability to exchange dialogue on just about any subject matter articulated at any given time, which in turn creates endless possibilities and opportunities for you throughout life. On the other hand, you need to know that life is universal in its thought process and not programmed to your philosophy or personal mindset only.

With that being said, understand that life doesn't surround itself around your personal beliefs. Based on your immediate circumstances life can embrace your experiences for a moment or not at all, it's all based on now you perceive things. If you are programmed to think inside a box, you can induce the life you live to embrace your personal beliefs for a lifetime and if you are shelter-minded that can be detrimental to you, your family and future generations. In relation to that statement, some people never expand their minds to the point of diverse understandings of life because they let people, organizations, social-isms and or uncultured doctrines dictate what they should study, read, talk about or not talk about. In life you must learn to overstand universal laws which are the laws of Creation and also understand everything that life encompasses is infinite even after death. With or without you, life will go on, down to the smallest organism. Life isn't just about you and what you believe; life is bigger than one microscopic person in the grand scheme of things. Life is about oneness with life and all the glory you experience and share. To live is to die but to understand life gives life everlasting meaning to all that embrace the comprehension of the thought.

The information in this chapter regarding your mind is vital because it allows you to understand why you think the way you do and why you do the things you do. It helps you to be more in tune with yourself and realize your strengths and weaknesses so that you will be able to create balance in your life through self-analysis. It would be in your best interest to understand the three parts of your mind and master yourself. Mastering yourself will evitable bring you closer to the Creator, and that's unequivocal truth. So remember when you hear that voice in your little head talking to you while in a self-induced trance; aka day-dream or you receive a premonition in your dreams, overstand it's your unconscious or subconscious mind in tune with the universe, which is in sync with Creation and in communion with you to stimulate your conscious spirit leading you in the right direction. This is all possible because; "Greater is he that is in you than he that is of the world"

On another note but looking through the same eye, when it comes to the way you react to spontaneous situations and the way the conscious side of information is processed is attributed to these examples. What you see when you look in the mirror and what other people see in their minds when they look at you is usually a different perception in relation to the concept of icebergs. For example, the Titanic did not sink because it hit the tip top of the iceberg: it was the larger masses of ice beneath the water that wasn't visible by the naked eye which did the irreversible damage. By the same token, when you look at this real life example and convert it into a metaphor and apply it to yourself, I hope it will help you understand how the mind works in relation to your actions, deeds, and thought processes. Throughout this book I ask that you keep an opened mind so that the icebergs you have won't give you "Chronic Voluntary Mind Block" meaning: you stop reading because you refuse to open your mind to new concepts. Therefore, you block out the possibility of what's being conveyed in the book because of the icebergs you had trapped in your subconscious or unconscious mind since you were a child. Those icebergs are isms and beliefs you held on to all your life. As a result you never challenged them due to the perpetual programming of information that was embedded in your mind via TV shows, movies, images, mis-education, society, popular opinion, religion, private organization, etc. Consequently, everything you were programmed to believe became your reality regardless of anyone presenting undisputable fact to dispute it. I ask that you lower your wall of impenetrable selfish reason and give yourself another chance to mentally see beyond your self-protected defensive wall of insecurity that's stunting your mental and spiritual growth.

I used Freud's concept to illustrate and point out the 3 parts of consciousness that we all possess and need to control for optimal focus and control of our mind. We need to gain control of our minds and stop letting popular social beliefs' and media dictate our thought processes just to feel socially accepted by the masses. THINK FOR YOURSELF! In the same light, because of greed on a large scale when referring to world government aka the power elite will not allow truth to be told to the masses on a massive scale. However, if you are sincere in your endeavors to uplift your families and yourself, it starts at home and with self. Renew your mind and if we all do the same, we will be one-mind, one collective body, with one common goal. We will be the manifest destiny of an integrated spiritually unified people who willfully freed themselves from oppression without physically coming together. It is definitely a reachable goal. All humanitarian *efforts outside of* disaster relief, philanthropy for organ donors, nonprofit organizations, International publicized crime victims, food water and shelter for some third world countries in direr straits is a far cry from the genuine realistic sustainment for human life. The real problems will never be addressed unless we take action as a collective mind-body. It's like having a pharmaceutical drug prescribed by the doctor and based on what you were taught and lead to believe it might help you with cancer, and at the same time the doctor tells you, that you have an incurable cancer. Now you can say, "What did he just say?" That exactly how all power elite talk to us, in circles, riddles, tax code, and we are left with the ball scratching our heads and we let them get away with that crap. For most of us most man-made drugs will never cure us. Initially they are not designed to cure any dis-ease they are designed to mask the root cause and alleviate the symptoms. The disease is still there even though you feel better but that's the intended illusion. Nevertheless, drugs will mask the origin of the problem and give you temporary relief until you die. The sad thing is you are already programmed and conditioned to believe these falsehoods by thinking a pray a day and the medication will save you. This is all part of your subconscious and or unconscious mind having faith in miss-guided teachings that became your reality because you never took the time to investigate and research for yourself. Most of us take the doctors word because he or she has a PHD "**P**ractice **H**elping **D**ummies" to practice medicine as a practitioner. Much respect to the doctors that are true to their profession and truly desire to help humanity, I profoundly respect your position and in no way would my statement encourage negativity regarding your professionalism as an upright expert clinician. Pondering that thought I reiterate, most drugs never fix the problem. Instead they pacify the issues you have until you mentally submit to the falsehood of being drug dependent which could be transformed as a life time truth in your mind because the doctor said so. The same concept is like what most governments do to the masses. The concept of conspiracy theories is a thing of the pass in the minds of the masses because when you program the masses through a covertly multifaceted corrupt manipulated media and an educational system, award the recipients with prestigious accolades and honors, they naturally believe what they learnt to be right and exact. Their way of thinking becomes a collective delusional thought through the cognitive thought process. It spreads like a contagious disease unbeknown to them; Churches, organizations, colleges, other schools of thought, etc. and the masses are blind as to what they propagate and stand for, the mind and spirit become voluntarily profoundly corrupt. This same mind set and teaching is duplicated over and over again and it becomes a way of life for all who are blind to the realities of the great deception. So you could never win the argument of a conspiracy theory, the masses would say you are one of those crazy people and stone you to death, burn you alive, well that's what they did in the past and it's coming back full circle trust and believe. Reason being is because you will allow it to happen if you don't start thinking for self. To add insult to injury, if you are thought to be one of those people who try to awaken consciousness and the masses follow your lead you will get assassinated, poisoned or locked away for life. In the future they will probably exile you and put you on another planet, "lol: laugh out loud." Remember this; to understand something is to be liberated from it. With that in mind it should be self-evident that governmental focus is never truly about the uplifting of humanity, world peace, physical & mental health, justice or spiritually righteous living as a whole and it will never be. "Absolute power corrupts absolutely" Sir John Dalberg-Acton. Governmental departments tell you GMO's "genetically modified organisms" are good for you and the environment and just as healthy as any other foods on the market; likewise, they say prescription drugs will help your health problems and in the same vein you acquire all types of side effects associated with the drugs, "allergic reactions" and even death. They play on your fears through the threat of major flu out-breaks; out of control crime areas, and most of us accept what they say as the gospel. With that in mind, we should take responsibility while we are still alive and teach our children and families what it takes to be real humanitarians for the sake of bloodline integrity and everlasting life. Where is our moral conviction for humanity, life, true-equality as one human family and where is lawful justice? Some of you might ask why some people are deprived of their history and others are not. What's the big secret? I won't get into the intricacies regarding that topic considering the focus of this book but on the surface, if each culture of people had the proper education and knew their true history and achievements of their ancestors along with their contributions to society that would give each culture a distinct feeling of self-worth, pride and dignity. By the same token, human nature would mentally and spiritually spark greater achievements as a mind collective that would inevitably start motivating people to respect and improve on their positive accomplishments through their ancestral legacies. As a result their cultural philosophies will in turn create positive spiritual motivation affording them the courage to strive to be better as a people and they would continue to grow in a direction of progression which ultimately enhances humanity as a whole.

. The result of this knowledge and understanding would decrease violence and corruption drastically and we as a people collectively would not be on a perpetual downward spiral to damnation by living a life of strife and oppression throughout the world. Duh! "SMH: "Shaking My Head."" The philosophy can even be taught through different schools of thought via making the lessons **sacred** and not **secret.** If the lessons are deemed **sacred**, a sense of pride, respect and ownership comes with that, which would make the lessons much more meaningful and heart felt. We can learn to be in control of our will and an accurate understanding of what will-power really is and how to execute it and control our minds verse having our minds controlled and programmed by governmental politics, society, T.V., peer pressure, religion and propaganda campaigns. "You say "God gave you a choice" so why are you a programmed Robot" Well I will give you the answer; there is information out there that would place world history into its proper perspective. Nonetheless, releasing these sacred ancient facts would not be advantageous for the power elite. The power elite have thrived on ignorance and coerced fallacies with the sole intent to keep the world in a deep sleep to perpetuate multi-level lies to maintain the illusion of dominance to rule and control the wealth of the world for a select few. This is nothing new and if you look at histories past you will see it throughout all the ages. By the way, speaking of greed, know this: it's enough natural resources in the world for everybody's need but not enough for everybody's greed. Back to the point; every culture has a story but you only hear of one dominate story as the tell all be all of cultural world history. We all have a significant role to play in life and if we didn't, nature would not allow us to be here, that's the laws of God, Nature, Universal law or whatever you call it. Everything and everybody has their rightful place in nature. So why can't every culture's story "his-tory" hold a place of important fanfare among the masses? You better know the answer by now.

Most people let their minds and their negative will control them. This book will give you the tools needed to start you on an eye opening journey that will change your life and the many lives that come in contact with you as well. "Change your mind, Change your life."

Keep in mind that there are 3 parts of consciousness but there is only 1 mind. If you are one of the lucky ones that's reading this book at the present time, then you have time to get some of your family in order. 1 by 1 we can help make the world we live in a better place, but it starts with you committing to yourself. "The word **world** in this book refers to the skin you live in as a spiritual being, you will understand why in the ladder chapters" Again you must commit yourself, if you lie to yourself, what good are you to your children, family and humanity. Ask yourself right now, what purpose are you serving here? If you don't strive to achieve divinity and a well-rounded understanding of life, 9'xs out of 10 the closest ones to you will duplicate your actions and this could go on for centuries until someone in the family breaks the chain. As they say, "a mind is a trouble thing to waste" Learn the three layers of the mind and get rid of those harmful icebergs. Again, if you are reading this book you have the power to change that. The overt secret is; "you must have a desire to change for the greater good and longevity of self before helping your children, family and friends. Remember, you are your own worst enemy.

Now that you are ready to open your mind to the concept of mental icebergs, the theory is that, only 10percent of the iceberg is visible and the other 90percent isn't. So what appears on the surface in most people is superficial to a degree. On the other hand, detonating most of who you really are remains is underwater and people see your representative instead of the real you, just a portion of you. Oddly enough and by the same token, they see the real you but you have aged-old issues that conflict with your sound judgment and emotional judgment overrides logic, these aged-old issues are what I also call your icebergs. If you can grasp the fact that you are programmed from birth by what you see, hear, smell, taste and are taught, you can start to understand your mind and how it works to a degree when relating to icebergs and their effects on your decision making and the overall outcome of any situation based on your choice or course of action.

I won't go deep into this subject because that's a different shade of gray "matter," lol. I want you to understand that you have a lot of programming in your subconscious and unconscious mind that appears out of the deepest darkest recesses of your mind and when you can enlighten that part of your mind, you will start to expand your mind and began to understand yourself more clearly. You will gain the ability to act and react with an above average logical and practical approach demonstrating clarity and superior confidence in self, verses an emotional confused irrational general consensus view when it comes to decision making and impulse actions. I will spread some light on the subject so you can see where I'm coming from. To enlighten your-self or to be enlightened, is basically light being shed on the dark part of your subconscious or unconscious self and that light is the revelation that created an epiphany. Some people reject it and some accept it. Depending on where your mental mind-state is at the time of acceptance determines your decision. It's the same with your spirit; they all work on 1 accord if you are balanced as a person. In the same vein, if your spirit is ready to receive the lesson it will and if it's not ready, the spirit will reject it. It all depends on your state of mind and your level of enlightenment. Your spirit and mind needs to be in harmony in order to grow. If you only feed your spirit and not your mind, you are on a spiritual treadmill. You are going nowhere. The same applies for your mind. There are extremely smart people who do not express a higher god spirit being exemplified through them. You can read about them every day or see them on the evening news. Honors student shoots classmates; CEO commits suicide, Priest arrested for molestation.

You have to embrace and identify with your icebergs and de-program your negative thinking by determining what was indoctrinated via a certain group or individuals as law in your own mind at the point in your life when you didn't know any better. As you get older hopefully you will realize that a lot or almost all of what you were taught might have been misinformation and hopefully if it didn't cause irreversible damage to your subconscious or unconscious mind perhaps it will lead you to question your current mind state and your level of understanding more and possibly open up your mind to explore and seek out more answers about life and yourself. Also if you perceive the education, doctrines and dogmas that you have read and learned to be true and you believe it, but something pulls at your spirit and it keeps you from growing spiritually and mentally and it doesn't allow you to think outside the box and or excise your ability to seek and find information outside of that specific agenda or place of fellowship, then wouldn't it be wise to look and learn via other avenues so that you can have more than one view point on a certain subject. Do you go to one doctor and believe his opinion is the one that's always correct? If you are only allowed to read what's in your house, how far can you really go if you ever decide to leave the house? Most people would be afraid to leave because they know nothing else. "It's like being on a job for over 25 years and your company goes out of business, what else do you know?" Do you think that life only consists of the information in your house? If that's the case, why isn't the world as a whole breaking your door down to come in? I bet you answered this with an iceberg answer for an excuse for those people. Maybe they know something you don't.

Jeremiah "17:9-10" the heart is deceitful above all things
and beyond cure. Who can understand it?
Excerpt from my KJV at home.

Emotional situations are not the time to answer questions. Sadly enough people who can't elevate spiritual and mentally 9x's outta 10 always answer with an emotional response, and then when the logic kicks in they regret what was initially said. Your heart will get you in trouble most of the time and as long as you understand that, you will be ahead of the game.

Study about icebergs and learn more about who you really are. Most people don't even know who they are, let alone the other person saying, "Well, let me get to know you 1st and we will see where that goes" You can be with someone for over twenty years and still never know who they really are, what a waste for both of you, That's sad, but it happens. How many times are you going to sleep with men and women you don't even know before you contract a debilitating disease or have constant heart break that drives you to hate or start relations with a different gender and you never realized you are the problem because you never knew you. Maybe you are so selfish that you lived a lie for so long that it became your reality and on your death bed you finally realized the truth about you and you want to confess it to the ones who loved you the most, the same ones you dogged out and treated the worst, the ones you burned bridges with, the ones you turned your back on and they still showed you love.

Lucky you, this is about light at the end of the tunnel; while you are still alive this book will give you the tools to change your life. By the same token, if you are well rounded and not consumed by isms, icebergs and certain doctrines and dogma, the chances of you being **consumed** by selfish people or people who are not mentally and spiritually mature is slim to none. The bottom line is there is more to you than meets the eye and you need to learn yourself. If you are always confused and over analytical about everything, you need to accept that you have major issues, deep under lying issues. Grab those issues from your subconscious mind and fix it so that you can make progress. You are restricting your growth and if people tell you this all the time and you even say it to yourself on occasion and you're doing nothing about it. You're in serious denial. Only you can pull you out of the hell fire. The truth will set you free, but you have to know that to be true. Only you have the power to fix you, but you have to know that. Strip yourself of all the excuses, and stop blaming other people for your lewd actions and be mature enough to be the man or woman you should be and look in the mirror and make yourself the responsible party for all of your actions, good, bad, or indifferent. I would rather be ashamed of myself than for someone else to be ashamed of me. I would rather have self-embarrassment than to embarrass myself around others. Don't you know most people see the games we all play and for the sake of not arguing they don't mention it and some just don't care if you make a fool of yourself, they just avoid you and you wonder why they always avoid you? Really, you really think people don't know you are full of crap? It's you that don't know who you are, and that's sad. The truth of the matter is, in the end you are only playing yourself.

Chapter – 6

Questions

1. If the Creator is our father why does he threaten to burn us in the hell fire for eternity and allow Satan, God's ex-best friend to be the gate keeper? Would you accept your biological father or mother punishing or burning you for what your older sisters and brothers did because you didn't listen to them?

2. If the Creator is our father why can't we question his actions? That's like a parent saying. "Do as I say not as I do," would you respect that kind of a parent?

3. Why would God create one man to have dominion over the earth all by himself knowing he would get lonely? Its human nature to yearn for companionship, right? On the contrary, how would human nature know it was lonely if it never experienced other humans?

4. Did Adam have a scrotum & penis when he was created because besides urination the sole purpose of a penis is for procreation combined with the scrotum, I'm I right? God could have had him urinate from another part of the body just like birds do. I'm just saying it wouldn't make sense to have a scrotum and you're the only man alive.

5. 5.   Why would God punish me and my family for what Adam & Eve did? I don't even know them. I guess forgiving them doesn't apply because Jesus wasn't here yet,

huh? He came and sacrificed his life for us, so why are we still being punished, and when is he coming back and what's the purpose, really?

6. If God sacrificed his self, meaning committed suicide for his creations, why come back again, you did your work, we can just meet you in heaven as planned.

7. Why punish the generations after Adam & Eve, a generation is twenty years long, five generations is a hundred years, why couldn't the punishments stop after that. Are you serious?

8. Why does our father threaten us with eternal damnation and Satan gets out of jail after 6000 years? Hell, there are flags older than that. Satan has been out eons ago.

9. Why did God kill everyone in the bible and Satan isn't mentioned one time that I know of for killing anyone, spreading plagues, burning cities, burning or killing new born babies or having people suffer to prove who's loyal and who's not. Just asking.

10. God knows everything so why would God punish Adam & Eve, knowing they would eat the fruit before Adam was even created. What's the logic in that? Don't ask, huh.

11. If Jesus taught people all those years, why didn't he write the teaching in a book like everybody else? Why didn't he write scriptures that reflect his teachings and deeds and why did other people talk for him in third party figures of speech throughout the bible?

For your information, I know some of these questions are to profound for some of us to answer but yet I had them on my mind and I'm sharing what's on my mind. Those are some of the questions that inspired me to write this book and simultaneously I'm hoping to open your mind's eye because I'm a child of the Creator just like you. Coincidentally I have the answers to the questions in this chapter.☺ If his son, Jesus *"our brother"* can make a blind man see I'm inspired to make groups of God's children see. Before you finish this book

your eyes shall be open and you will be like **gods** knowing good &
evil. Stop believing & start knowing.

12. We know what was taught but I have to ask. Why would
the Almighty impregnate a mortal woman to save us from
us, descending down to our level to prove a point regarding
humiliation, *"and still threaten to burn us"* when contrary to
that logic, I was taught to never come down to your level but
bring you up to mine. Is it me or what? I'm just saying who's
teaching this stuff. It's like God belittled himself to save the
people he created knowing we would be unruly and give
the unruly to his ex-friend Satan to watch over them as they
burn in hells pit of fire.

13. Would you stoop down to your children's level as a parent or
would you bring them up to yours.

14. If God is everywhere all the time why does he need Satan
as the Guardian of Hell, just kill his sorry ass, ultimately he
can't kill Satan if he wanted to. I'll explain in another chapter,
wait until you read that stuff. Also it is said that. "Jesus sits on
the thrown next to God in Heaven while Satan is on Earth
wreaking havoc on God's children." Hum? A spirit has eyes?
Spirits can sit on thrones? God makes itself flesh as a person-
savor named Jesus and watches itself, talks to itself up there?
God let's Satan torture his children while the two that are
supposed to be one Jesus and God, watch and wait? Wow!
If I did that to my children the "Department of Human
Services" would put me under the jail and my children would
denounce me forever, but my children wouldn't do that to
God because it's ok if God does it.

15. If Satan is so disrespectful and evil, why is he still alive
and why does he have the right to watch Gods disobedient
children burn forever in the Hell fire? Does my soul-spirit
have nerve ending? Are nerves the reason why we will feel
pain while burning forever in the hell fire? I thought my
spirit was energy trapped in a body to give the body life and

to be returned back to the essence meaning; the Creator after the body dies, so how could energy feel pain; it's already fire/ energy? Right?

16. One of the worst ways to die is by fire. But to be alive and burn forever is so inhumane but we won't be human at that point so I guess it's cool and you people accept it without spiritual recourse. My child does and he said to me he's cool with this as long as God does it, but if I told him I would do the same, its abuse and he won't tolerate that from his father only his father God.

17. Why would God separate everyone and cause confusion and change all languages at the "Tower of Babel." It is said the reason for that was they were building a tower to reach him. What language did everyone speak before they spoke different ones? Oh that's not important huh? Why? What language did God speak, even though spirits don't have vocal cords, lips and tongues? "Don't get so uptight, free speech is our 1st amendment" That's the funniest lesson I ever learned about. God is too great to reach. The physical form of "people-flesh" could never see him anyway and the Creator's spiritual essence is on an entirely different Godly plane. To top it all off we can't even breathe at very high altitudes. The air is to thin, If you don't acclimatize properly you will eventually develop High altitude pulmonary edema, or high altitude cerebral edema, who would have known that back then but God so it wasn't necessary to cause such a calamity at the top of the tower, People have so called, "tried to" "fly to the moon and other planets," nothing is happing to them.

Think of this as well, most cultures have their own native tongue and each cultural tongue has a different language and meaning of words that are in contrast to the next cultural language. Some cultures don't even use words that other cultures use. In that respect, translations will vary drastically. So that would mean interpretations vary as well. We should realize by now as a people whatever culture is dominate in a particular geographical area will most likely be the one to tell his-story.

18. Why Christians have Church on Sunday which is the 1st day of the week and the 7th day God rested and said, "**Remember the Sabbath Day Keep It Holy**" people argue about working, washing clothes, cleaning the house etc. on Sunday. I have to bust your delusional bubble. Saturday is the Sabbath day, it's the 7th day of the week and God rested on the 7th day. To enlighten Christians who don't know why they go to Church on Sunday, it's because Jesus rose from the dead during a time now called, Easter the 3rd day which happened to fall on a Sunday so in commemoration of Jesus being risen from the dead, The "Counsel Nicaea" Church decided to have Church on Sunday even if it is against what God said, but who questions the Church. The other reason is because they still wanted to emulate the worshiping of the sun, which they probably will not admit. The Counsel of Trent had a lot to do with Reformation, read about it when you have the time. Now that I opened Pandora's Box, I have to go hard or go home. I hope I opened your mind a little for what you are about to bear witness too.

One of my objectives in writing this book was to find a way to present the information without offending anyone. What I have learned in life is that people run from that which they don't understand or feel threatened by. You should never never-ever run from adversity-trials and tribulation-tests whatever you call them. I elaborate about adversities more in the chapters ahead. Brace yourself for a high speed ride. Fasten your seat belts and put on your thinking caps. It was once said, "The goals set as a youth may not have been reached but one weighted with years feels it is useless to strive to achieve them." I beg to differ, why? I'm living proof that the goals I have set as I sit here and write this book have not been reached, this is true, but the power of the Creator in me will not let me quit due to old age "whenever that comes" because Universal law helps those who help themselves and I will never stop traveling and seeking light, not until the dirt is thrown over my physical face and by that time I will be light in its purest form, God-body, back to my essence. I thank you all in advance for your desire for knowledge wisdom and the quest for understanding. For you are the ones chosen to carry and pass the torch. Destiny said so or you wouldn't be reading this book. The next chapters are spiritual modus operandi and ways to evoke your will power vested in you to triumph in the battle between good and evil and how to abandon your F.E.A.R.S. in regards to fighting this spiritual war. Remember that f.e.a.r. is; False Evidence Appearing Real, sorta like the blue sky, aqua blue water, a yellow sun, white water, the boogie-man, ghost, monsters, Wizard of Oz and the dark but that's nothing to fear, it's all just False Evidence Appearing Real.

CHAPTER – 7

COMMON SENSE VS BOOK KNOWLEDGE

There is a huge difference between book knowledge and common sense. Let's say an extremely huge difference. You can't find common sense on the internet, at the library, in a class room, at a lecture hall, a biology lab, intellectual conference, or in a book. But you can find book knowledge in all the places I just mentioned. You will never learn common sense or anything related to it by reading or searching about it. The way you acquire Knowledge is by experience, reading, have a degree of intellect and through academia but not common sense. I call people who are smart or well versed in a subject with no clue of common sense, "smart dummies" we can agree that they are smart but they lack the greatest gift of all, common sense. They really are clueless. I don't think I could survive without having common sense, I really don't know how they do it.

Common Sense is all through this book. I have to say this, when I was in college I remember people in biology and psychology class doing experiments straight out of the books and not factoring in circumstances that wouldn't be in the books. I would tell them you can't do it that way because it won't work unless you do x-y-z first. They all say the same thing, "but the book said." I looked at these people like, you can't be serious, are you for real, laughing my ass off (L.M.A.O.) on the inside. Bottom line is, people with common sense can learn knowledge and become intelligent but it appears to be that most people with intelligence can't learn common sense. People with both are well-rounded and avoid more pit falls in life and are more likely to be out going. While we are at it, I will tell you what wisdom is. Wisdom is the combination of Knowledge, Experience and Understanding. When those three experiences bond together as one it produces wisdom.

I said all that to say, the same thing applies to religious doctrines. The Hebrews wrote the Old Testament and the Greeks wrote the New Testament. You have two entirely different groups of people from two different periods of time, education, knowledge, history, language, dictatorship and common sense who all played a vital role in writing and translating the bible, Sunna, Koran, Quran, and other religious books as well. Prime example are the words, Koran and Quran, they both mean the same thing. Depending on where you live, your belief system and what you are taught will lead you to spell the word one way or the next. People will argue over which spelling is the correct one, which Koran or bible is the right one. Which sect of Islam was the first to spell it correctly? Which religion came before the other, to prove religious authenticity? You name it and the argument will ensue. All of this is superficial in actuality but people lose focus on Allah and focus on the doctrines and superficial isms. I will get back to the topic of common sense.

Common sense would tell my spirit the truth based on what I have witnessed in my lifetime thus far regarding religious differences, wars over who is right and wrong and also what I have learned over the years about ancient history, law, language, etymology, the Kings who ruled and made the laws during their reign to suit their lifestyles. Last but not least, the different origins of religions left me with the thought that there could be a considerable amount of room for human era regarding translations, transliterations, conflicting philosophies, and false or mis-leading information. So with that wealth of information, common sense would tell me to check it out **before** I personally take any religious books for face value or make it self-evident in my mind as absolute unequivocal fact. So I went on a pain staking quest to find out for myself the truth about life as a whole. I considered dealing with three major aspects of life, well major in my eyes, you may see other aspects of life more important, but that's your opinion and you are entitled to your opinion. My major three are; Health, law and ancient history. If you don't know about health based on how the medical industry focuses on the business aspects of health and not the physical aspects of medicinal healing and the pharmaceutical industries focus on drug selling instead of disease and chronic disorder prevention, either you will die young, in agony or take medication for the rest of your miserable life. Are you praying God willing help you get better? Your family will be the same way. I want to die of natural causes like my great grandparents did. How many people die that way now? Some people never even heard of natural causes and the ones who did, forgot they existed. We all have to go, but you don't have to go in pain. I had to study law and for me not to, law means: wal backwards. If you don't know the law, any unjust act can be your demise and you would never know because you didn't study the law. My people are destroyed because of the lack of knowledge. The lack of an overstanding of law and the "color of law" system that you are subjected too is pulling certain cultures apart and slowly breaking down your will to overcome adversity.. That's why most people keep running into a brick wal and also the reason why most innocent people are incarcerated as we speak. I found out that studying law and his-tory is synonymous and so is health to a degree. You can't study one without the other. I noticed a trend with all three, each time his-story was written so was new laws. But the only laws that never changed throughout his-story were the law of the Creator. The Creator's laws are always a constant as it still is and as it will be. The Creator's laws are the true "Cardinal Law" the laws I'm referring to are not in the book, if you think I'm talking about the "Ten Commandments" Not the laws that were given to you, Nature's laws and the laws of Creation. Read on you will find them in another chapter if you don't know. The crazy things about divine laws are, that they express common sense not rocket science and you don't need a book to know about them. Once you read the laws, you will see. ☺

Question, wouldn't it make sense to have knowledge and experience of the subject you are engaged in with the understanding that most of the time common sense must play a role in your thought process in order to get a true full overstanding of the subject matter based on the, "what if" factor. If you read a book on how to play football, cook, build a house, or fix a car, there are factors that come into play that are not in the book. Playing strictly by the book without any common sense factored in place sets the tone for the possibility that you will lose, get seriously injured or have a fatal accident. You hear about it all the time because people always say, "Why didn't they just do this or they should have done that. Again, "My people are destroyed for lack of knowledge" Use your God-given gift of common sense and stop being so naïve and tenacious.

Life is a process and to live is a process. When it come to your passion to defend your position about your religious doctrine and say, that's what the book said, that's what Abraham said, that's what Mohammed said. Most of the time, those statements are weak because there is no true foundation to stand on besides what somebody else said. Just because they said it and its popular belief, doesn't mean he or she is right. That type of attitude reveals you are; close-minded, selfish or lazy or all three because most of you took a passage that someone else said for face value and never questioned the other factors based on the content. Do you examine material you read or do you take everything that is deemed credible by society, the media and the powers that be at face value? You don't know the processed they went through to arrive at their answers or the mindset or intention of the people who translated the words. The people who translated the words ages ago definitely were not versed in linguistics to the degree that we are now and possibly made translation errors. If you never studied variations of a language, dialect, syntax and or etymology you would never know if the translation is correct or incorrect and you still take what he or she said for face value. That's equates to being subject illiterate, having "chronic voluntary mind block," closemindedness, selfishness and lazy. This is another way to show you that faith without works is dead. You might have faith in the word you read but you never did the work-research to figure out the process that it took to understand why Abraham, Mohammed or whoever drew their conclusions about that particular subject matter or if it was conveyed in its original syntax the way it was communicated to you.

With that in mind, you need to understand the processes of life in order to understand God. Take this book for example; if you go straight to the chapter called "Who is God" and assume that you will know God and make a statement defending your position about God because you like the book, you are sadly mistaken. The whole book is written in a specific process for you to understand totally that God is more then what you were taught or what that one chapter is about or much more than what you conceive and believe. The only way you can get the full overstanding of the Creator is to read the whole book from beginning to end and understand the processes of spirit, higher-self, lower-self, mental and spiritual focus, the bio-chemistry link between you and God, religious psychological programming, social programming, attributes of God, Creation, Nature and Universal laws, image indoctrination and other aspects of life which are explained in detail throughout the book. Before I proceed remember this, constant exposer to redundant application of false doctrine and history which is coerced and overtly demonstrated will generate a subversive reaction to true doctrine and history causing the masses to view what was once true as false and what is false to be true.

In order to understand, "Who God Is or Who Is God" going straight to that chapter is cheating yourself of the reality and the purpose of this book, life and the fact that you will never know who God is. If you notice, "Who is God" is not the last chapter because there is more to the Creator than one chapter and I purposely added other jewels about God in the chapters preceding the, "Who is God" chapter to teach people who like to cheat too stop cheating their self in life because you will always **miss all the Heavenly glory**. The way you will know you didn't understand who God is, is when someone who read the book, talks about the aspects of God you didn't read about or if you stay seated in your old ways and your spiritual vibration doesn't elevate to a higher level after reading this book. At that point, you have to go back and read this book again if you care to get the full overstanding. Cheating is not in the process of a peaceful life, laziness is not in the process of an abundant life. The process of a life takes work; the process of living a fruitful life takes work. You need to work smarter not harder and you will reap the benefits, cheating gives you the allusion of easy. But when you cheat you never reality understand or know about the subject you cheated on and if that subject comes back in your life to enhance you as a person or to advance you or your family to a higher level in life, you wouldn't know nothing about what you should know because you cheated yourself from learning when you had the chance to understand. You just lost the opportunity to grow because you cheated and you wonder why your life is so hard and people like you blame everybody else to justify your **self-inflicted ignorance**. You need to learn to exercise your higher spirit and be a leader and your world will be a better place and so will mine. I will give you the benefit of the doubt and say, most likely, like everyone else, you were taught wrong. You should have been taught to sacrifice and to work hard as a young adult so life can be easy as you mature later. With sacrifice and relentless focus comes reward. Once rewarded, then you will have found one of the secrets to life everlasting and your reward would be to read this book in its entirety.

Now that you overstand a little about common sense vs book knowledge, I would like to share my views about Déjà vu and reincarnation. This would also appear to be common sense in my book. Wow! This is my book and with that in mind. If you have déjà vu you are most likely experiencing a spiritual epiphany. You couldn't have been in the same place you are in now and have been in the same place in another lifetime because the place you had your déjà vu did not exist in the state that it is now or the previous life. Neither did the furniture or scenery that you see, it wasn't there either just as you see it now. Nothing in this lifetime existed in the previous one except the Creator and the people, places and things that came with that era. How do I know, because the people who lived in those times showed pictures of people, places, things, clothes and etc. of what that era looked like, common sense. What you have witnessed in a *déjà vu*, none of those items or moments was in existence. If you see a person that looks like a person in a crowd next to you or whatever and the scene looks like you saw it before you are most likely experiencing a spiritual epiphany. No one has ever recalled the exact events before or after a déjà vu. It's possible that time as we know it stops for a couple of seconds in your conscious mind and your sub-conscious mind takes a snap shot and a split second later the snap shot appears in your conscious mind without you being aware and that triggers you to have déjà vu. I can't phantom any other logical explanation. Nothing else makes common sense. You picking up what I'm putting down?

Déjà vu means you somehow have already witnessed something in your mind that happened for the first time, which leads me to reincarnation because déjà vu in regards to reincarnation would appear to have a spiritual connection. If you were reincarnated from a previous life it would make sense to have a recollection of your previous life via déjà vu so you can make progress in your future life which is the present life. Déjà vu if logical would trigger occurrences that happened in your previous life to help and support you in your reincarnated present life so you would not make the same mistakes and or *déjà vu would warn you of dangers you should avoid. I'm stating this from a universal law prospective because that's the only constant that doesn't change. Also universal law is pro-life, that's the stand point from which I'm referring to in respect to a positive outcome regarding déjà vu in correlation to reincarnation. I had to break-down the reason for my hypothesis because I know the nah-sayers are being who they are born to be.* Any who, if those factors aren't expressed, it is safe to say that reincarnation doesn't make sense and the only possible way reincarnation can be relevant is if you are reincarnated and/or recreated as the same life form or a different life form to perpetuate life via universal law. I express this to a slight degree in my commentary regarding, "The Beauty of Death"

CHAPTER – 8A

EXPERIENCE & AGE

Experience: Something Adam and Eve did not have. Direct observation of or participation in events as a basis of knowledge, that statement is undeniable. Experience is also the fact or state of having been affected by or gained knowledge through direct observation or participation, the act or process of directly perceiving events or reality. Thank you (Merriam-webster.com) for helping convey my message. The word experience spawns fact in my book.

Experience

Your experiences of a particular situation or events and/or different aspects of life dictate how you perceive things in your own mind. Not what you were taught as a child and or adult. What you are taught and what you experience are to different things. What you have seen as a child and the same things you see as an adult are very much different. But nothing changed except your perception. The more you are exposed to different things and events, the larger your perception. The less you are exposed to different things and events, your perception narrows. If you read one book all your life, your life will be centered on just that, "one experience." Life is more than North America, South Philly, the Masonic hall, your Church, Masque or the city you live in. Life is different all across the globe and once you experience more in life your perception will adjust to the experience. Your belief system is simply that, "Your B.S." To expand your mind you need to experience life to see what it has to offer and once you start your journey, you won't see life through just one book or one experience. Everything you understood about life will have a new perspective. The more you understand life the easier it gets. The more you understand yourself through experiences, trials, tribulations and adversities the easier it gets to cope with life on your terms because you came to understand yourself and how to handle different situations virtually stress-free. It's like a relationship, the more you understand the person you are with, the bond between you gets stronger, or you depart because your perception changed from what you thought you saw in them in the beginning. Due to the fact that when your experience was limited because the relationship was new, you couldn't see everything you needed to see, you needed time to be exposed to the actions of that person in different circumstances to see how they perceive and handle situations. If the actions are acceptable, you stay, if not, you leave. The people that stay any way waste years in a relationship that's going nowhere. I did it. I'm glad I'm out of the stage in my life! The message I want to convey is simple. Be a sponge in life, absorb everything you can, ask questions and always seek to understand instead of wanting to be understood all the time. If you always want to be understood you will never learn the lesson being taught because you will always over talk the teacher. By the way, no matter what age you are that's a sign of immaturity, insecurity and a lack of confidence.

When it comes to experience, here's a parable to help you understand life through my eyes. Life is like a massive door with a combination lock. There are a billion combinations to each lock but only 1 combination will open the door. Once you pass the 1st door you have other aspects of life beyond those doors with many other doors that have combination locks as well. There are countless facets and experiences behind each door. Once you have found the combination-experience through a particular door, you can advance to the next because the area of life that you just experienced has elevated your spirit and mind to the next level of understanding, which in turn changed your perception and or gave you a new comprehension and self-identification that there was once no factual understanding. To sum it all up you just experienced what life and maturity really is to a degree and for your information, I also broke down maturity again in a different chapter.

Age: The times in your life when you are mentally brought to maturity. The legal and or physical age is really superficial when considering the level of maturity someone has. So don't form prejudice opinions about someone based on their chronological age, be mature enough to give people a chance to show their maturity level to create the best possible outcome.

Chapter – 8B

Age

They say, "Age is nothing but a number" that's true in regards to experience. But when you look at it from a legal prospective, the problem with the age of 18 & 21 as an adult is the fact that most people know right from wrong at those ages but for some reason most are still immature. You can get charged with murder and tried as an adult at 18 but you can't drink alcohol until you are 21. "Huh?" Most 18 & 21 years still don't have a clue about accountability, most of them are not taught to take responsibility for their own actions and have no idea what it is to be an adult. We as adults need to educate our children at a young age and show them responsibility, how to honor leadership, leadership, integrity, self-esteem and family values. They say, "It starts at home." We as parents need to remind children to stay in a Childs place (stay in your lane) hold them accountable for their homework, their word, actions and deeds, studying, small chores around the house, the up keep of family pets and cleaning their room, instilling these qualities will help your child become leader driven, mature and responsible. Also, make them earn allowance; don't give them money just because you were deprived of money when you were a child, or because that's your first child you want to spoil them. Rewarding children without sacrifice makes them lazy, physically and mentally and eventually most of them become burdens on you and the government and that trend shamefully continues generation after generation. Teach them to be leaders early in life, teach them about finances and instill courage, independent thinking and show them what it is to be well-rounded as a person so that they will be grounded in life with a strong mental foundation and resolute self-constitution. There are amazing children throughout the diaspora who have diverse social and economic backgrounds who are taking accountability for their actions as well as being responsible at young ages and their chronological age has nothing to do with it.

Proof is all around you. There are eight & ten year old entrepreneurs, sixteen year old geniuses and twenty year old adults whose maturity levels are much higher than some thirty year old adults. In the same vein, you have thirty-six year old immature adults, irresponsible adults, adults who act on impulse before thinking of the consequences, so on and so forth and when you look at the big picture age really is, "nothing but a number." A lot of parents are the blame for the way these children behave in this day and age. Reason being is because of the same qualities I just stated you need to teach your children. Either you were not taught or you simply lack the discipline and leadership to teach your children properly. They are probably acting in the same manner you did as a child too their children. If you consider a young person that's out going and not restricted to experiencing life because of their age and who also mingles with an older crowd, more than likely they will mature faster than the average teen their age. Engage them based on their level of maturity and don't treat them in a bias way because of their chronological age or because you are old than them and you feel they don't deserve the same level of respect. That same person might be able to offer you a job, help you financially, etc. The lesson is, don't burn that bridge because you never know if you have to walk back across it or not, so don't talk or treat people with an assumptive prejudice because of their chronological age. Treat them with respect and equality know matter what their age is and engage the conversation based on their level of understanding and the content of their character. It's all about activating the god in you for the greater good of humanity as well as yourself. Don't be superficial in your judgments. Beware of their actions to make sure **they are not** the actions of the representative but the actions of the true person, this will allow you to make a sound judgment call based on your perception; "Young, old, good, bad, or indifferent." Yes this also applies to what ignorance might categorize people as being a particular class or race. The Point is, be fair and treat people accordingly and don't be judgmental, it hinders your mental and spiritual growth and the growth of your children.

CHAPTER – 9

AGES

Ages: Understand the ages and the meaning thereof because this will support you in elevating your level of overstanding life. **Don't shun** astrology; its important is regards to your spiritual growth. With that being said, an astrological age is a time period which astrologers claim parallel major changes in the development of Earth's inhabitants particularly relating to culture, society and politics. Thanks (En.wikipedia.org). Remember everything created naturally by Creation is interwoven in you and is a part of you. Just so you understand, there are twelve astrological ages corresponding to the twelve zodiacal signs in western astrology. Alkebulan and Kemet have a much more accurate astrology system so use that version. For all intend and purpose I will refer to commercial western astrology. At the completion of one cycle of twelve astrological ages, the cycle repeats itself. If you didn't know, astrological ages occur due to a phenomenon astrologers know as the "precession of the equinoxes." You need to know that one complete period of the precession is called a **Great Year** of about 25,920 years. "Which breaks down to the number 9" 25+9=34+2=36 3+6=9, Are you picking up what I'm putting down?

For most of you, what you are about to read, will be an entirely different language, I know that. But you need to be exposed to other avenues of knowledge as this also relates to the Creator. With that being said, I want to show you the correlation regarding **2,160** which you can breakdown to the lowest common denominator, 9. Nine in numerology also relates to completion. You will understand the whole concept as you read on. I want to mention the <u>precession of the equinoxes</u> and how it's relevant to a new beginning. "The age of Aquarius" is the age in which we are living in right now. Is it possible that whoever wrote about 666 (6x6x6) *"which equals 216"* knew things in life that psychologically might affect you as far as your mental programming which could cause most people too be afraid to study about the essence of 666? As you read about the answers and meanings of 666, there is another answer included in this equation. Approximately every 2,160 years the Precession of the Equinoxes appears to rotate the spring equinox from one constellation to another and this is how the Mayan determined that the world would come to an end in 2012 and they were right! The age of Pisces came to an end and the birth of the Aquarian age was born. The media & "the powers that be" had all the people who are ignorant to Egyptian and Mayan sciences petrified. Again, "My people are destroyed by lack of knowledge" If you are the type to dismiss this information because of your beliefs, the devil is your friend in disguise and you will never grow in truth, you will become stagnate and continue living a life of lies. All it takes is a little research; if you are too lazy to do that, don't complain about how the world is so sinful. "It starts with you, Mr. or Miss holier than thou! The age of Taurus is in relation to; the female which borne the matriarchal cultures, goddesses and customs of that era. (Much respect to Allat) After that came the age of Aries which is in relation to; masculine energy and Aries is ruled by Mars. Hence the cliché, "Women are from Venus Men are from Mars. This is the time period when men started the takeover and also change the meaning of religious beliefs and customs. The age of Pisces is in relation to; Material and emotional focus, the "I believe era" dawn of religion in a new light, the Christian era started; approximately 4 BCE. The old ideologies of religion are shifting and that shift started when the world "Pisces era" came to an end in 2012. The new dawn ended the Mayan calendar in 2012, spawning the present day, "Age of Aquarius" which is in relation to; The, "I know era" "era of knowledge, logic and quicker advances in technology."

CHAPTER – 10

THE LAST REVELATION

Quote: "Holy are you" by Rakim, "What this will do is help you get to your spiritual pinnacle." I quoted a line from Rah the God MC. I know the song by heart as well as, "Who is God" by Rah

"United we stand" "We can't exist without the unity of 1." "Divided we fall" "Division is the separation of 1; meaning 1 unity, 1 union, 1 universe, 1 mind, body & soul." Power of one or Power of the people is not in the individual, "in-divide-dual" it's in the union of **two or more** becoming 1 mind to accomplish 1 common goal. I will use the example of marriage to get the point across. It's what's needed in a marriage, if two individuals become one mind as a couple, 1 common goal and 1 mental accord, the marriage will prosper and grow strong. If the two think as individuals, there will always be opposition and the marriage will never work. As an individual, you are powerless unless you unify your mind, body and soul as one unit daily to function as a well-rounded person and or in a relationship. If you are not willing to do that, at this point it would appear that you have issues so don't blame your spouse as the one with issues. Nothing will get accomplished as it should because you both are separate mentality and spiritually with each other indulging in superficial non-sense. Which only amounts to nothing ventured, nothing gained, which amounts to wasted time in life and years of reflection about why I stayed in that relationship so long knowing it was not healthy. Overstand this "opposites attract," only in science, electric and magnetism, so stop believing that misnomer, since it doesn't apply to us in relation to that phenomenon. The laws of attraction with people would obviously be, "Like minds Attract." The crazy thing is, most people are never honest with them-selves and play on people's emotions and weaknesses to avoid acknowledging their own weaknesses because they are selfish and or can't handle the truth about self or just choose to ignore their own weaknesses because being strong and honest is too much work in their own mind and they start the cycle all over again with someone new. They always blame everybody else for their short-comings and they think no one can see the game they are playing. Soon they burn all their bridges and some start pity parties to help them-selves cope with rejection and the hardships of life. They live the lie they created for so long, it becomes their reality. Some people even convince you to live their reality. Overstand this; reality is perception and whatever you perceive from your experiences is expressed through your actions which denote your reality. What you need to overstand is that reality is not always real. Your reality is just that; "your reality." If we experience the same exact thing, my reality might differ from yours based on how I perceive that particular experience. If something is real it will never change. The only thing that will change is your perception of it. Example: your perception of life, people, places and things as a child changed as you progressed into an adult but the essence of life is still the same. The places are still the same places, regardless of construction and renovations. Center City will always be Center City. The North, South, West and Eastside of town will always be the North, South, West and Eastside of town. That aspect of life is real and the perception of it can always change. Outside of that thought, perception will have you believing illogical truth and you act on that illogical truth. Regret is one emotion that expresses acceptance of and illogical truth. In some instances, acknowledgement of and irrational action followed by apology is another form of illogical truth, meaning based on your perception your actions caused an undesirable effect and you realized your perception was not real. Lastly, we have the emotion of confusion, the distortion of what's reality and what's real. As we delve in the concept of reality vs real, answer this; is this next sentence self-perpetuated reality or is it real fact; some people die thinking that the whole **world** is against them. Was the whole world really against them? What exactly is considered the whole world in their mind? They never accept truth as an option because no one ever taught them about a higher self or the real facts of life. They might have insight about life through someone else's reality but again that's someone else's perception. Most people, who live carelessly, live by one extreme to the next, they always have excuses and or put the blame on everyone else and never accept responsibility for their own actions or they walk around like, Duh! We know them by certain characteristics we call people like that, zombies, sleep-walkers or snakes. Some people might say clichés like, "the lights are on but there's nobody home." "He or she has two loose screws." I call them transparent fools who believe their own bull★★★★ Bottom line is their mental state and spiritual propensity is not (1) in harmony with the universe or their higher god-self. Everything about you as a person should be in sync all of the time. We fall out of sync at times but most of us use our will power to come back to true reality. Some people don't know they have will-power. Not to go too far off track, I want you to fully understand the concept of oneness.

We live in a galaxy called the, Milky way Galaxy that the Creator made. The galaxy is comprised of everything in the universe that the Creator made; the universe is united with everything in it; which formed the galaxy and universe that the Creator made, including you and I. The power and gift of life that the Creator gave women is the most profound gift of all. Creation gave women the power to give life-birth. The only true natural way to procreate is the union between man and woman. Two must become one to create one: 2+1=3 hence the Trinity. The universe encompasses and represents life in many forms and fashions. Women have the universal power to create universes, metamorphically speaking. With that in mind ponder the possibility of this sad mind set.

Imagine if a certain group of elite people found out that the more melanin a particular group of people have the less susceptible they are to diseases and this same group of people don't have many fertility issues, they also have a dominant gene, they have the strongest cell integrity for stem cell production and cell reproduction, stronger bone density during space travel, they were born with high volumes of melanin and also produce the most amount of melanin to protect them from ultraviolet sun rays, their pineal gland has a higher percentage of carbon than any other human species, not to mention some of these people reside in one of the richest geographical areas for natural resources on the globe. Based on that information, a power elite group of people that realized this are questioning their existence as future elitist and are in fear of remaining the minority and someday losing cultural identification as a people because of multicultural mixing. So these groups of Power Elitist infiltrate the heart of civilization. Let's say Alkebulan and they branch out to Alkebulan of the West, Turtle island, North, South and Central Americas, Mexico, Tasmania, Kemet, China, wherever and compromised the lives of the women, men and children by spreading Ebola, HIV, syphilis, and other life-threatening viruses to possibly annihilate the melanin rich people all over the globe to ensure domination and everlasting life for the power elite, and or maybe to see how fast viruses breakdown certain blood types, weaken or strengthen DNA of certain people over a period of time at the cost of your life through involuntary vaccines and unjust wars. I see that people are that gullible that they really believe HIV and Ebola started in, Alkebulan-Africa. I guess the people there are so dirty and malnourished in your minds that they created a virus through their own DNA and are the host of the virus and at the same time they die from the same virus they created and their own immune system can't create antibodies to neutralize the virus huh? Mother Nature would allow that? Oh really? Are you that naive? Like Brill said in Enemy of the State, "your either incredibly smart or incredible stupid." Maybe you read too much of his-story and you are an uncultured book smart wannabe, I can't tell, no common sense, yes I can tell. So where do you put God in this equation. Prayer, pray for the less fortunate, will that fix the problem? Pray for those people and or the virus so it will never make it to your country. Do you seriously think that will fix the problem? We have been praying since we created religion and what did it fix? I'm just asking you to tell the **world** what did it fix? "Faith," faith without works is dead, so how do you make that work without being interactive or proactive? Some would say we can make it work by being devoted religious people and that will help the situation, what is that exactly? Some would say let's fix home first and then venture overseas. Seriously, if all those things could help, don't you think it would have been fixed before you were born? Let's look at it from another perspective but in essence, the same light.

Imagine if a group of people or one person of power was taught that their nationality is superior to all other nationalities in the world, but this group of people had a recessive genetic defect. The defect would cause extinction of that nationality if they have intercourse outside of their bloodline. So in order to ensure everlasting life for this group of people, the king in power declared a decree that stated, no more fornication unless it's, **F**ornication **U**nder **C**onsent of the **K**ing. F.U.C.K. "Origins of the word, phrase, and acronym vary" This decree would control the population and help stop the possibility of extinction because now you have semi control over your subjects. Now what if the King added the fact that you can only have one wife or go to jail for polygamy *"**Most all men in biblical text, no matter what book it is, had multiple wives, a harem, concubines, etc.**"* If I had twenty wives, I have the power to impregnate all twenty at one time. I would have twenty children in one year, instead of one child in one year. Looking at it from another angle, if I lived in a village, city, state, or country that you lived in, and we had two different nationalities and you had one wife and I had twenty wives and your gene is recessive and my gene is dominate and we both had children once a year. Who do you think would dominate that area? "Keep in mind, it's is not because of the dominate gene that I would dominate the area, it's due to the twenty wives and my twenty children verses my neighbors one child. Who do you think would rule, not to mention the fact that if the men in my family had intercourse with your family, eventually one family would be endangered? "That is due to the dominate gene factor" The combination of the F.U.C.K. Decree and one "in-divide-dual" wife would change the direction of the people as a whole when you relate that to the controlling element-dominate nationality, of the world. Each Nationality of a people has their own cultural customs and religious beliefs and if you are the dominate nationality in your city, country, etc. most likely your belief system would be the most dominate one. If you want to increase your nationalities chances for everlasting life, you might start to impose your principles or belief systems "B.S." on other nationalities around the **world** as well.

Example: If China took over the United States, we would be communist as a government and a people. We would start to speak Chinese as a primary language. If the majority of government and people are Confucianism, Buddhist, and Daoist or Islamic, whichever one is strongest in their cultural beliefs, you can bet your "**sweet baby Jesus**" they will impose that system of beliefs on you as a people. Maybe it already happened based on what you believe now, because there are no people called, "white people" in law or as a nationality. I know of no known people in law or as a nationality called, "Black People" African American, Colored, either. What country is called, "white?" What country is called, "Black" Matter fact, look up nationalities and or cultures and show yourself where black or white exist as a country or people on the map. I'm just saying. This is all to illustrate how we could have the power of one collective mind to uplift humanity and the illusion created by one collective mind or group of people called the Power Elite, Devils, Satan, whatever you want to call them who spread degradation and oppression amongst the masses via separation, segregation and overt linguistic programming. That group I just mentioned has so much mind control over a multitude of people it's insane. We have to unite as one mind as they did in order to form a more perfect union.

We must have one universal mind to enhance our quality of life to achieve our fullest potential as a people as we did when Kemet was thriving as a nation. Again, "Like minds Attract" and if other cultures see a positive change in us as a people, the like-minded one will be attracted to join us in our quest to uplift humanity because that's the creative forces of nature. Satan's nature is to reverse that so Satan would appear to be attracted as well. As long as we evoke our higher power via the principles of Creation, wisdom and discernment, we can acquire serenity.

We need to stop thinking as an individual mind. The teachings of most religions allude to widespread systematic thinking in the dogmas of their text and rituals. That thinking will hinder your understandings of life, as well as God and also your primary purpose in life. This is why most people who think outside the box or throw the box away and have so many questions. People, who ask questions, have a desire to know more. People, who don't ask questions, think inside the box, don't think for themselves, listen to their doctrine only, are sheep-people that need a shepherd to lead them, or they didn't comprehend the material and or are too embarrassed to ask questions for fear of looking stupid. Remember, the only dumb question is the one you don't ask. Understand this; the word know, is the first word in the compound word, know-ledge. Remember, "My people are destroyed by lack of Knowledge." Don't let the doctrine you believe, hold you back from knowledge. There's more fish in the sea besides the one you catch. There are more books on the shelf besides the one you read. It's not about 1 as in an individual, it's about all of Creation being 1 and being 1 with creation. God is 1 and I am 1 with God. If you agree, then who are you?

The Creator breathed the breath *"God's spirit"* of life into every living body and your body became a living soul. So every time we breathe, we are celebrating the breath of life via the Creator. "I can live with that" On the contrary; when your pores breathe, that's your fleshly lower god-self celebrating his existence as well. The beast in you is the representation of falling man; your lower god-self; 666. Your flesh has to breathe to stay alive and so does your body. The biggest overt secret of all time is that, Satan has and inevitable fate called, "death" remember, "the wages of sin is death" My question to you is, if you acknowledge this to be self-evident, why would you think you will burn in Hell? Any whoo! Satan will pass-away, Satan's **will**; will die when your flesh ceases to breathe. The perfection in you; the **god** in you will live forever and return back to its original owner, "The Creator" Maybe you didn't catch that. The lower god-self will be deceased, dead, gone, non-existent, poof. How many ways do you need to see Truth? You need to see truth, one way! With an open-mind that is not tainted by religious dogma and isms. "The only way to hear truth is through the spirit, which spirit are you following?" If you answered that question with, "the spirit of god, answer" you are confused to a degree. You should be leading your spirit of god and cultivating your spirit of God to be the god you are born to be. The spirit of god is the seed, you still have to cultivate it, water it, pick out the weeds from time to time and prune it so it can grow for you to reap the benefits.

So what actually will be burning if you are an un-righteous person in the eyes of your God and or religion? Because the Skin you're in is sin. **Again,** the **skin that your higher-self lives in** is **comprised of sin.** "Your god-self-higher energy-life force" The wages of sin is death; to live, is to die. You don't take flesh; 666 to heaven, to God, to the Creator, to paradise, to hell or to be reincarnated. Energy produces energy. Life produces life. Life needs two elements to be everlasting in the physical **world;** it needs spirit and flesh. Spirit is the quintessence essence; the life force; the energy that produces life and spirit has an intricate synergistic relationship with science. "1 Corinthians 45: *The Scriptures tell us,* "The first man, Adam-Atom, became a living person, but the last Atom-Adam— that is, Christ—is a life-giving Spirit."* We recreate life in science, not spirit; spirit is the essence of life that needs a physical form for animation. God, the Creator-higher intelligence used science to create you; most religions say that the only way life is represented is when God breathed the breath-spirit of life in your nostrils and you became a living soul. So I use this analogy throughout the book so I don't lose you. I want you to maintain your focus in regards to one of the main points of the book. But let me say this, When half of you were sperm and the other half of you were the egg and before the two of you met in the womb, intelligence directed you to come together as one and that intelligence was alive and it would infer that if spirit exist, it's synonymous with intelligence and intelligence comes from nothing and nothing is alive. Nothing is something we can't see but it doesn't mean it doesn't exist.

1. Corinthians **42:** It is the same way with the resurrection of the dead. Our earthly bodies are planted in the ground when we die, but they will be raised to live forever. **43:** Our bodies are buried in brokenness, but they will be raised in glory. They are buried in weakness, but they will be raised in strength. **44:** They are buried as natural human bodies, but they will be raised as **spiritual bodies**. For just as there are **natural bodies**, there are also **spiritual bodies**. "Keep in mind spirits don't take the shape of your physical bodies like you see in the movies or on TV"
2. Corinthians 42 43 44 & 50: This is proof to you that you will not burn in hell. Enough said!
3. Corinthians 50: What I am saying, dear brothers and sisters, is that our physical bodies cannot inherit the Kingdom of God. These dying bodies cannot inherit what will last forever. "Your physical bodies cannot inherit the Hell fire either unless the devil takes them out of the caskets" I'm just saying, maybe you believe in miracles, I mean magic.

How many ways must I say it, for you to understand that you are a Child of the Most High and your Creator doesn't burn flesh-souls-spirits in a place called, "Hell?" Your spirit goes back to the essence. Spirit is energy; light, eternal life and the Alpha & Omega, which will never die. If your spirit dies, so does God, god, the Creator, the Almighty, The Great Architect, the Universal law, all there ever was and all that is. "The universal laws that are bound by the Creator of life will not allow that to happen." I pray that you are starting to get the picture and understand how simple it is to overstand how society and dominating religious agenda makes understanding religious doctrine complex. It's turning people away from their own spirituality and the truth about the Creator. Our spirits are the essence of life! That's how we became living souls. Don't you find it weird that the focus is on the doctrine and not spiritual integrity? When you go to church or the Kingdom hall you learn about the scriptures and are taught the proper translation thereof. When you go to the Mosque you learn about Surah's, Hadiths and follow the Sunna. Why are you not learning about whom you are and your direct connection to the Creator? Learning about religious doctrine gives you this type of mind-set; if a person isn't in my circle of beliefs I need to shy away or chase them away before they try to corrupt my mind. The deep-rooted fear within you subconsciously allows you to think that people outside of your religious beliefs wants to harm and corrupted you with their doctrines, or possibly brain-wash you and you might be right. But that's not always the premise. You become conditioned to believing only the doctrine according to your religion. Life is not just about religion. There are many facets of life and religion is just one of them. You are told that if you doubt your religion it's likely that you will burn in hell, so obviously you become afraid of pursuing knowledge in other areas of life. You stop searching to find the truth because you accept what you were told or what you heard. You learn nothing else and stop spiritual and mental growth as a human being. "Zombie"

Quote: "Same love" by Macklemore: "When I was in church they taught me something else, if you preach hate at the service, those words aren't anointed. Everyone else is more comfortable remaining voiceless, rather than fighting for humans that have had their rights stolen." This quote reminds me of the Martin Luther King quote I stated at the beginning of the book.

Some religious teachings are like money in your wallet, God is like the identification in your wallet. If you lose your wallet, you don't care as much about the money. But your identity is everything to you. The point is this; focus on your relationship with god that's the substance which is truly important; along with your **ability** to **identify** with the **Creator** and become **one** in thought and deed. Embrace your higher life-force and build an overstanding of your identity with god and not your identity with your religion. Religion is not the foundation of god, **you are**. Religion can help set the bases for understanding religion, but you will never understand or know god from a religious perspective, only a spiritual perceptive. You will never know god if you focus all your energy and time on the doctrines of your religion. Someone once asked, "if all the Catholic priests are so holy, why are so many of them pedophiles?" My answer is, "because of the power that's given to them from the people who follow them and because of their adapt understanding of the faith they propagate along with the power they know they have to lead people in any direction they choose, leads them to feed their lower god-self due to a higher indulgence in the dogma of religion verses focusing on the identity and relationship with Creation and your higher god self. Absolute power corrupts, absolutely. Quote by, "John Emerich Edward Dalberg-Acton" They look at the superficial external values of gratification instead of internal spiritual will power to resist the temptation." "In actuality their physical gratification becomes stronger than their reality of damnation." "In this case the battle of Armageddon-holy jihad is won by the god of their lower self." In the same vein; I would say, "The spiritual power they possess is dominated by their fleshly desires like anyone else and in time it will create blind faith and self-righteous behavior as to who has absolute power, them or the God they serve." These are the same type of people who lay in their death beds and decide to apologize and confess for all the wrongs they have done. Look at it this way, if your devilish lower-self wanted to trick a person or convince them to do whatever you wanted them to do without using drugs or force, you would pick the innocence, naive, docile, obedient ones. Eve, Adam, and little children, get it? Overstand this and you won't go wrong, once you start your quest to be a leader of self by exercising your higher power and not a follower of the flock, the Creator will start to reveal God's hidden colors and you will have revelation upon revelation and purpose will start to be clear. You can then warn and teach people like; Adam, Eve, little children, the naïve and obedient ones to summons the power of god in them and never question who they are as gods. In doing so, it will build mental and spiritual strength as well as confidence and they will have no doubt in their minds whose spirit they are fighting against. The power to say no gets easier when you know who you are and what you are up against. If you don't know who you are, you are lost. If you don't know who you are up against, how can you win the battle, you lose again and again and soon you will lose your life. Now that you have an overstanding of your potential as a child of God you need to understand the programming of the image you see when you think of God because it will alter your reality if you are not aware of the deception and mis-education thereof. Again you need to know who and what the Creator is, one thing is for certain and two things for sure, before you finish this book you will know who God is.

As I stated above based on the concept of how most people view the Creator it will have a strong impact on the way you think. People tell me they talked to God and God physically answered them. They said they heard God literally speak in their ears. The Creator speaks to me to but in my head or in my heart. It's sad some people want to defend their diluted way of thinking so dispersedly that they create new medical terms such as; self-induced schizophrenia.

Your depiction of the Creator is so far from reality if you've seen and heard God speak, but maybe you did, maybe you make up lies just to defend your doctrine and maintain your view point because of your programmed isms about your religious belief system will not allow you to accept the truth because your spirit is not ready to receive the word, sounds familiar. This book is written to save your life not to destroy it. Most people can't handle the truth and that's part of the problem. If you have conviction for the Creator and your spirit is thirsty for knowledge and truth, you will read the book in its entirety without prejudice. The God in you will not get offended about statements that are not common place in your religious doctrine, above all if you have a humbling higher god spirit you are already where you need to be. I will give you a better overstanding of spirits in another chapter as for now I would like for you to absorb the material.

Spirits do not have vocal cords and the Creator is not the image you were taught about, thought about or fought about. The image you all portray in your mind of Allah is that of a spirit-being in the celestial form of a human body. "Stop watching movies and tel-a-lie-vision!" It's obvious some people believe that because they are the only ones that can see or hear God physically talking in their ear. You are so special in all of creation that Jehovah only physically talks to you. That's prejudice; God you love me too, right? You need to acknowledge that this type of flaw can be mentally and spiritually toxic. This view of what the Creator looks like taints and clouds your judgment as a child of the Most High. It causes you to assume you will see your dead relatives once you die, you will walk on streets paved of gold and you will be eating fruit, nuts and berries with Jesus, Peter, Paul, Moses and the rest of your so-called dead brothers and sisters. Adam and Eve might be in hell because they sinned so you might not see them. Jesus didn't die when they committed sin, plus they didn't get baptized to be saved like you did, I might be wrong but moving forward. The image you have of Yahweh ben Yahweh also leads you to believe you will be in an actual place called heaven with people who died over three million years ago etc. oh really? As they say, "To each his own." If you like it I love it.

The way I see it is simple, the Creator is a life-force manifestation of energy perpetually transforming in and out of different states of matter seen and unseen to perpetuate life everlasting. If life stopped in heaven, life would cease to exist on earth. If you truly look at the principles and laws of the Creator which is all around you, you would clearly see that life is a never ending cycle full of beauty and splendor and human-kind is the only hindrance to life. Everything in life was created before humans. Humans were the last to be created and the first to terminate it with ill intention. Did you ever stop to think? We are the only ones on the planet consciously aware of a God presence. The sad thing is that all animals, reptiles, fish and insects live by universal law and respect life but know nothing about a Creator. The dawn of a new beginning is mounting.

If you don't overstand what I'm conveying about the image of God, I will break it down. The emphasis in relationship to acknowledging an image of the Creator, expresses that all your energy and focus will be in the wrong place with respect to building a relationship with the Al-mighty and aligning your spirit up to be 1 with the Al-mighty and excise your will for the greater good of humanity. Life is based on your actions and deeds and if you are sincere in your actions and deeds, wherever you end up after death is of no consequence because you served your purpose while you were alive and if you are a true child of God, again wherever you go after death would not matter because you fulfilled your destiny. With that being said the image also distorts your perception of the judgment day as well. On that day you still think Allah will be talking to you "the dead person with no capability of hearing, inoperative ears, no living physical body or eyes and you would really think God with no vocal cords is asking your spirit that has no auditory canal if you were naughty or nice. He's making a list and checking it twice, you might not get the gift of heaven if you lived a naughty life. The irony of it all is that you will come to face your iniquities through the conviction of your heart and soul while you are still alive.

On judgment day you will answer to your guilt by the conviction of your soul, if you do not die instantly. You will confess your sins to your spirit. If you are spiritually convicted enough and you have the time to make amends with the people you wronged or the bad things you have done as you lay on your death bed knowing you will depart from flesh, your head shall bow, your knees shall bend, you will submit and your tongue will confess. By the way, it's sad that you are so selfish and thoughtless that you wait until you are about to die to admit your wrongs but for the selfish that's just the nature of the beast, the 666 you represent. "Now is the time you confess and ask for forgiveness." Once you have released all of your burdens, judgment has been met and thy will has been done. I will give you an example.

Let's say you have a family member, family etc. who wronged you all their life and you go to see them in the hospital or where ever they may be and they know they are about to die soon. This is when some people finally want to tell the truth and lift that burden off of them so they can, "Rest in Peace" If you notice, most people that make a testimony of confession die soon after. They did not talk to God literally as you would think. However, their soul did convict them and the spirit of God moved thru them to state their last, "Will and Testament" before returning back to the essence of life, which starts the recycle of life all over again for the next student to experience life as we did.

CHAPTER – 11

THE BATTLE

War time people, I hope you have all of your spiritual ammunition and studied the word to the fullest extent along with your faith and belief. If this is what you have been programmed to believe that's all you need for the battle. I know some of you weren't even taught that much. Let alone the fact that some of you are the battle is literally between God and Satan and you would just sit around and watch. Know that if you were taught in that context, you were miss-educated like the rest of the followers. Once you recognize the fallacies in some of the teachings, you will understand universal law and know that he laws of creation are constant. Universal laws that govern all life never change for the worst. Universal laws adapt too and compliments evolution without waver or choice. Choice is not an option. Even the concept of God giving you a choice is flawed. We will discuss it later and you will overstand. For now, you need to understand the necessity to engage in the everyday Battle of Armageddon with well-rounded strategic actions which encompass; focus on overcoming adversities, maintaining objectives via your higher power and mental conviction for the purpose of spiritual success.

What else will you need to fight the biggest spiritual war in history? When you come up with the answers add them to the list. When was the last time you prayed for strength to carry you through? Well for the people that are fearful of Armageddon- holy Jihad, like I said earlier everything isn't always what it seems. Understand this, the battle can be easy or you can make it hard, the choice is yours. Know it or not we all have a personal relationship with our Creator. If the Creator **only dwelled outside** of you (in heaven) then it would not be personal, all spiritual energy would come from one source outside of you and that is not the case, understand that the creator is the one source of all things created and all things not. I'm speaking from the prospective that some of you are taught that your God is in heaven with Jesus by his side looking down on you and never considering the fact of God is dwelling in you, only outside your body for all intent and purposes. *You picking up what I'm putting down?* *"Even though you are taught to pray to* **G**od *in Heaven"* If **G**od is only in Heaven as you were taught who's fighting Satan down here? Did the fight start yet? Where is heaven? Where is Hell? "You are programmed to think of a down here, as opposed to a Heaven up there, Right?" Since the Creator created everything that is and ever will be, the Creator is everything you are, and everything you're not. Most importantly **G**od Dwells in you, I, everybody and everything else based on the teaching and your perception. Not all beings are conscious of **G**ods' presence but yet **G**od is there. The list of spiritual ammunition you need is not what you were told it is and what I mentioned in the beginning of the chapter is what most people are told. "LOL" I just said that since most of you believe that's what it takes to win the war. For the reason that, that's what most of you are taught.

Essentially knowing who and where **G**od is by evoking and excising your **g**odly self in Spirit to reach divinity are the only keys it takes to win the Battle. **G**od is in you and **G**od is with you all the time, so if you know that to be true, **G**od is literally in you. "John 4:4 Greater is **he** that is in you, than **he** that is in the world" **He** that is in you is **G**od, **he** that is of the world is your flesh, flesh is the fall of man and falling man is sin, sin equates to Satan, Satan is in you too and that's the imperfection of man and the unperfected spirit eventually dies. Why? Because the unescapable truth is, "the wages of sin is death!" Not the act of committing the sin, sin itself which is you as a living soul. We are the spiritual beings that animate our physical bodies. To my knowledge spirits are not seen by the human eye on this plane. Spirits are usually only seen through the actions and deeds of the humans that animate them. Most of you are taught that the Devil is on the earth as a separate entity other than residing in you and also the Devil lives in hell, flawed focus, the focus should be on self. Question; you don't see the actual Devil and God running around creating chaos do you? Well that's a trick question depending on where your head is and the level of programming you were subjected to. I just explained that spirits need a body to animate them but I know programming and B.S. belief systems tells some of you to look at that statement as unacceptable. If you don't know your body houses the spirits of the Creator and Satan I will prove it to you. We will explore the probability of your conclusion in another chapter. Your higher-self is the **supreme god** that you are. Your lower-self is the **inferior god** that you are. "John 10:13 Jesus answered them, "Is it not written in your Law, I have said you are **g**ods" "Psalm 82: I say, "You are **g**ods; you are all children of the Most High."" "Psalm 82: **G**od stands in the congregation of the mighty; he judges among the **g**ods." The distinction is in the upper case and lower case **G**ees.

Whenever **G**od, Jesus or an apostle talks of us as **g**ods, we are always referenced to in lower case gee. **G**od the Creator, the Almighty, the life force is always referenced to in upper case **G**ee. The distinction is identical to your higher self and your lower self. The **Almighty Creator-God** is your life force source, "**The Alpha & Omega**" "If you don't know where you came from you won't know where you are going" If you know you came from **G**od, once your physical body dies you are going back to your original essence, The Creator, the **God** that created you and who you are connected to by quintessential God born intrinsic nature. John 4:6 We are from **G**od and whoever knows **G**od listens to **us**; but whoever is not from **G**od does not listen to **us**. For your information, us; can't be Jesus because if you think Jesus and God are the same, that would mean Jesus is God, not with God, so it's only one entity, not two as in Jesus and God are side by side. **Us;** means more than one, so you think about that next time you give false answers regarding who us is."

Basically, God recognize god, real recognize real and game recognize game. That is how we recognize the Spirit of truth and the spirit of falsehood. Also overstand that some scriptures, hadiths and surahs do not apply all the time when you are in a battle because circumstances are always different. When you are in a battle always remember that you have the will power mentally and spiritually to win by excising your higher power because the battle of Armageddon-holy Jihad is continuously present and it will be until you physically expire due to the fact that you are mind, body and Soul are all connected as one body and this connection will die and your higher spirit will return back from which it came, the Creator.

Explore this as an example of people that are from God, know God and recognize the Spirit of truth and because of social pressure they live a spiritual falsehood. Single men & woman are pressured by the church and society to get married before they get old, so they get married for all the wrong reasons and pray to God to fix it. People get pressured into marriage because they have children out of wed-lock and pray to God to fix it. People of the faith get married because they want to uphold a false reputation as a heterosexual to save face and their careers. When the skeletons come out the closet they pray to God to fix it. The point is; know who you are as a child of God and know the power you possess as the little gee, knowing this **will** help you win the battle. Hopefully this will help your focus on self; at least I hope it will. **Think of the world**, in regards to religion; God or Spirit whatever phrase you feel comfortable with **as flesh,** not the physical world we live in, because that's taking away the attention of who you're **really** fighting in the battle. It's not the spirit of the devil on the planet you need to be concerned about, it's the spirit of the devil in you that you need to be concerned about. The spirit on the planet doesn't exist as you were taught in Sunday school, bible study, at the table etc.

With that being said, I wanted to try and give you a crash course in the fundamentals of God, god and flesh to mentally prepare you for battle. Are your eyes open now? If so know that in spirit **eyes open** is a metaphor for an **open mind**, if you look at it any other way you will lose **the battle**. In spirit to be **born again** is to open your mind to a new understanding of life and how use **god** as a compass to lead you in the correct direction. In spirit the Blood & body of Jesus is the word, as in the conviction to your **higher god-self** you thirst for. Any other way is symbolic to the ritual that vampires perform by killing humans and drinking their blood for everlasting life. It also eludes to cannibalism by eating the body of Christ. "See what I'm saying" "Focus on **g**od-self not the ritual" spiritually and mentally you understood or physically you only comprehended the words and context of the statement. Please tell me spiritually and mentally you felt the spirit move and understood, let's go!

FOR YOUR INFORMATION: throughout the bible you will see **G**od spelled with a capital **G**ee and a **lower**-case **g**ee, understand why that is. Embrace the essence of your higher and lower self

The battle of Armageddon-holy Jihad is within you, the world we live in. The planet we live on is external, outward, and superficial when relating internal spirit, get it? The sky will not open up and the spiritual war between God and Satan will not began, "erroneous" again the only thing that will open up is your mind if you **will** it too. To have spiritual power is the same as having God's **will**, if God's **will** be done, so be it, you have the power. *"When in doubt check it out!"* You **will** become stronger through the practice of excising your **godly will** to over-power your fleshy **will** "Satan." Since birth you were in the battle of Armageddon-holy Jihad and if you knew the right battle to fight your life would possibly be different at this moment and time. The spiritual fight between your higher **god-self** and lower **god-self** "Satan" is the true battle. Most people live a superficial existence and cater to the exterior aspects of life. People for the most part look for a leader-Shepard to guide them along the path of life and when that leader no longer leads for whatever reasons, the people come lost again and the cycle of ignorance starts over again, time after wasted time and because of this we as a people who are truly the majority will always be the minority. When critiquing your higher godly power it's a matter of knowing your heart and the actions that follow. It's said only god knows your heart, well act like you know.

The one you feed the most **will** win the war and coincidentally have the most impact in your life and control your actions. **Warning**; never lean towards one extreme, you need balance between Satan-**god** and God and in this physical world you need both to survive. I will talk in-depth about that in another chapter, but for now bear with me. Keep in mind that **God** is spiritual-Spirit and Satan is spirit and physical form mixed together. The fleshly I want what I want lower **god**-Spirit. You heard the cliché; ""*Matthew 26:41*" **the "spirit is willing but the body is weak"** (*my KJV I have at home*) keep that in your mental rolodex. When you are ready to give up, remember the **God** in you gave you a higher **g**odly power to fight your lower **god** power. Also it's important to understand that sometimes **the "body is willing and the spirit is weak"** due to the natural default called flesh which is natural born sin. You really need to be able to recognize which God you are serving at any given time and if you mentally extract **g**od from self and place **g**od in the outta limits of space-heaven, you are headed for self-destruction. If you use this spiritual philosophy you **will** reign supreme over your **lower god-self-Satan**. The spirit of God is always stronger than the spirit of Satan as long as you consciously bring **God** to consciousness and spiritually feed **God**. By doing so, the battle will get easier and easier. You are endowed with the innate ability to defeat Satan if you **will** it to be. You are **god** so how can you be defeated by flesh and flesh will pass-away but the **god** in you will live infinity, How do you think **G**od will burn all who disobey him, it surely won't be flesh burning and Satan told Eve she won't surely die, He never lied because at the time Satan made that statement she was without sin except for flesh, so there was never a deception. I'm just saying. She's probably burning as you read this chapter and if you are tortured in the superhot flames by God and are burning forever and you can feel the pain, something in your **G**od-spirit is surely physically alive, which doesn't make since or maybe spirits have nerve ending, I'm just saying.

Let's talk a little about balance; having a 360 degree intellectual, spiritual and mental balance is equivalent to being a well-rounded individual. Without balance you tend to be and extremist in a negative or positive sense and that creates losses. Balance gives you the edge in life. Being well-rounded as a person allows you to adapt to almost any given situation. Sorta like knowing when to pull back or knowing when to push forward, knowing when to walk and knowing when to run, you get the picture☺. You **will** learn later in this book. Everything living is connected in some form or fashion, meaning all life is connected as **1 and 1** is connected to all life. What the hell? Let's learn about it now. It's a profound subject dealing with polarity, I won't elaborate but here's a small fragment. I will use this number line to illustrate **oneness** to a degree. Hopefully you will over-stand the concept. Ok here we go, obviously when you look at the number line, the left side is negative the right positive. In the center is zero, the zero represents the mental and spiritual balance of you, me, him, her, it, us, them and little gee If I lost you, start reading from ok here we go. Suppose you are a girl who likes attention from your boyfriend, husband or whoever. Nothing is wrong with that. Well let's call the girl Tanocki and Tanocki's boyfriend, Zealous calls her at work to say he misses her. Naturally, Zealous gets kudos and moves from zero to 1 notch to the right "positive side of number line" two hours later Zealous calls again to say he misses her and cannot wait to see her, Tanocki tells him that's so sweet but you can't call me at work because I might get fired and Tanocki moves Zealous 2 more notches to the right because of his thoughtfulness. That means Zealous moved up to number 3 on the number line and in Tanocki's heart. Tanocki gets off at 5, Low and behold Zealous is outside waiting for Tanocki with flowers and a card; she can't believe this, so she moves Zealous up to number 6 because she hasn't seen

this much attention since Obama got elected. The next day Zealous calls Tanocki at work to tell her how he had such a wonderful time together and he can't wait to see her again. Now the red flag raises and Zealous moves down the number line a notch because Tanocki told him not to call her at work. But she likes attention, Right? So now Zealous calls Tanocki at lunch and she's like, what the hell! He goes straight to negative 2 on the number line and now Tanocki is about to send him packing. In the mind of Zealous, he was showing her attention and how much he cared for her. LOL, The problem is that Zealous is and extremist and doesn't know how to balance his motions. This is the epitome of, "The same thing that makes you laugh, makes you cry" or "It's a thin line between love and hate" Most importantly these are examples referencing extremes of the same thing. Sadly enough, we are taught that they are total differences and one has nothing to do with the other. You need to understand that there is no duality in the physical or spiritual plane; like hot and cold, night and day, good vs evil, man and woman etc. There is only one acceptation to the rule; the combination of spirit and the physical body are separated at death allowing the spirit to make the transition back to the astral plane and the essence of life. Case and point, Zealous did what Tanocki wanted and that was give her attention but when Zealous couldn't control-balance the emotion that made her happy, that uncontrolled emotion had adverse effects and triggered a negative out-come. The number line is here to paint the picture and give you a visual distinction regarding **oneness and balance**. Nothing changed in the situation except Tanocki's tolerance to handle the **extreme** action Zealous displayed that she held so dear. Again, there is no duality in the spirit world; there is only oneness, Spirit is spirit, God is god, and they are 1 in the grand scheme of things. No matter what shape or form it's in, it's the same intelligence that spawned creation. Oneness in respects to the union of universal principles represents a constant union of laws that will never change. If these laws change by a slight fraction of a degree, it would alter the eco system of universal laws and have catastrophic consequences concerning creation.

The enigma of CHANGE is intricate with a touch of simplicity. Two of the few things in life that are consistent are change and at the same time, continuous perpetual obedience. We as a species have the ability to think and create; we think creative thoughts and bring those creative thoughts into fruition through action. Our thoughts evolve into an action; the action is an experience, the experience promotes change. Change happens through the process of time, time is infinite and change happens in infinite time. We need to accept change because change is evolution and your mind has the capacity to think; therefore you are an integral part of the eco system of evolution. The people who can't accept change become stagnant and eventually stop the process of evolution and start their demise, meaning; you can't teach old dogs new tricks because they are not receptive to evolution and revolution. You must have the student for life mentality which will allow you to accept change and continue to progress until your existence "as we know it" is no more. In the same light we have, continuous perpetual obedience which is the ultimate law. For example; the sun will always shine, planets will always revolve around the sun, the waves will always flow in the ocean, to live is to die, people will always have ears, eyes, noses and a mouth, etc. Creative intelligence will always have a bond that will never be broken.

The consecrated bond between us and Creation is that God created us in God's image and likeness so we are a part of Creation and Creation is a part of us. So ask yourself what does that mean to you in the grand scheme of things? If you are a child of God and God said he is your father and you are created in his image and likeness, who are you? Your actions and deeds define who you are. When you look at the positive attributes of a deity and the negative attributes of another and look at your actions, which deity do you represent?

For Your Information– If you don't know who you are, you will always stay in conflict, maybe lose your life, which means your purpose for living was all for naught

CHAPTER – 12

ATHEIST VERSES PAGANS

For all of you who have been miss-guided as to what these terms really mean, is why you should be a leader instead of a follower. "Don't be the sheep, be the shepherd" you heard of what an atheist and or a pagan is, or you were taught what your religious teacher thought an atheist and or pagan is. Contrary to popular belief neither one is evil or bad. I will not get into the complexes of either, for sake of an argument by people who think in the box and can't see the big picture. I want to get the main idea across. This book is about, resurrecting the birth of spiritual revolution and the upliftment of humanity, that's the focus. One thing is certain, you never hear of a Pagan or Atheist groups murdering people, bombing people or blatantly causing harm the humanity. The only groups throughout history that does that are, the Christians and so called-radical Muslim groups. It seems the radical Muslims do it out of retaliation for what and organization has done to them as opposed to random acts of violence, but that's just and opinion and everybody has one so don't get bent out of shape because propaganda has tainted your mind-set.

Pagans derived from polytheism most people will say and they worship life, the sun, moon and stars, mountains, Gods and Goddesses etc. It is associated with a connotative meaning; which is misleading and deceptive. Meaning that, most religious groups infer that paganism is devil worship. Most indigenous people were pagans until foreigners invaded their lands and imposed their ideologies and customs on those people. So for the new ideologies to take form and flourish they would have to give the original customs of the original people a negative connotation. Pagans do not believe in 1 God as you see God because it isn't their custom. It has nothing to do with turning their backs on the Creator or devil worship. Wake up! Pagans are manifestations of the Creator just like you and I. They just see God in a different light. So what is wrong with that? Unification is the primary objective; it's about unity of a people who all relate to the same spiritual and mental frame of mind. The differences of perception are only based on culture or preference, not superficial doctrine. Speaking of lost teachings, Voodoo is not what most of you perceived it to be and it has Catholic and Christian origins. Wicca also has its roots in Christianity but it is mostly a Pagan religion. Again you never hear of people who practice Voodoo or Wicca as a whole, murdering people, causing harm to humanity or oppressing the weak and idolizing the so called strong.

Atheist is used in a connotative sense by most non-atheists. As a matter of fact most people need to understand what, connotative and denotative means. Because most people are deceived by quasi truths mixed with connotative terms to appear relevant. Once you realize these terms you can start to decipher for yourself the validity of a passage or statement. The term atheism: *originated from the Greek, meaning without* **gods**, applied to those **thought** to reject the **gods** worshipped by a larger society. Thank you Wikipedia.com

Here are some atheist groups you read see and hear about everyday but I can bet it never occurred to you that they are atheist; Hinduism, Jainism, Buddhism, Raelism Neo-pagan. Here are countries in which the majority of the populations are atheist: Sweden, Russia and Japan and that's just to name a few.

The atheist viewpoint is primarily based on their respect for logic, evidence and science, and yes that represents a valid and vital value for their system of thought. So what's wrong with the system in which they have? When you have an internalized perspective that encompasses all life and logic outside of your own, the foundation and want for existence is greater than any religious belief. So embrace them as you would any other creation of the Creator and come together for the sole purpose of everlasting life and stop publicizing and advocating negativity which indirectly creates self-destruction. At the end of the day logic and science are still derived from intuitive Creative and universal laws, so accept the atheist as your brothers and sisters and embrace them for who they are.

A note for all scientists out there that see life in a unidirectional scientific structure, my statement to you is this. "It's the only thing that intertwines with logic, evidence and science; it's the higher intelligence that borne logic and science, one of the many things we can't create, **Spirit.** Our spirit is the permanent perpetual complex existence of energy and awareness which can't die or pass–away. **1** can never exist without the other **1**, so logically spirit and science synergistically come together as **1** to create **1**-life in all of creation." There is a spiritual kinetic connection in mitochondria or it could not exist, you are the living proof, we are more than conclusive and compelling evidence. As a student seeking understanding, **will** yourself to **embrace** what you don't **understand** and you will **gain** understanding. How is a stem-cell created? Not from scratch. It's only 1 genome that holds the power to withstand the process of creating a stem-cell. Do the research yourself to find out who stem cells are originally extracted from.

Connotative: something suggested or implied by a word, the secondary meaning of a word **in addition** to its **primary** meaning. Basically I'm pointing out that most of the terms used in everyday language are unknowingly use apart from its literal meaning and for the most part, the meaning within itself expresses **deceit and prejudice.** Thank you (Webster's Ninth New Collegiate Dictionary)

Denotative: This term clearly gets to the point and expresses the positive side of a word or phrase by stating the explicit or **direct meaning** as in **denotation:** a direct specific meaning of a word, as distinguished from the associated idea. (Webster's Ninth New Collegiate Dictionary)

Chapter – 13

Prayer Verses Meditation

Xternal: of or pertaining to the outside or outer part; outside of a body; superficialities; from *ex* out of. Thanks to the free dictionary.com the meaning I'm presenting to you is for purposes of expressing the mindset of most people who pray and who they are praying to. I would like you to keep in mind of your thoughts when you pray and the conviction you have for God or yourself or God and yourself when praying.

Prayer: Pray would imply a sign of weakness and instability by which there is nothing wrong with that. But requesting assistance, confessing sins, or to express one's thoughts and emotions to God and then looking and waiting for an answers is something that puzzles me. The action that seeks to activate a rapport and action of a deity God or thing, I would like to know if you all hear God's voice and/or does God give you a sign and that sign signifies your answer. Thank you kindly en.wikipedia.org/wiki

Note: there are different forms of prayer, but for all intent and purpose we are referring to you praying to God who **art** in heaven; meaning outside of your temple; church; the body of Christ; the flesh and blood individual; or the life form that houses the god–spirit that stimulates the mind, Body and soul. Overstand this; the point of making you aware of external projection is the fact that projecting your prayers outwardly takes away your power to evoke the god in you. That is like waiting for a magical miracle and it's pertaining to

JAHI ISSA JABRI ALI-BEY

the surface qualities only; superficial: "outward appearances." You should be inflecting your spirit to get a favorable reply from Adonai, God, Allah, Jehovah, Elohim, super sub-conscious, Allat, Athena, and Yahweh or any other name you call your deity. Again when you project outwardly to God it cripples the power of the god in you, rendering your prayers impractical, to a degree. Note, I said, "to a degree" not totally, don't read into it, read it for the intent. Remember, two hands working can do more than a thousand hands clasped in prayer. With that in mind, when you pray, who are you waiting for to perform the actions of the prayer? Of course the God you are praying to because why else would you be praying except for thankfulness? So again, who is actually preforming this action if there is any action being performed? You can make all kinds of justifications, at the end of the day, if you are not performing the action, it will not be done.

Internal: internalizing thought brings about a certain unparalleled personal power that helps you build a stronger personal constitution. Internal means; of or pertaining to the mind or spirit; mental; spiritual: the inner life; intrinsic: Also internal represents having a since of internal logic. Existing in the interior of something Thank you, thefreedictionary.com

Meditation: The spiritual introspection portion of this definition is the focus which would support the subconscious in manifesting your strength in a weak area. Meditation simply means; devout religious contemplation or spiritual introspection; to train the mind, body spirit to induce a mode of consciousness and build internal energy. This form of reinforcement would seem to be the most productive because it builds inner strength and inner strength is what you want to progress as a spiritual being. Thank you Dicitionary. reference.com

I don't know about you but weighting the differences between, external prayer verse internal meditations. The latter wins in my book, but that's just my book. You have your own book to write. If you are an active Muslim in Islam it takes about 25 minutes to finish all five prayers. That isn't long for devoted Muslims "to easy." So in essence you pray for the rest of your physical life which is religiously right. The problematic dilemma is, you recite the same words forever and in doing so, what are you actually reinforcing? There are plenty of issues you are faced with surrounding your life and the prayers do not cover all the issues. If the prayers are only used as a guide through Allah's word, then who is helping you with your issues and short-comings?

Moreover, with the over-standing of prayer vs meditation **would it be safe** for us to conclude that praying outwardly towards God in Heaven, having faith, belief and hope in a miracle, that something will magically happen is counterproductive for most of the populous? By the same token, this type of ritual could possibly have an adverse effect on your faith and or **B**elief **S**ystem. If you pray for issues to go away, problems to be solved, for the sole-mate, husband-wife of yours dreams, for your life to get better, for all the persistent bad things to stop happening in your life, etc. and none of those prays are answered, you might turn your back on the Creator: Your Life Force, and the sad reality is that the Creator had nothing to do with those issues or wishes. If you look at the world as a whole and consider all the religious people on the planet who pray religiously on a daily basis and consider how the people of this planet continue to get worse, how can you think that prayer really helps or that a God is answering your prayers? Question if you are taught that God knows everything you are thinking, why do you have to pray outwardly? If God is the spirit within you, why are you praying to God in heaven? Because your thoughts are executed before the words are formed from your lips and God already knows what's on your mind and or in your heart. I just wanted to give you something to think about. On the other hand, there are multiple benefits from meditation.

Meditation also helps with your ability to breathe properly and focus your energy at the core of your energy source, your spirit. It helps the flow of oxygen to the brain via the blood flow. "Your brain uses 70percent of your oxygen intake to maintain cell integrity" It opens your vortex to a higher state of consciousness. It balances your chi and aides in the healing process of bodily function. These attributes of meditation out weight prayer by far.

In a different light, internalizing your thoughts and aspirations in the form of meditation by which your god-spirit can be feed, nurtured and cultivated would be extremely affective as an alternative approach to divinity. Your sub-conscious mind is a powerful tool that you need to tap into and activate its potential to the fullest capacity via meditation. The point of this dialogue is to point out the mindset of people who pray vs the spiritual power of people who meditate and the disassociation with God and Creation from an internal and external perspective.

By no means is this meant to deter you from prayer. My goal in this book is to elevate your conscious and subconscious mind-spirit and show you that internalizing your focus on the god in you would be much more advantageous in the battle of Armageddon-Holy Jihad and in life. Life would be lived much easier and peacefully. This will give you a much more well-rounded appeal spiritually and your bond with the Creator will grow stronger and faster, in the same vein; you **will** get to know yourself even better and people will start to see a spiritually healthier you. You **will** start to feel the presence of God, not just on Friday, Saturday or Sunday but every day of the week. The more you come into self the closer your bond gets with the Creator and you start to look at life in a brand new light.

Don't try to change just do it. If you try you already failed. FOR YOUR INFORMATION, throughout life you should be a student. Always seek to understand instead of trying to always be understood. If you practice this philosophy you **will** reach new heights in life continuously, stagnation will cease to exist for you.

For Your Information: I put these definitions within the chapters for you to use as a reference instead of the back of the book to make it easier to overstand and access so you can keep your focus on the subject matter. I do encourage you to research whatever you like to get a better understanding if need be. Please don't research just one source for information.

Faith: Strong belief in God or in the doctrines of a religion, based on spiritual apprehension rather than proof. (Oxford Dictionary) it's a belief in the teachings of religion; something you can't see, feel, or touch. FYI faith is not concrete and to rule out a shadow of a doubt in life or anything else I experience I would rather have certainty which leaves no room for doubt and it's concrete and totally reassuring to be certain as opposed to having faith or belief.

Belief: A state or habit of the mind, an opinion or conviction. Something considered. Thank you (Webster's Ninth Collegiate Dictionary) FYI belief is not concrete and leaves room for a shadow of doubt in life or anything else we experience, I would rather know for sure which leaves no room for doubt and it's concrete and totally reassuring to be sure and it also show your strength and confidence

Hope: considered to be a person or thing in which expectations are centered and a desire for something good in the future. We should all know placing expectations on someone is basically setting you up for a down fall. The exception to the rule would be your best friend because you expect them to be special as a friend or they wouldn't be your best-friend. The dilemma is the fact that there's still a possibility of the infamous let down. I'm not saying hope is bad, just acknowledge the complexity and risk involved and accept the outcome good bad or indifferent so the impact doesn't have an adverse effect. A good truism to remember is, "hope for the best but expect the worse"

Knowing: would imply that you are astute; something meaningful; knowledgeable and intelligent. Based on the word association of knowing, wouldn't you rather have confidence in knowing as opposed to faith and/or belief? Thank you (thefreedictionary.com) Look at the power it holds.

Will: force, power, impulse, energy, and desire; inventions are manifestations of **will** and so are your actions which are based on your perceptions and beliefs. Thank you (Thesaurus.com) Will is what most people lack because most of you go against your will because it's easier to accept predestine fate rather than use your will to change it.

Will Power: **by which a lot of you don't use it;** the power of control over one's own actions or emotions, passion. Thank you (Webster's Ninth New Collegiate Dictionary.) Invoke your will-power and stop making excuses. How can most of you know that smoking cigarettes, using drugs or eating certain foods and/or **not** losing weight will kill you or cause serious chronic issues which will ultimately kill you prematurely or induce a illness that leaves you cripple and/or in pain until your demise. Most people acknowledge the facts of your demise and say I'm going to do the right thing. Eight years have passed and you are still saying the same thing. You justify your lack of Will-power by making excuses and that selfishness hurts the people who love you. More importantly the ignorance of your actions are passed down generation after generation and you all pray to make it better, YOU ARE KILLING ME!

Manifestation: Is considered to be an outward or perceptible materialization:

Disembody: I know it means to free from *physical form* and we possess the power to disembody the negative attributes of our spirit and manifest our higher-self based on our thoughts, again do you know what you think or do you believe what you think? You are **what you think!**

Quote: "Our lives begin to end the day we become silent about the things that matter"
Dr. Martin Luther King

Chapter – 14

The Game

You think you're invisible huh?
What if I told you most of college is a sham and the institution is based on financial gain and financial status as well as institutionalized thinking for the progression of one group of people to insure their survival as a species, (farfetched right?) If you go to school and get loans to pay for your education and when you graduate you work to pay for your education for the second time, outside of the fact that based on your financial status you can get a top notch education if you can afford it. Temple verses Harvard, Community College verses University of Pennsylvania and Widener University verses Yale. It's obvious that levels of education are based on financial status and the college reaps the financial benefits because of the social acceptance of a piece of paper that is supposed to dictate your level of intelligence. There are more college students out of work and in debt <u>statistically</u> than most people who never went to college. On the financial side, the college is paid regardless and the national deficit continues to rise. With that being said, you have to take prerequisites which have nothing to do with your major (*spend extra money*) by the same token, at some colleges it's a possibility that if you never took the S.A.T. or A.C.T. test and you want to attend college, you are deemed a non-matriculating student and you have to matriculate, you have to take part-time classes before you are accepted in the college of "Arts and Sciences" (*spend more money*) Some college people say that

you take all those extra classes and electives because it makes you a well-rounded **individual** and preps you for the work environment. (**An divid u al**). I thought experiences and the proper up-bringing did that. Are your thoughts dictated by an institution or the higher spirit that resides in you? What if I told you that people of color are the majority of people who make up the world's population? Not the so-called Black population, the melanated people all over the globe from all walks of life. But the minority is portrayed as the majority to help sustain power and maintain control. You would say you know this to be true and think, but what can we do? We can't do anything about it, that's just the way it is. That's the thought process that shows you are programmed and controlled and don't even realize it. What if I told you that Religion was corrupted and purposely miss-communicated to distort reality for the purpose of power and control? What if I told you that an elite group of wealthy people realized they could control the world by psychologically programming you through propaganda, education and religion? What if I told you that this same power elite group has plans to take over the entire world by staging wars, spreading the idea of democracy, one religion via religious missionaries as fronts to infiltrate 3rd world countries by aiding and assisting via medical and quasi financial aid and the hidden campaign is to persuade these people to adopt a new Christian way of life? What if I told you that Islam is the biggest religion on the planet and the elite Christians are setting up mass propaganda campaigns to weaken the number of followers and have them convert to Christianity all for the sake of world domination?

I asked all those questions to spark your consciousness and awaken your curiosity to research the questions, personally I won't go into that, it's for a book someone else can write. All in all, I would hope that you investigate those allegations because it's real and that's a part of the game of life and the fight for world supremacy and everlasting life through the process of, "Divide and Conquer." Remember "The wages of sin is death" and this is "do or die" for 666, the nature of the beast. You have the power to destroy the beast or the ignorance to be destroyed. Due to the fact that it might not be your nature and the fact you have been living a lie for so long, you might deny those statements to be true. Hopefully you can step outta your shoes for once and give it some thought. Seek and you shall find, knock and the door shall be opened, ask and you shall receive.

When I look at the teaching of Christianity via the bible, I noticed how it works better for the people who look like the image of Jesus and what that really projects on a subconscious level. For the majority of Christians that look like the image Christians portray Jesus to be, life works great because the governmental structure is setup in such a way for them to succeed with less resistance. So it would appear that God is doing his job and there is no reason to have doubt about the teachings or to reconsider the concepts of who God is. So I can see how they "believe" in God the way they do. Looking through the same eye, if other people slid through the cracks, then that would be a perfect disguise to legitimize the appearance of a diabolical plan for global supremacy. Take into consideration the fact that if the same Christian Power Elite groups setup their own educational and judicial systems as well and implemented and instilled in the people who attended their schools of thought, their beliefs and ideologies, those Christian beliefs and ideologies would rule out any other cultural and/or Nation's practices and philosophies. **Note:** "following some ones philosophies and ideologies is not a problem if it's for the greater good of that culture or all of humanity." Proof being, if you introduce any other forms of philosophy they are inclined to disagree or tell you that's wrong; homeopathic medicine, esoteric science, meditation, etc. The system is setup so that everybody can be on the same negative mental wave length and bypass the hidden agenda. Their program is brilliant because no one can say it's a conspiracy against humanity and prove the allegations and everyone that continues to sleep wake and be a follower will be a sacrificial pawn that perpetuates the lie. Living the life of Jesus for these people is a beautiful thing for them to implement their scandalous program. Because some of them work hard and receive their blessings, it's nothing wrong with that. Life for them isn't about bearing the cross their whole life or living a life of oppression as Jesus did. They are not Living to suffer their whole life as Jesus did. They are not fighting a corrupt government as Jesus did or lying down their burdens to the Lord and sitting and waiting for the Lord to make it better as Jesus did. In their minds and in their teachings, Jesus did all of that already so they don't have to. As a whole, for the people who look like Jesus, life is not that oppressive in the least. On another note, the ones who refer to themselves as, "White trash" "no pun intended" your own people could care less about you too, but I'm 100percent sure you already know this to be true. You are the people who are the tokens they need to justify the allegations of a conspiracy theory.

By the same token, when I look at the teaching of Christianity via the bible when dealing with people of color all across the globe, I see the same image of Jesus we were taught to follow and acknowledge but with a different meaning; the Jesus that is subjected to retribution, the Jesus that is whipped and beaten by his oppressors, the Jesus that fights for a just government but is always denied, the Jesus that speaks in a non-violent manner for justice and peace but is spit on and humiliated, the Jesus that modestly witness's to the world the injustices that take precedence over spiritual reverence but is ignored and discredited. The Jesus that ask, "Why Lord is Caesar's heart hardened" and the same Jesus prays for Caesar to be an upright man and Caesar laughs at him. The same Jesus that asked (his-self), (*scratching my head*) "Lord God why has thou forsaken me" while being put to death. The same Jesus who had to hide from his oppressors in hopes to avoid assassination so he could continue to spread the truth about the evils of an elite group of people who bleed greed and practice insanity on humanity. The character of Jesus is the epitome of all the leaders in the world who stood up for oppression. Not to mention all the homeopathic doctors who created cures for major ailments and mysteriously disappeared or died unexpectedly or in a plane/car crash. Hum. "Libation for Dr. Wyatt"

"Dr. Wyatt never rest in peace until your work is done. Invoke the return of your spirit through your most devolved student to finish what you started and when you see what you worked for over the years manifest into success, then, only then may your spirit rest in peace, love and respect, your brother in spirit."

Let's move forward to another characteristic of games. You are a child of God but you play games with your family, friends, God and worst of all, your god-self. I mention you worst of all because you all say the Almighty Creator is merciful. Contrary to that, if you allow yourself to do dirt to people and act as if you don't have a conscious, your lower god-self **will** allow you to make justifications for the dirty games you play. You are now making your lower god-self-Satan that resides in you stronger. Money & Power; most played game of all time, People owe you money say things like, "you are that bent out of shape over a couple of dollars? "10.00" – "2,000" dollars, most of the time it's not about the amount, it's usually the principle of the matter and not the money. Most people who don't want to pay their debts try to convey a false sense of guilt on you, pretending that you are harassing them for what they owe you, they say things like; you keep harassing me over a couple of dollars, oh I forgot, wait until I get paid, I didn't forget to pay you, knowing they got paid yesterday. Every time they see you or talk to you they never mention when they will pay as if you forget. Smh: (Shaking my head) or they make up countless other excuses. When someone borrows money or loses a bet, you take them on their word and when they renege, it feels like they intentionally deceived you and took advantage of you, and they probably did, that's what hurts most people more than the fact that the person didn't pay the money back. What makes it worst, the person that owes the debt starts to live the lie that's in their head created via Satan who is none other than their lower **god-self** and lives a falsehood based on deceit to justify dishonesty with excuses and the intent to be excused by everybody they deceived or try to deceive. You are some of the same people that, when the table turn you want justice. People like you are selfish and irresponsible, you killing me … most of you people never mature and you think the world owes you something.

Worse than that, when you have problems you can't fix you turn to God to fix it, when it doesn't happen, you blame God or resort to other destructive vices and even drugs to relieve the pain of your reality that you created as god. What kind of insanity is that? It's the kind of insanity that most people live with most of their life because of misguided teachings or lack of an ethical foundation in spirit and in life. It's not the world that's in shambles, it's the worldly people "satisfy my flesh people-the **lower-self satanic god spirit people** who deny there devilish ways because they can't face the truth and they're too lazy to take responsibility for they own actions. The crazy thing is that you are probably reading this and saying that's right but you are one of them and are so far gone that you're in denial just as a drug user denies being a drug abuser.

Here's a game that you play on yourself that jeopardizes you, your spouse, your children and your future as a family, not to mention "Nation building as a whole." Most people get married for all the wrong reasons. If this were not true, it would not be a high rate of divorce throughout the country. The fact is, most of the time it's because of society and or religion pressuring single men and women to get married once they reach a certain age. This causes you to second guess yourself and rush into marriage when logic or your spirit tells you not to do it. But you go against the grain and do it anyway, or you get married because of society and or religion pressuring you due to the fact that you are pregnant and you don't want to have a child out of wed-lock and disgrace the family, or you want financial security from the father or whoever might be the bread-winner. Some people even get married because of the pressure that's placed on them by society and or religion because of their sexual preference, and lastly, some people get married because of their belief in their religious doctrine, period or the selfish tradition of a family arranged married. All these factors lead towards anxiety, regret, loneliness, anger, resentment and the notorious questions for some, "Why am I going through this God?" "What did I do to deserve this?" "Why me lord?" The god's honest truth is that, that's the road you took because of the peer pressure imposed on you by the falsehoods of society and or religion. Another reason some relationships never work is because you are so caught up in your own selfish world of what you want the relationship to be that you will go above and beyond to make it work when you know it won't. You spend countless hours, days, months, weeks and years trying the make it work and everybody is calling you a fool and you know it's true but the selfish part of you keeps justifying your reason to live the lie. You try even harder to make it work because you want to prove the world wrong and this pushes you farther away from reality, so out of desperation you accept whatever is presented to you in the relationship; good, bad or indifferent. Years have passed and you said that you have invested too much time and money so you are determined to make it work. Now you justify your insanity by using the scriptures that tell you how you should be faithful and loyal because your good deeds will be recognized by God and you will get what you worked so hard for all your life. So you dig deeper into the falsehood of reality and pray and hope it will work. When the hard drive crashes and reality hits you like a tons of bricks, you blame the person you tried to mold into your perfect model of perfection for all your heart-break, you blame them for all your; woulda, coulda, shouldas. After that you start to resent God for not answering all your prayers to make the relationship work. You feel God turned the other cheek so you turn the other cheek on God. You blame everybody but yourself for your unescapable demise that you created because of your selfish fantasy that you wanted to have. You question the fact; why me, I am the nicest person alive, I will do anything for anybody. Maybe you would but you didn't consider your actions as to why you allowed yourself to be victimized by your own selfish behavior. The truth is most people in these situations find out early that the relationship won't work or they realize from the start that it won't work. The problem is; what they want is more than the reality they refuse to accept. So they go through the pain hoping to make the other person change and it never happens. The irrational phycology is that after a while some people are still in denial and start to blame themselves for what they've been through, but the blame is justified with ridiculous reason; like maybe I did something wrong, maybe I shoulda tried harder, etc. So you set out to do the same thing all over again. It's all based on your selfish superficial actions to get what you wanted and you don't even realize the game. I hope this message will wake some of you up so you can understand yourself and grow as a child of the Most High and by the principles governed by the laws of the universe. Take time to learn yourself and be a free thinker, become a leader that's enlightened by spirit and not doctrine. The doctrine is stunting your growth, it's like being in the 8th grade every year learning the same thing but in different words and you never pass the 8th grade, but you think you are learning something. You are learning something, learning how to accept that level of understanding and you justify it in a way that only you understand.

By the same token, you were a follower and not a leader, meaning you were a follower of selfish pride and superficial wants and desires. As a leader you should have followed your logical thought and not the emotional heart; (**logic** is to **know** and **emotions** are to **believe**) the god that told you not to continue hurting yourself is the thoughts you should have manifested into fruition. I know the truth is a hard cross to bear but that's the cold hard facts. Understand, the truth will **set you free** and you will elevate to the next level of understanding once you **accept the truth**. I have to bare the same cross because I'm no greater than you. The only one that can make it right is you. You are the one that put yourself in the situation and you are the only one to get yourself out. Praying will not help you fully understand the answers to your problems or magically make it better so don't turn your back on who you think God is when you don't get an answer because you are only hurting yourself. Once you overstand who god is, **you will be free and you will have the power to make a change**. By the same token, when you rely on specific vices like prayer to strengthen your weaknesses it shows you're spiritually and mentally weak. Examples; alcohol, drugs, stimulants to lose weight and other issues that you have the power to control to strengthen your weak spirit and weak mind but you chose a substitute your power and relinquish it to false vices to do your job shows you are weak and it takes away the will power/God power within you to overcome your weaknesses. In essence you live your entire live based on a false ideology that becomes a legacy for generations and based on your indoctrinated teachings and the mind set of popular belief (based on the life of Jesus) you understand why things are always grim for you, so think it is supposed to be that way and you accept it and teach your offspring to accept it. The game gets deeper and deeper until you dig so deep that you can't get out of the internal hole you dug. But as long as you are breathing and you read this book, you have a chance to change the game, so be a game changer and live a better tomorrow today.

Understand that you have the willpower to overcome but when you are inundated with Unnatural supplements … medicinal crutches and philosophy outside of yourself to help you be spiritually and mentally stronger … you become powerless and unaware of the power you possess within. Again greater is he that is in you than he that is in the world, Throw away your resentment, anger, selfishness and pain because it's holding you back from the fruits of life, it's creating unwanted health problems, and it's stopping you from growing as a child of Maat. Life isn't about you, it's about us. It's not about 1 thing; it's about all things living as 1. As long as you hold on to the past and the negative aspects of it; by making comments about it, constantly talking about, using your pass experiences as an excuse not to move forward in your own mind, you are keeping yourself stagnate and depression will always haunt you. It's time to grow and seek out a new experience and execute the power of your positive will to take you to the next level of understanding. If we both train for a ten round fight and you train ten times harder, who do you think will win? "You of course" But do you know **why**, it goes beyond the harder training even thou that would be the initial path to winning. It starts with consistency, your desire to succeed, your will to want more, your focus on success and the extra 3% that out weights the law of averages. The **why** to all goals and answers are the root to motivation and true understanding which empowers your will and subconscious mind to stand firm and be consistent in all you do. **Why**, will enable you to be the best in everything you do and allows you more victories than failures. Failures should be embraced as lessons learned not as defeat. Remember, **you never lose** either **you win** or **you learn**. The more you overstand the closer you get to the Creator and you experience liberation every time. Personally, I love the high of being liberated, it happens over and over again. Remember, **you can only see as far you can think**. The games you play on yourself for selfish reasons might be for the same reasons people don't wanna hear the truth about their "BS" belief system and are in denial about that as well. A man named, Friedrich Nietzsche once said, **"People don't want to hear the truth because they don't want their illusions to be destroyed."**

"Pain is weakness leaving the body" This statement holds true to every aspect of life. Working out your muscles for the 1st time, you will experience pain because your weak "cells" muscles are dying and being replace with stronger cell tissue "muscles." In a relationship your broken heart is weak to new negative experiences and the adversities you have will pass–away as long as you learn from them and not look back like Lot's wife did and turn into a "pillar of salt." Meaning; **grow through** the pain so that you don't have to **go through** the pain, again and again. (thank you Les Brown). Don't look back on life and get stuck in a time-warp, or become a "pillar of salt" as Lot's wife did in the story of Sodom and Gomorrah. Keep mentally moving forward and let your pass stay in the past. **"If its dead don't dig it up"** As you get stronger life gets easier and you learn how to handle all relationships better. You are living history, meaning every time you witness or experience and event, whether you are part of it or not, that's history that you should learn from. History for all intent and purpose is a lesson of learning and developing yourself. His-story should be just that, his story. All people should learn about their own culture and be told of their history. If you learn about another sociality's history thought-out life and never learn about yours, what contributions do you make in life regrading someone else history. Your experiences and mistakes in life are learning lesson. If you don't learn from your past experiences you are bound to repeat them. Never look at a situation as a bad experience always look at it from the prospective of a learning lesson because that's what it truly is. If you see it any other way, life will always be harder for you to understand and deal with because you did not learn from your experience for the simple fact that you do not see it as a learning experience. If you never understand that negativity is an adversary that initiates your growth your life will be the epitome of a living hell.

While we are talking about game I feel the need to express this point in hopes parents who seek money-child support designed for malicious reasons above their children's parental welfare, mental state of being and by the indirect injustice perpetrated by some parents who exploit their children will understand the impact of being selfish and greedy will have on their children's life as a whole as well as the future generations if they duplicate those selfish ways. "Mostly women" "Men do it to, but I see mostly women who do this selfish act" For the people who use their children to spite their other half is the worst. You are hurting the children and teaching them to be just like you. Look at generation X. Who do you blame for their disrespect and ignorance? **"We are!"** Our children of today are ignorant about who they are, health, law, history, religion, life, job applications, economics, morals, respect, spiritual deities, etc. Most of them show no spiritual drive to enforce their high god-self. I doubt if they even know who god is. They most likely believe in God or heard of the idea of God but I doubt if they truly know who God is. They don't even have a spiritual foundation because you never represented yourself as an example. As long as you are still living you have a chance to change yourself. Hopefully through that change, maybe your children will be inspired to learn who they are and become the gods they were destine to be and make their **world** a better place.

It's so much game out there I can't get into all of it, but its ridicules. People tell you they will do this and that, never do it and when you see them, they never mention anything about the topic. The point of this is not to go into all the games, it's too many. It's to show you how the lower self-indulges in non-productive activities and life is too precious to waist on playing games on people. People who live long enough to reach 3 score and above, see how lonely it is at the top, the top of their game that is. You die lonely and are easily forgotten. A note about the game of life, people tend to say, "Life's a game, you just have to know how to play it" The problem with that is, the game you think you are playing is serious and it's not a game. You can't even use the term metaphor for life and game. Unless you call it, "The game of death" If you are in a game you call life and all the players, play like you, those players need to be cut from the team or find a new game to play because you keep coming up with Ell's. (Losses), the only game of life that is relevant is the one you play 1 on 1, you the person and your persona, when relating to your lower and higher self. If you lie to yourself about your weaknesses or believe falsehoods and live them as a reality you put yourself in jeopardy and the lives of the people you love. That selfish spirit is the devil without a shadow of a doubt.

People tell me all the time, "oh no, the devil isn't in me, I have God in my heart, I fear God, I am saved and I know the devil isn't in me." They get so offended and make excuses to run away, run from the possibility that it could be true because it's easier to live the lie, because everybody is doing it. "That's sad and scary at the same time." The easiest fix is to admit your shortcomings to **yourself** first "internalize it," ask self to help self. Procrastination is a spirit called, "I'm my own worst enemy" remember the **Battle of Armageddon-Holy Jihad** is the **Trinity, "Me myself** and **I"** not outside the body. You are 1 mind 1 body 1 soul-spirit with Allah, the Creator, Jehovah, Yahweh, Yahweh Ben Yahweh, the Universe, The Great Architect "she is great" God, The Almighty and The Morning Star of the East.

Quick Note: throughout the book I highlight will, god and

God, the drive home the fact that there is a distinction between God and god and that when using certain words, like; "will" you are willing a particular action to happen. Gods **will** be done, its God's will … It's your **will** to do **gods** work … God's **will** be done on earth … **by god** as it is in heaven" **by God**.

What you do in the **dark** comes out in the **light**." If you don't acknowledge your sins & transgressions and no one else doesn't either, that doesn't mean they didn't see them. For me personally, when people run game, play stupid, think they are slick, try psychological games or whatever games they play, 10 out of 10x's I know what they are doing but I don't want to deal with the drama or I don't care because they are not that close to me anyway, or after years and years of trying to help and support that person they just don't want to change for the better because they choose not to. "**god** helps those who help themselves" you are the one that's helping you, no prayer or magic moment will help. It never did and never will. Wake up now! The funny thing is some people really think their game is invisible and supreme. I just laugh and keep it moving or become conveniently unavailable to avoid all the drama. I know as long as I live there will be opposition; Flesh can't have it any other way.

Dark: "my defining thoughts and the manifestation of knowledge"
Light: "knowledge manifested" (Jahi Ali-Bey)

Here's a side bar about money because most people think it's the root to all evil. It's not!

The reality of money is, it gives you a superficial feeling of power if you are not grounded in your higher **god** spirit and have the understanding that the spirit of greed, power and lust are the dominate factors that prevail if you already have them present within you. They are lying dormant for the chance to emerge. Meaning; if you are, who you say you are but your middle name is, "incognito" you won't be able to hide your true essence because money enhances the real you. "You have the power **in you** the defeat that spirit," but if people-society and your religion teaches or uses the excuse, "Money is the root of all evil" the lower you **will** subconsciously justify that bullshit and run with it" If you're an asshole, you show your whole ass. If you're a giver you have the ability to give without condition. Bottom line is whatever spirits you have hiding in the closet they **will** reveal themselves without prejudice, if you allow them. Take charge of **yourself** and destroy the, **I** part of *you* to be the, **me** that, I am. Me, Myself and I, we are **1** with **G**od and **g**od is **1** with *us*. When the trinity is in balance, meaning: 1 me, 1 myself, and I, we fight as 1 god to defeat our lower god-self.

Future lessons in sacred geometry 1+1+1=1 there are 3 points to a triangle but there is only 1 triangle.

Here's a side bar about Users, whether they are users of people or drug users the spirit of most users are all the same. They are Selfish and self-centered with a Bladen disregard for everything else. The spirits of most of these people think their game is superior and all others inferior, lol. What a joke. When users are not confronted right away, they take the rope and run with it, burn bridges and when you give them an inch they don't take a yard they take the whole darn mile. But when you get tired of them trying to use you and you confront them about their issues or addictions 9x's out of 10 they **will** try and reverse the blame to avoid the shame.

People from all walks of life can be users, no matter what background they come from. We can go on and on about people and their selfish games but I don't want to invest my time or the patience, most of you know who you and or they are. The focus here is twofold; if you are taught or have the mental capacity to self-teach yourself and build self-awareness of your fallacies you **will grow** through situations vs **go through** situations. Learn what it takes to be spiritually mature, have a strong foundation and reprogram you "**the higher you, the god in you**" to be a responsible person by dealing with your issues and shortcomings via the person in the mirror *"face to face,"* before pointing the finger at other people for false justification. Remember, when you point 1 finger 3 point back.

All three point at the 1 person who's truly at fault. All heads shall bow *"humiliation"* and all tongues **will** confess *"self-conviction"* You need to know who has the power, wake up! Enlighten your god self. Don't believe you have the power, know it, don't hope you can do it, just do it! "Thine **will** be done."

CHAPTER – 15

BAD HABITS

I want to talk a little about bad habits because its and integral part of your spiritual and mental weakness when you don't acknowledge bad habits. Bad habits are like excuses most people have them. When you have a strong higher **god-self**, you find it easy to **break** bad habits. Bad habits express **Satan's**-lower god-self. You might not be aware of a bad habit because you've been doing it for so long it became second nature. Your lower god-self tells you, you can't quit instantly because it's a habit and old habits are hard to break. That's what you were told and/or taught, Right? That social construct weakens your higher god-self and advocates selfishness and weakness. This is the type of attitude which develops the weak mentality that justifies the actions of your lower god-self.

With that in mind, if you allow yourself to believe that crap, your lower spirit will use that to keep you captive and stagnate. The spirit of selfishness is the obstacle that's keeping you from moving forward. This is the id side of your psyche/consciousness which revolves around your fleshly desires; satanic selfish wants. You have the power in you to defeat Satan but you need to know that and know it with full conviction! Be adamant in knowing who you are! For the simple fact that you're fighting for your life! Do you understand the forces you are up against? Please understand this is not just words on paper. We are talking forces seen and unseen. Your physiological and psychological states of being are constantly in opposition. Know this, the only reason you are not perfect is because you are a mixture of flesh and spirit. Not because you are not God because you are god and once you return to the essence in your spiritual form, you return to perfection. So you are who you are and with that you control the power to over-throw Satan-the bad habit.

I've often heard people who have fought with addiction mention that everybody has a bottom: meaning they had enough, they can't take it no more, I reached my breaking point, etc. and now I'm ready to go in a rehab. But why wait until you hit rock bottom to do something about it? Answer; you lost your **will** to win. (*Psychological warfare*) You don't know yourself enough to take pride in yourself and lead yourself out of the storm. (*Psychological warfare*) You feel you are a failure. (*Psychological warfare*) Also due to the fact you didn't know bad habits and excuses are bad spirits and you didn't know you have the power to win that battle of Armageddon without medicine *"in some cases."* (*Psychological warfare*) Question, are you doing this to yourself because of selfish reasons. Are you saying you are a victim of society and the system and you allow yourself to be a puppet that can be controlled by strings because you are too weak to control yourself and you use bad habits to justify your-self-induced self-pity? As long as you are still breathing and your spirit animates your body you have the self-induced will power to take charge of self and change your situation via your higher god-self. Be strong in knowing who you truly are and use the power vested in you to your advantage so life can be lived much easier for you and your family. Teach your children the same principals and instill leadership qualities in them so that the spirit of procrastination doesn't become their own worst enemy. Teach your children that adversity is a great tool for acquiring mental and spiritual strength and it promotes maturity as well as well-roundedness. Teach them to embrace adversity and accept the challenge. Teach your children and yourself to be responsible for your actions and understand you are hurting more people than just yourself by being negligent. Bad Habits can lead to bad health or death if there not broken in adequate time. Some people ask me from time to time. What can I do to fix my debilitating condition because the doctor gave me ex-amount of months or years to live? My reply is this; first you need to listen carefully to my instruction, you must do everything I tell you, dig deep and pull every ounce of mental strength you have left to the surface and we can get started. Their response is; I don't have a choice!

Quote: from a song by, **"Mary Mary"** "What is it that you think you see? **"It's the god in me"**

I personally despise the idea of teaching that the Creator gave us a choice because it's in conflict with my spirit and opposes everything I know the Creator is, was and ever shall be. Let me explain. If you who are in stage 4 renal failure or any other stage of life which constitutes expiration and you tell me that you don't **have a choice** after I lay down the laws of survival. That means that you submitted to the **will of god.** From that point forward, you **will** do everything in **your will-power** to live. If I was told I had a choice to do right or wrong because I have a **will** and whoever told me that, would still condemn me for my choices, they are dead wrong and it means that I never really had a choice.

I want you to look at these two definitions and you decide which one fits the teachings and doctrines of some religious schools of thought.

1. **Ultimatum:** "I see negative outcomes based on the meaning of ultimatum;" a demand whose fulfillment is requested in a specified period of time and which is backed up by a threat to be followed through in case of **noncompliance.** Thanks Definitions.net

2. **Choice:** "I see positive outcomes based on the meaning of choice;" Choice; of a grade between prime and good; Thanks you kindly (Webster's Ninth new Collegiate Dictionary) also

implies the chance or ability to choose between different things. … I would like to know why we are taught God gave us a choice. I know why but I want to plant the seed.

If I had a choice to pick, choose or do whatever I wanted to do, there are no negative repercussions behind my decision based on the meaning of choice. On the other hand, if I was given an ultimatum, the threat is reasonably evident. It would have made total sense if I was taught that God gave us an ultimatum as opposed to a choice because ultimatum sets the tone for the fact that discipline or punishment is enviable. But that's sounds too much like the truth so the Church must have omitted it or translated the Hebrew incorrectly and the Greek, given the benefit of the doubt, Smh "shaking my head." I guess the Sunna and Quran's interpretations are somehow inter-connected to the same miss-guided principles. In the laws of creation and life there is no choice, that whole concept is so far from the truth that it pisses me off to know 99 percent of the religious people who follow that religious doctrine really believe that B.S. belief system and never used common sense and the god spirit that was bestowed upon them by the Creator to pick up on that non-sense. Furthermore, for all you theological scholars that teach your sheep how to argue your doctrine by using the word aka scriptures, surah's, etc. whereas, "God gave us a choice" quote unquote in your biblios? For all intent and purposes, don't say **freewill** because **will** is not **free** if there is a **price to pay** for using it based on having a choice. If ultimatum was used instead of choice it would be totally acceptable and my spirit can receive that concept without question.

If you were taught that you never had a choice from birth, it **would not** be so easy for you to succumb to your lower god-self because your higher god power would hold you in contempt as a child of the Most High. Knowing you don't have a choice would have a greater influence on your decision to do the right thing **as god**. But if you are taught that you have a choice, subconsciously you make excuses and continue your bad habits and consciously pray for forgiveness. By which you're never forgiven because you are intentionally defiling yourself and selfishly and **un**knowingly feeding the **wrong god**. Again, "My people are destroyed for lack of knowledge," Not having a choice in certain avenues of life is spiritually healthy; it doesn't make you a robot it keeps you from being a fool. Open your mind to common sense and if you don't have much in common with your higher god-self, then it doesn't make sense. Unless you are the devil and you've been ever since. Honor thy father and thy mother: that thy days may be long upon the land which the Lord thy God given thee. I think that verse came from, **Exodus 20:12** If you know this statement to be true it's synonymous with obeying God's natural laws. To honor your mother & father is not a choice, "You do have a choice not to do it. Doing it is not a choice. For all you street scholars, if you don't honor your parents you die at a much younger age or live a life of chaos and your children will do the same. God doesn't curse you, you curse yourself by the life you live in regards to thinking you have a choice. Look at the news and compare the 50's, 60's, 70's, 80's, and 90's up until now. The progression of death keeps climbing; I'm not making this up! The point is that our teachers, friends, family and parents as a whole, instilled a God fearing mindset along with a parental understanding of total respect for all elders. Where are these principals now? So it's easy to understand why there is more death and corruption in the world-Flesh. It's more of everything negative escalating at an astonishing rate. With the help of your local, state and federal governments changing laws and taking power from god and giving it to man and you as a child of God allowing the ruler of the world's lower god-self to conquer the world as he should because you let him. We are the Mark of the beast by default "flesh" 666 your last Revelation

Its power in numbers but most of you forgot who god is and you are duped into thinking you really know. For it is written, "I will deceive the whole world" "all flesh" Do you not think that you are a part of the whole world? Or are you an alien? Contrary to Satan talking all that jazz, I'm not deceived. So I must be an Alien or maybe common sense over powered my willingness to be a follower. What about you?

Back to choices; if the sun had a choice to shine and decided not to. We would die instantly. Did the Creator have a say so as to the sun making a choice not to shine? If the planet earth decides to stop spinning we would die instantly. Did the Creator have a say so in that as well? What if what we call gravity and or magnetism decided to demagnetize or gravity become anti-gravity, we would die instantly. Who made that choice? Flies come out in the summer, if they had a choice to come out in the winter they would die the same wintery cold day they transformed from maggots. All insects that are naturally made to breed in the summer, it would be foolish to disobey mother-nature, by not honoring God's law. There is no choice in that reality. The point is this, everything on God's great earth obeys natural laws except the most intelligent beings living, us. For the most part, the only time we consider obeying god is when we are on our death bed. Most people become humble, start apologizing about mis-doings, wanting to see the people they did wrong, so on and so forth. Again you should understand that if you **decide not to have a choice** you are building the higher god in you to destroy the lower god in you and the battle will be won by the creator. At that point in your life you will have no doubt in your mind that you are going to Paradise, Heaven or you will be reincarnated, whatever divinity is yours, you will get there without a conscious question.

Be careful about who you pretend to be
because you might forget who you are!
"Unknown" Much respect to whoever
conceptualized this quote, OMG!

CHAPTER – 16

SALVATION

EVERLASTING LIFE

Salvation: Think of woman when you read the definition of salvation and relate the aspects and characteristics of woman and witness the similarities. **Salvation:** deliverance from the power and penalty of sin. Thank you (Webster's Ninth new Collegiate Dictionary.) Salvation is also considered the act of saving or protecting form harm or destruction.

Savior: someone who saves something or someone from danger, harm, failure. Thank you Merriam-Webster.com Note: If Jesus and God are one in the same, why doesn't the definition reflect Jesus or his other self as God the savior and not the word someone? I'm just asking. My parents were my savior when I was a child and as I matured I have grown to save myself as a child of the most high through my actions and deeds.

Eternal: There were cultures of people on the planet thriving and living just as every other culture did. But for some reason some of them are nonexistent. So where would the meaning of eternal life fit in the way we are taught what eternal life means? **Eternal:** having no beginning and no end in time: **lasting forever.** Thank you Merriam-webster.com

Parable: A parable is like a metaphor; perceptible phenomena to illustrate abstract ideas. Thanks En.wikipedia.org My question is why would religious scholars teach us that God speaks in parables and then justify scripture by insisting those same parables are literal meanings?

Remission: I was taught about remission and I do not understand how some of us will still burn in a so-called hell when some of us repent, pray and practice communion along with the fact that remission means; release, as from debt or obligation.

In this chapter I will answer your question about what is the purpose of life, on a spiritual and physical level. Any other purpose, you got me, because outside of these two principles I don't know of any other purpose. Before we explore purpose, as always I have a couple of questions to ask. If God speaks in parables why do most people take studying religious doctrine to the extreme and come up with 40,000 different meanings and explanations of what the Hadiths, Surat, sahih and scriptures means? "K.I.S.S. Keep It Simple Stupid" Ok let's look at simple. Your purpose in life is to keep mankind from self-annihilation by enforcing your higher **god–self-will** of, love, truth, peace, freedom, justice, equality, knowledge and understanding to all life you come in contact with. In doing so, your lower god–self will stay harmless in the grand scheme of things. Remember, because we have the spirit of God in a fleshly jail called the human body, there will always be opposition from Satan. As long as there is God there will be Satan. The battle of Armageddon will never stop because all people can't be on the positive side of God unless you are called back to the essence. It's not easy bearing the cross when you don't have the right ammunition to fight with. Your second purpose in life are the goals you set on the physical realm of life, meaning; your major goals you would like to accomplish before reaching perfection, the creator.

Ok this is the part where I say, "Stay with me." The woman is our true **salvation.** The **savior** is the union between man and woman coming together to procreate to give us eternal life. "Stay with me."

Due to the fact, that women have a menstrual cycle. Which by far, is the Creator's greatest gift to humanity, via all women? The blood sacrificed by woman every 28 days is proof of everlasting life as well as remission. The representation of this is, "Holy Communion" which occurs once a month in some religions: "the blood and body sacrifice of Christ for salvation and eternal life." Like the scripture says, **"Hebrews 9:22"** and almost **all things are by the law purged with blood**; (KJV) and without the shedding of blood there is no remission. Women purge involuntarily through the flowing of the blood and without that process she could not ovulate. By the laws of nature and yes, nature is created by God. All women who have a menstrual cycle pay the price for the sins of mankind month after painful month along with the agonizing pain of birth to ensure that we live forever and we need to acknowledge them for the life bearers and life saviors-savers that they are. With that being said, I will extend light far beyond your cable toe-umbilical cord so endure the pain. Remember, "Pain is weakness leaving the body." This will be intricate for many and hard to swallow for some because most of you stay in your mental comfort zone four-cornered box and dare to come out. I know I should not reveal this but I will break the rule this time because I am not bound by the halls of men. Throughout my travels in life, E Pluribus Unum particular philosophies I studied introduced me to the Heaven and Earth connection and the vortex from which semen travels through. This is called the Kundalini, initiating the heaven and earth connection called the "triple stage darkness" evolution of mankind. "Surat 86:6 He was created from a fluid ejected 86:7 emerging from between the backbone and the ribs." **Semen** has the same fatty acids in it as the brain does, docosahexaenoic acid and arachidonic acid are the dominant essential fatty acid components of the brain and these are the elements that pass through the "Blood Brain Barrier" induced via sexual stimulation and carried by way of seminal fluid down to the Kundalini "Backbone and the twelve chakras"-Serpent chamber "prostate" to unite with a male's **sperm** in the testicles and become united in the 1st stage of darkness. The sperm is then ejaculated in the uterine walls; it swims inside the cervix to the fallopian tubes to be received by the egg which is the 2nd stage of darkness. When her egg allows the strongest sperm it wants to fertilize it, through her earthly gates, she then electrifies her walls around the outer perimeter of the egg putting up a plasma force-field so no other sperm can penetrate her barrier to fertilize that egg. Fertilization begins and that is the 3rd stage of darkness called life. And out of the darkness came the light-knowledge-born. In other words, it's intrinsic intelligence manifested by the act of procreation into human form to animate life and express it as a physical being.

This is your revelation of being saved by your savoir. When your body is in the ground, what are you saving? Oh yeah, your spirit from burning in the Hell-fire, I forgot I mentioned earlier that your spirit must have nerve ending and your father will burn you forever ever, forever ever. Know that the 7 primary chakras and 5 subprime chakras for a total of 12 chakras are what make up your spirit and your spirit is 1 with the Creator; your spirit is a spinning ball of burning fire inside of you. "You have your own personal sun that keeps you at 98.6" That's why when your flesh dies you get cold and your spiritual god-self returns back to its origin which is the same universal energy that created it. So how could you possibly think you will burn in hell? The Creator-God I know would never do such a heartless act. It still boggles my mind to think that people believe that a spirit which is energy-light-part of the Creator can burn in hell forever when in reality the chakras in your body are representation of the spirit burning as you live each day.

With that in mind, I would like to shine light on the distinction between your spirit and soul. Your soul relates to the burden of proof regarding your conviction to truth. Your soul convinces you to do a righteous act and your spirit leads the way. If your spirit is in the wrong place it will lead you in the wrong direction. Your soul comes into play again to convict you to do the righteous thing; hence, "The Battle of Armageddon." Some faiths believe your soul is the part of you that burns in hell. That is not the case. Your soul is attached to the physical plane and is synonymous with emotions which are also on the physical plane. The only substance that's not on the physical plane that resides in you is your **spiritual essence** borrowed from the Creator. Your spiritual essence is that part of your higher-self, energy that transcends back to the essence and recreates energy-life when your physical body breathes its last breath. Your soul can not burn in hell. Please understand that the physical elements of life breed physical properties and the spiritual elements of life breed spiritual properties. The two of them are like oil and water, one stays on the surface and the other is underneath, they never mix. The Creator does not have a soul for those of you who believe this **non-sense**. It does not make sense due to the universal laws of Allah, emotion and logic cannot mix. The Creator is not emotional, humans are and if you refuse to know this truth to be self-evident, maybe you have "Chronic Voluntary Mind Block." It could be stemming from an inescapable misunderstood religious educational system of teaching that programmed you to be afraid to think freely and independently as a leader. This could cause you to acquire "Sheep like tendencies" and conform you to being a follower for the rest of your physical life which stunts your mental and spiritual grow as a spirit of the Most High. Start from the beginning of the book and try to grasp everything once again. Please get a pen a paper, take notes and research what you must. I really want all of you to travel in the true guiding light so you can see more clearly.

I hope you over-stood the reasoning of **soul**. I had to touch on it because it's one aspect of religious dogma that's mis-understood by many. With that being said, I want you to understand the other side of salvation in regards to how the government and big commercial business (The Central Banking) agenda is waging war at the price of our salvation and eternal life. When I speak of waging war on our salvation, I'm speaking of our Godly principles and moral constitution as well as our obligation to humanity which is contrary to the laws set in place by man (Big Business). It's an abomination with regard to the ethical principles of life itself. In business there is no place for ethics or morals, it's all about business. Here's salvation with a twist. On a life threatening scale, salvation is losing momentum in the grand scheme of things. This is where we as a people need a collective thought process due to the big picture in regards to greed by big business and everlasting life as we know it. I said that to say, big business is set up for an elite few and they don't care about humanity as a whole, only fiat currency and power. If we as a whole act as a team mentally and spiritually to save ourselves, eventually big business will implode and self-annihilation will be inevitable. As a child you witness the aspects of life and are taught what the realities of life is supposed to be like, but as you grow up to be an adult that picture you had of life changes and your spirit tells you that something is different and or wrong but you can't put your finger on it. Most people you know have the same common interests basically because everyone has been conditioned to be submissive and follow the agenda. "living the lie and accepting nonsense and or truly believing the nonsense" so you go on about your life like everybody else, totally ignoring the truth because you feel you can do nothing about it, so you accept it and some of you join circles and organizations that accept hypocrisy as reality which gives you a false identification with self to help justify your so-called reality so you can fit in. Then you raise your family to do the same and in the same breathe you wonder why the whole world-flesh is in shambles "how hypocritical is that?" How crazy is that? Again, if you tell a lie long enough, you start to believe it; it becomes your reality. The same thing applies if you hear a lie long enough you start to believe that as well. If you read this book in its entirety and do nothing for your family's survival or even start to learn about your true self and god, you are perpetuating mass murder through Satan, your lower god-self. Most of the world is living a lie. How do I know? How can I say that? "You are killing me!!!" Simple; almost every culture complains that their government is mis-treating them. We even fight other governments-countries that abuse their citizens. We make statements saying, "The world is getting worse," "People are turning away from God." Pray more, Etc. First of all, they never knew Allah, God; still don't know Allah or most importantly, the power of self.

This is one of the reasons why I wrote this book, we as a body collective throughout the national and international diaspora need to know and understand who and what The Life Force is. If most of us really knew Allah, The Almighty, the Higher Power, The Life Force, Jehovah things would be moving in the opposite direction because we would be imposing our universal powers on Satan as 1 mind. The people would have their power back where it belongs, with god. *"You can't hear me thou"* All religions will never come together as 1 mind. Religion was created to keep us weak-minded, separated, segregated, and infuriated with each other. The distraction is working for the ones in power and it has been since the writings of the first biblical books. Proof is all around you I'm not making this stuff up. If this was not true there wouldn't be books written way back then that talked about government tyranny, burning cities because of sinful people, killings of the first born because of heartless kings, famine, locust eating all the crops because of disobedience. And the infamous one of all that is mentioned every so often, "the world coming to an end."

Most of you don't even know what the word "world" means or what it is. If you did, businesses would not make so much money off of the masses because of propaganda and scare tactics. One example is the Mayan Calendar that ended the world in 2012. The Mayans was right about the end of the world if you study astronomy and astrology but most religious sects deem that aspect of life taboo. "Think outside the box you will learn more." They were referring to the end of the 2000 year Piscean Age which ended officially on November 10, 2011. November 11, 2011 ushered in the Aquarian Age. They were talking about the end of and Age in reference to the mindset and philosophies of a people "us" as I mentioned in the Ages Chapter of this book. Let's get back on the issue of salvation. Understand this; when you die, the world just came to an end for you, "the dead person" that's what that means. "Your flesh will cease to exist, Satan is dead" Remember flesh is sin, "he that is of the world"-Satan is sin, your skin breathes through your pores but the breath of life comes through your nostrils and mouth. The Almighty breathed the breath of life into your nostrils not your skin. Satan's breath is through your pores, again when you take your last breath; Satan dies with your physical Mind, body and soul. The wages of sin-Satan is death. Can you truly comprehend the profound meaning behind the simplicity of that sentence? Universal law, Jehovah, Yahweh, Allah and Mother Nature, took the breath of life back. That breath is everlasting on a spiritual plane because it comes from the source that created it and truth can never change, die or pass away. The Creator can never be destroyed only the creation. If the **source of creation** is destroyed life will cease to exist and so will creation itself. Intrinsic Intelligence will not allow that to happen. With that in mind, Satan is part of the creation not the source. Some might say why am I putting all this energy and focus on non-sense. Because I care and I want you all to grasp the over-standing and stop understanding what is being conveyed. Every little bit of knowledge gets you closer to the overstanding of who god is and before you finish this book, god will be revealed. Swimming in ignorance allows the power elite to hold the power and take everlasting life from us. "My people are destroyed by lack of knowledge." How many people in your family died since you have been born? How many do you keep alive by celebrating their anniversaries or talking about their ancestral tree every year, make family day for them, pour libation to show respect for your ancestors in the valley of the dead. Probably none and if you do your family might think you are crazy, Right? Well our country celebrates dead presidents and rich people who died all the time. "Keeping their spirits and traditions alive in the hearts and minds of all of you" Hum? It's not about the money, that's a smoke screen. The only way to ensure everlasting life is to join forces outside of your religious convictions and become 1 mind as a people and 1 with your god spirit. By the same token we need to focus on self-sustainment as a people. If we do that, salvation is inevitable and no weapon formed against us will prosper!

Quote: "The worst drug known to man, it's stronger than heroin, when you could look in the mirror like, There I am and still not see what you've become" (Jay-Z)

135

I feel the need to explain judgment from a different prospective due to the fact that it's some many aspects of religious education that is miss-represented that it leads you in the wrong direction and that's why so many people are confused. Open you mind for spiritual reception and take down the walls of religious rejection. When it comes time for judgment it's not about what the prophet or the priest said, it's not about how well you are versed in all dominations of Catholic scriptures, Quranic surah's, Sunna, Buddha's Pali Tipitaka, or the Christian fraternal twin called the Torah. It's not about what Peter, Paul or Jesus said. It's not how devout you are as a religious leader or a religious person. It's about your heart, your actions and your deeds. That's what you will be judged on at the last day of religious reckoning. So for all of you who are defending your religious B.S. belief system by saying, that's what the Hadith said, that's what the Bible said, that's what the Pope said.

What I am trying to get you to overstand is this. Research, study and accumulate you data from different sources so you will have a boarder prospective on the subject matter. You can't research inside the box because everything that's in the box validates the box. "Get It!" You can't live and base your life off of what someone else said, you need to be a free thinker, be a leader and take responsibility for your actions as a child of the Most High. Don't wait for someone or something to save you, Save Yourself. Waiting for a savior is a true sign of weakness. As a child your mother was your **savior** and your father should have been the protector. Look it up and while you are at it, look up **save**. I also gave you the biblical meaning of savior and salvation. Correspondingly, the first meaning of a word is usually the original one. But if you have, "Chronic Voluntary Mind Block" this whole lesson went over your head.

Question; Yeah I'm full of these, did you ever stop the think that some of what you were taught could possibly be pain-staking wrong? Did you ever think that even the devoted people who teach you could also be wrong? It's like the possibility of the blind leading the blind. I really don't think they purposely misguided people but they might be so devoted to what they believe that they don't know they don't know and think they know what they know as truth and it's possible it's not truth and I am here to show you the truth. It's ok to be wrong, but it's not ok to be wrong and not acknowledge your faults, make amends or correct them. That's not conducive of your higher god-self or life.

I have another question and I purposely saved it for this chapter. And I say this with all due respect! Monks as I understand do not fornicate, correct me if I am wrong. So if all men decided to be Monks what would happen to civilization? **Civilization would cease to exist** and who decided that there should be Nuns who are only married to God? Note: *"No way shape or form am I disrespecting your religious believe or your devotion to God as Nuns or Monks"* But the Creator, Universal law, Inanna, Allat, Mother Nature and Ishtar; enabled us as women and men to create life through each other forever. God is a spirit; a spirit cannot impregnate you. Virgin Mary served her symbolic purpose so why would you marry a spirit and not flesh to do what you are made to do by natural Universal Law. If my memory serves me correctly, "Hebrews 9:22" (KJV) According to the law almost everything is purified with blood and without the shedding of blood there is no forgiveness. "Forgiveness verified through the gift of life via ovulation and your menstrual cycle: the cleansing of the body via the blood sacrifice and the ovulation process for life ever-lasting" If our whole planet of women were Nuns and Priest **life would cease to exist** and that's contradictory to what the Creator's will is for humanity, insects, animals, reptiles, plants, flowers, stars, planets, fish etc. If all living creatures, plants and insects decided to marry God or abstain from the procreation process, life would cease to exist! Creation is everything and the majority of people only see God in relation to human creation and this is a major mis-conception and it's causing spiritual disruption and religious confusion. Creation is bigger than human existence and with that in mind, people cannot be born homosexual. When you look at the natural laws of nature and the want for creation it would appear that your personal desires, emotions and focus along with other factors cause you to go in the opposite direction that is contrary to the natural processes of gender. If you produce more estrogen than the average male or more testosterone than the average female, that simply means you have a chemical imbalance that needs to be corrected before it gets out of hand. At two and three years of age you don't even understand the concept of homosexuality. If Creation made you gay that would means trees, wind, water, clouds, planets, stars, fish, lions, bears and etc. would be born gay. Why is it that only people can be born gay if all things are created by 1 universal creator? So the god you believe in just singled you out and made you gay huh? Are you saying God/Creration is prejudice? God went against the 1st rule of, "Be fruitful and multiply" Creation itself went against its laws of Creation to eventually prohibit the act of creation by making people gay huh? Intelligence would not indulge in self-annihilation by creating gay off-spring because logic would not allow creation to destroy itself without the ability to reproduce. If you feel you are born gay those feelings are feelings you would need to acknowledge your own identity and justify your actions to get acceptance with your higher self. I personally have nothing against homosexual people; some of them are the most loyal straight forward people I have ever come in contact with. The ramifications of certain cultural existences would be devastating if we continue to act irresponsible by showing a Bladen disregard for the "Laws of Nature" because of our selfish behavior. Caveat; if we as a people do not conform to the Laws of Nature and continue to conduct ourselves in an immoral manner and ignore the natural process designed for us as the ordinary heterosexual beings that we are, we are predetermining our destruction.

People listen! If the good book says whatever it says and the higher authority you respect and admire translates, transliterates, explains whatever lesson, scripture, surah, hadith or passage, can you please use the common sense, understanding, your capacity for knowledge and logic you were bestowed with by the Creator and draw your own conclusions sometimes? It is ok to think outside the box, that's not a sin. Think about this, why isn't the Black Madonna with Child that's on display in Rome publicized worldwide like her duplicate Virgin Mary? And she existed thousands of years before Mary; I'm just asking the question. Why did the power elite (the ancient Greeks) change Auset's name to Isis? Auset is the mother of Heru; Heru's name was changed to Horus. Thoth's real name is Tehuti and there is more deceit and lies, more than I care mention. Do you know what they are a representation of? I'm asking you to research it. Why haven't local governments throughout the diaspora donated funds to reconstruct all of the Kemetic statues and other statues around the globe that were defaced? The secret is out about the defacing of statues and what ethnicity you were trying to hide by applying acid to the hieroglyphics inside of some of the pyramids (Pro-Neters) and Tombs to fade the brown color skin depicted by the glyphs and turn the color of the glyphs white, so why not do the ethical thing to correct it? For what it's worth, I will give you the answer. This is how the power elite-devil operates with respect to changing words, names, letters, meanings of scripture, translations, transliterations, abridging dictionaries and other books, etc.; if you do not speak the original language, you can never possess the power to understand the true language of your culture or cultural iconic glyphs-symbols and meaning that connect with your specific culture, Linguistics and Semantics, you cannot truly understand or translate your language and get the proper meaning or concept and your spiritual connection to your ancestral heritage is severed, making future generations weak and hybrid. So how can you teach me history and religion about my people and you have ill intention and you are not part of my culture and you don't truly know my heritage or language? If you do know about it, you hide from me and claim to be a child of God. With that being said the devil creates a total disconnect with my culture, my God, who we are as a people, my ancestors, my spirituality and my freedom. The truth will set us free but it will also give us salvation.

Quote: I'm for truth, no matter who tells it. I'm for justice, no matter who it's for or against. "Malcom X"

Here's out the box again; I hear people saying all the time, "if you didn't get baptized with your whole body in the water and they only dunked your face in the water, you were not truly baptized so you are not saved. Baptism is symbolic of being born again in spirit, mind and a willingness to submit to the will of the Creator. To be baptized doesn't save anyone from hell. OMG! Baptism is like a wedding ring. Weather I wear the ring or not, will not dictate if I will or will not indulge in infidelity. The ring and or contract in the form of a marriage certificate does not make me loyal, trustworthy, honest, righteous, or a saint and neither does a baptism. Every attribute I just mentioned comes from my soul and my willingness to act on those principals, not the superficial ceremonial ritual. I'm not saying that the ritual is wrong. I'm saying, understand the meaning of it, don't read into it and don't add to it. "It is what it is, so let it do what it does" "God knows your heart" and if you're telling people that quote, then a baptism should not be your concern, leave the superficial crap for shallow people, Still waters run deep. Either you are shallow or profound; there is no middle ground, that's an illusion. Action speaks louder than words. Show me your intent through actions and deeds and I will show you god. Good, Bad or Indifferent. Women, **thank you for your menstrual cycle**, "the blood of salvation and symbolism of everlasting life" if it wasn't for the god of salvation, I would not have existed to write this book and I wouldn't be able to have offspring that would carry my spirit in them to continue my legacy to help fallen humanity. Again, **I applaud you!**

When it comes to everlasting life everyone doesn't have that luxury due to the fact that certain groups of people want to secure their presence and ensure everlasting life for their species. It stems from the scientific fact that certain interracial mixing would eventually diminish some nationalities as we know them today. This is due the dominate genome that certain groups of people have and if interracial mixing increases, the progression of evolution would change the face of the world. By the same token, that's why the power elite had to annihilate quite a few cultures of people who possessed the dominate gene by means of deliberate cultural genocide. I explained it in detail to drive home the fact that, everlasting life can only be obtained through the presence of life. The nations and cultures of the past that were destroyed will not have a chance for everlasting life because they are not here to be **fruitful and multiply**. Cultures of people have flourished through the ages for hundreds of years but at some point some cultures will die off or get annihilated by a power struck dictator, selfish greed, or ignorance. This fact tells me that, we can't possibly have everlasting life or live in a so-called paradise after death based on religious doctrine because the people-cultures that are deceased are not alive to procreate. It would appear to me that the teachings of everlasting life are mis-guided and or mis-understood. I implore that you are absorbing the vibration of light in the form of overstanding. I also pray that the revelation of god is being received by your higher god-spirit by now. Outside of that, it's in my nature to ask questions, I see asking questions as a form of learning and a way of understanding. So the question is this;

Why are my Muslim brothers and sister fighting about which sect prays five times a day and which one prays three times a day and whoever doesn't pray all five times a day is subject to the hell fire and we refuse to speak or break bread together because of our indoctrinated differences and Chronic Voluntary Mind Block. Question: Praying 5 times a day is noted in the Quran? Three of the Salats' are in the Koran and the other two are not. Salat Al-Fajr, Salat Al-Isha, Al-Salat Al-Wusta. The other two are; Maghreb and Asr in the Hadith. My statements are not to judge anything regarding what you do religiously. My focus is to point out the stigmas and displacement of people because of religious beliefs from my observations throughout the years and how it pulls family, friends and people apart as well as confuse you. It's not your place to judge as a Muslim brother or sister or to indulge in the dogmas of any other religion. To condemn people because they don't see things your way or do things the way you do them is not conducive to the progress of humanity. Embrace them as a child of Allah and allow them to discover truth in their own time, make Dua for them and/ or show an open mind the path of light that will guide them, that's how you help your sisters and brothers learn. Arguing over your religious doctrines is one of the many obstacles that's pulling us apart and keeping us from divinity. You should embrace each other and unite as one for the greater good of Allah. It's basically your personal ceremonial ritual once again and because it's a religious preference and it's not law by Quranic principles that we to pray five times. We need to stop concerning ourselves with dogmatic perception and walk in the direction of spiritual perfection. Even if you argue the fact now, it doesn't change who I am or who you are, we both have freedom to voice our views on life so don't get bent out of shape. Breathe easy! I'm just writing my views in hopes to enlighten some of you so you can stop the non-sense and realize there is much more to life than a personal stance about your religious beliefs. This book was written to help you **grow** through it, not **go** through it. We are brothers and sisters in Maat, can't we just all get along. ☺ The Hadith says wear your trousers at calf level or at least above the ankle, so to speak, if not you will be pulled in the hell fire. This principle is based on conceit or the negative mind-set of greedy rich men, whatever analogy you choose to use. Allah considers your heart, actions and deeds. The way you wear your pants has nothing to do with Maat deciding if you go to paradise or burn in the so called Hell-Fire. That passage is a metaphor explaining the heart of a conceited man or a wealthy, greedy and heartless individual whom you would not want to emulate. It's nothing more or nothing less, your spirit should show you the common thread and relevance of this passage should be clear. Spirits do not indulge in material issues, only the intent of your heart and soul, which is akin to your spirit. Only man indulges time with materialistic values as in conceit because of how you look or the status you hold in this materialistic world and or the wealth you have that might have tainted your mind to the point that you disrespect, abuse, and hurt people and abuse the use of authority, these are the actions and intent that will be judged by Allah that will have you burn in the so-called "Hell-Fire," not the way you wear your pants. Also while we are discussing the appearance and issues concerning clothes; Ladies, if you have a bad hair day please stop acting as if you are Muslim by wearing a Niqab to hide the fact that you are too lazy to take the time and style your hair because your conduct is inappropriate and ill-mannered. There are seven different ways to wear your headscarf and sometimes it depends on what sect of Islam you choose to represent and with that being said, some of the sisters in New Jersey, Delaware and Philadelphia who choose to wear your Shayla, Kemar and or full garb need to re-read or read, Surah 24: ayat 31 because you are disrespecting yourself, your religion and you are putting out the wrong message to the rest of the community by wearing tight jeans with your Al-Amira, Shayla, Hijab, Kemar, Chador, Niqab and Burka, and smoking cigarettes while in garb, using profane language etc. You stick out like a sore thumb and because of that, the people that are stereotypical superficial swallow minded individuals look at the Islamic culture as a whole and condemn and criticize the Islamic religion and Muslim community which in turn creates a negative outlook on the religion as a whole resulting in negative out-lash and opposition. Wearing Muslim attire doesn't confirm you are Muslim; your soul must be convicted, and spirit must be motivated by the, "Five Pillars of Faith" and the "Principles of Islam," which are exemplified by your actions and deeds. The Islamic religious community should reinforce a type of corrective discipline to those who disrespect the Islamic attire as they did when I was a little boy and if Church and State are really separate, then the State should stay in its lane when it comes to Islamic discipline and allow the unimpeded practice of Shariah. All who practice Islam should take pride in your religious attire and also be mindful of who you are as a child of Allah when conducing yourself in public. Actually a good percentage of sisters that I see wearing the Niqab and Burka respect and represent Islam well. I would like to thank you sisters for doing the right thing. If you are not practicing Islam you certainly need to take your garb and kemar off!!! All the devolved Muslims, why do you allow this to happen? Some things change and some things don't. If you have a bad hair day, the niqab-kemar is not a scarf or a fashion statement. As a Muslim knows, you don't look at the person that's committing haram acts; you look at the truth in the religion. But it's hard to do that when you have ex amount of people operating outside the scope of Islam. The problem is, if all people looked at the characteristics of the religion instead of the people who misrepresent it, everything would be in accord. But if the people who follow Islam are not conforming to Islamic principles and you can't help but look at the people because that's all you can gauge the religion on. The people whose intentions are not of Islam, those issues need to be dealt with on an individual basis. These types of issues should but addressed but that's just not the case, that's why Islam has a bad reputation even though it's the world's largest religion.

The wearing of religious attire is well respected; this is in reference to people who have little regard for their religious apparel or issues that do not concern Quranic law. Because no matter what religious attire you wear it does not build or strengthen your connection with the creator, it just shows a physical distinction in regards to what you believe and your religious preference. This is not about dressing modestly, covering your breasts or genitals as a devout person who submits to the will of Allat, covering should be automatic and by the book. If you want to model yourself after Mohamad's wives so be it. I'm referring to the non-sense regarding religious dress that is not Quranic law and a lot of westernized Muslims make a big deal of it. I see too many people arguing about what is the proper attire and who you will give the greetings to and who you refuse to greet in an Islamic fashion because of what they may have on. That in itself is haram. How can you as a Muslim even think that way? I under-stand correcting people, who are blatantly disrespectful regarding how they dress, or act, but the petty arguments and bickering need to stop. It's parallel to the wedding ring; the ring itself doesn't show fidelity or loyalty to your spouse it just distinguishes you from a single person. Fidelity and loyalty is in your heart, Allah is in your heart not in your religious attire or the wedding band. That's superficial and you should have your focus on Allah and building a relationship based on the principles of Islam, learn to exercise "As salamu alaykum" the meaning and not the formalities of the greeting. The world is watching, show some honor and dignity as a person first. As one who is a part of the largest religion world-wide, you should be proud of what and who you are. Stop verbally bashing your brothers in Islam. Islamic wear doesn't make you a Muslim, your heart does. If you can't "show and prove" via your actions and deeds, your intent is not that of Allah. How could you expect Allah to bless your Salah or your Zakah? Remember, you came here with nothing and you will leave with nothing. But by the same token, if you truly study Surat 20 75 76, that might help you to be a better person in life and you will leave knowing that you were a role model for your children and you show them the righteous ways of Islam so they will not get caught up in the system and that will be a blessing from Allat.

Find Allah in your own proper person quick, respect yourself and other people will respect you. You should never demand respect, because that's not real, demanding actually leans towards fear, resentment and envy. The only genuine respect is the kind you earn. Lastly for the astute Muslim brothers and sisters, what is the difference between, Allat & Allah? I understand that pre-Islamic doctrine considered Allat and Allah but modern Islam only acknowledges Allah, but Allah and Allat existed at the same time, "from the beginnings" so why take her out of the picture? Is it due to the reconstruction of Islam that she was removed from the modern day teachings of Islam as the Christians did certain woman of the Bible to show male chauvinistic dominance? It's a question of equality in relation to 1. Without going on a tantrum and some long drawn out explanation, there is a reason why or is it that you can't answer that question because if a devout respected Islamic scholar was to reveal supporting evidence that the Allat deity is equally important as the Allah deity, it would raise question about Islamic doctrine?

Because in Islam the woman is second to the man and not essentially equal, that's why she walks to the rear of the man or did that change? I understand the concept of submissive actions of the woman, I'm past that justification. As you can see this sparks question and sheds light deep inside the male and female aspects of Islam. Let's create a healthy debate so that all can be enlightened. By the same token, if you give Islamic women spiritual equality, the doctrine that states Allah is 1 would still prevail and the women would stop defecting. My other anxiety is the fact that the Shiite and Sunna fight like crazy. It would seem that as a child of Allah you all should have put those physical difference in the dirt and spiritually matured by now and embrace Islam as 1 to united in the faith and leave the war ridden pestilence for the infidels? All of Islam agrees that the supreme divine law is the Quran so why are you killing Islamic brothers and sisters, would that be haram in the eyes of Allat? Where is your higher God spirit? Lastly, why do you as a Shiite, practice the ritual of beating yourselves with chains and cutting your heads with a dagger for thirty days? Your Imam who was Hussein, "May Allah have mercy on his soul" is in a garden of paradise, so by you preforming the ritual in commemoration of his assassination and thinking you will receive forgiveness from Allah for an act you didn't commit, that spiritually is perpetuating oppression and paying homage to a person outside of Allah, wouldn't that be idol warship, I'm just asking?

In science and in Universal law, it takes two to become one. That's revealed in the beginning, middle and the end of this book. Allat and Allah merged as 1 deity for the 1 common cause, they are 1 in the same when you look at their spiritual purpose. Remember spirit has no gender on the spiritual plane. There's a much larger meaning to the names but I won't go that far, you can do that on your own time. Understand this concept and the world we live in will be different as we know it. Make 72 equal one: 1 God 1 unified belief, no duality, no segregation or separation of 72. "7+2=9" that symbolizes completion in our science called sacred geometry. So make 9=1 "Maat is 1 but I see 72 and if 72 only see 72 as 72 how can Allah be 1? I'm just saying …

My Moorish brothers and sisters who only practice the religious side of our culture are deterring away from the primary reason Nobel Drew-Ali initiated and erected the temple. "Birthrights" There is nothing wrong with what you do religiously and that goes for everyone reading this book. To be clear, again I wrote this book to point out the possibility of mis-education and ignorant teachings of most religions and reveal to the world, "Who is God" Now as I was saying, what happened to the teachings of the seven liberal arts which consist of; rhetoric, grammar, logic, arithmetic-,"numbers within itself," geometry-,"numbers in space," music-,"numbers in time" astronomy-,"numbers in space and time" and just as equally important, civic lessons and the rights of all indigenous people-humanity? Because we are not Black History, we are World History and Columbus did not discover America, he exploited it, so did the Greeks, Romans, Persians, the French and most of the super powers on the globe. The seven liberal arts are our foundation as a culture and somehow they fell by our waist-side. What happened to focusing on the freedoms that were took from us as a people and the, "Rights of the Child" it appears that Nobel Drew-Ali died in vein because the only thing that came out of his struggles and hardships were Temples. That breaks my heart and I can't be the only broken-hearted one. The most devastating heart breaking actions of all is that some of the so called Moorish governments "outside of the Temples" set out to exploit Moorish brothers and sisters by nonperformance of services rendered in the arena of the civic, estate and criminal law. If you take funds from people for services rendered and guaranteed remedy for that group or individual and you defaulted on the performance to guarantee remedy, by law, you as the responsible party should pay back that client in good faith. Based on your actions you are acting in the, "Color of Law" capacity that we work so diligently to refute. You are no better that the judiciaries that hide behind the cloak of the black robe who practice, "Admiralty and Maritime Law" via a corrupt justice system that thrives on deception and codified legalese.

You are wicked and should be put to death via a firing squad. If it doesn't apply, let it fly. Where is your moral conviction for the uplifting of humanity? You should take off your Turbans, Kemars and Fez and never speak of, Truth, Love, Peace, Freedom and Justice ever again. If anyone should be pulled by the pants and put in the, so called Hell-Fire it should be you.

CHAPTER − 17

SPIRIT

I will start off by saying; spirit to a degree, is synonymous with heart and soul. If you feel it in your heart, you also feel it in your soul. Soul is the negative attribute of spirit, negative in this sense is not denoting a bad thing. Remember that two become one which manifests life for a specific purpose. Example (1) night is the negative aspect of twenty-four hours. By the same token, that same day is the positive aspect of twenty-four hours and together their specific purpose is to form 1 day. Example (2) we have a left and right side of our brain and they have distinct functions, but each component does its duty and together they create balance as 1 unit called the brain. We have a left and a right side of the heart, whereas one side receives blood and one side pushes it out. Again they both work in sync as one unit to do a specific job. We have five fingers that can do different things as a team; hold a pen, pick up a bucket, hold a broom, brush your teeth, wipe your buttocks and all five fingers come together to form a fist. In the same light, your toes enable you to maintain balance when standing and walking. You would not be able to run without your toes. With that being said, I will break it down like this, spirit is the positive component of soul. Your soul is attached to the physical realm via emotions and controls your spiritual convictions that triggering your emotions creating the motivation which causes your spirit to react. Emotions, soul and spirit are the trinity of the spirit body; meaning all three come together as one.

Your soul is the connection between body and spirit. Maat breathed the breath of life into your nostrils and you became a living soul; hence, mind, body and soul. Everything within you is connected as 1 and when a part of you becomes disconnected or out of balance; dis-ease, viruses, bacterium, mental disorders, headaches and other abnormalities emerge. When speaking on or referencing a Godly plane, everything is always 1. We as physical beings make distinctions and separations on this physical plane to simplify life as we know it. By the same token, some of us also know life on the spirit plane is 1 and our spirits will go back to which it came as will your flesh. The physical plane is the lowest form of intelligence. Your spirit is the supreme form of intelligence that creates the balance in life for us to exist. When Maat returns to take back our breath, which is synonymous with spirit-God-body, life on the physical plane will cease to exist. Keep in mind that the soul and spirit are synonymous with each other and at the same time they play distinct parts in our creation that allows for a balance in the physical realm. If you can overstand Matthew 16:26, you are making progress. Matthew 16:26, "for what is a man profited, if he shall gain the whole world, and lose his own soul?" "Or what shall a man give in exchange for his soul?" Notice it's not talking about spirit because you can't exchange spirit in regards to life, you can live as a lost soul in the **world, meaning** your soul is still there but its warped, at the same time, you can't live without spirit in the **world and spirit** is never lost. Spirit could possibly get trapped but never lost. And for all the master-minds who know that their interpretation of soul is in relation to being a material person and your heart isn't in favor of God and for that reason God takes your soul and burns you in the eternal flames. Once you die, you lose everything anyway! The only thing that never dies is your holy-spirit-holy-breath and your soul is not attached to your spirit. Your soul is only attached to spirit in conjunction with the physical attributes of life, God breathed the breath of spirit in your nostril not spirit and soul, but I hear you genius.

Now that you have an understanding of what your soul, spirit and emotions are and how they are inter-related and connect as one,

I want to show you how issues and situations affect your spirit. In western culture, we have a system called, Welfare which is supposedly designed to uplift impoverish people to the point of common place financial independence. But from my observation it basically locks most people in to governmental dependence and some of the reasons are; it targets woman to be pseudo bread winners, breaks up the family structure, makes the man feel psychologically inferior and promotes lazy minded people who think they are getting over on the system when in fact it would appear that the system is aware of your mindset and using welfare as a tool to keep a mental stronghold on the weak and at the same time complaining about welfare is contributing to keeping North America in a deficit. With that in mind, the ever rising inflation rate also plays a role with people who desirably want to relinquish the benefits of welfare, because most jobs they qualify for doesn't afford them enough money to survive on the current economic level and or the job doesn't offer medical benefits and this to has a physiologically effect on your higher spirit. With all these obstacles and others it seems to infer overt psychological warfare which is draining people spiritually that are reliant on the system to survive by any means necessary and possibly resort to a life of crime due to a weak mind, weak spirit and a lack of education.

By the same token, if we have differences between each other on a large scale and or with a group of people, or groups of people who despise you for whatever selfish reasons and you are bombarded with an onslaught of degradation and humiliation and in addition; that person, group or nation constantly intimidates you in anyway shape or form as in; threat, duress, coercion, murder and other acts of violence which forces you to submit to their will and customs. The physiological and psychological aspect of those actions not only alter present and future DNA code, those actions also took your **heart** and **soul** which takes your **spirit** which in turn deprives you of your **will** to act, which lowers your **morale** and **courage** to fight, which makes you feel **worthless** and that breeds **negative** psycho-kinetic energy which strengthens your lower god-self to justify **self-pity** which drives you to be **wreck-less** in life, give up on life and think that there is no chance to be an achiever and consequently you start to indulge in activities that's not conducive to your higher god-self. This is the creation and manifestation of weak-minded, mis-guided, animalistic, lower intelligence that we need to correct NOW. (Read the statement above again and let it sink in. 9 minutes is good enough, now change your world.) The sad reality is that this process is what the power elite reinforce through education, social fear tactics; media based propaganda and other overt forms of deception as well as chemical compounds in certain foods that alter your biological process. This is the primary reason most of us can't make the spiritual connection with our higher-self and when people of higher intellect try to educate you on their level, you can't grasp the information because you are indirectly programmed to dis-believe it and slaves only think what their masters programmed them to think. If you think outside of your master's box you think you will be reprimanded, possibly fired from your place of employment and or socially attacked by friends, peers and or the media. You lost your heart to stand up and fight for truth and what is right. The power elite continue to reign and laugh at your ignorance. In the same light, we are programmed to focus on other issues unrelated to god so the higher-power of our **will** is diminishing. You have just witnessed another aspect of the "Battle of Armageddon" and how your mental and spiritual attributes can be deprived right in front of your face. If you don't overstand what I'm conveying, the characteristics of what causes your spirit to become weakened are expressed at the beginning of the Chapter. You must admit a little bit you are really sick of the crap, get your swag back daddy, where your focus at. "Jay-z" Get your spirit back in order. One messiah, messenger, leader or shepherd will never get you to the promise land. There can never be 1 leader because the records reflect that there is no power in 1 leader or shepherd of sheep in relations to uplifting people that has ever been successful. When the head-leader falls, the body-people will follow. Here is a list of falling heads based off of one that was imbedded in your brain to have you think you will be saved. In your subconscious minds you are still waiting for Jesus to come back in the form of himself or another one like him. You don't even realize the deception from the "Decepticons" Jesus is the psycho-kinetic savior in the form of; Denmark Vesey, Fred Hampton, Stephen Bantu Biko, Malcom X, Marcus Garvey, Martin Luther King, Mahatma Gandhi, Medgar Evers, Nat Turner, Mohammed, Honorable Elijah Muhammad, Carmichael Stokely, Noble Drew-Ali, Halie Selassie, Harriet Tubman, Nelson Mandela, Tsali, Olaudah Equiano, Huey Newton, Rosa Parks, Ella Baker, Harriett & Harry Moore, Desmond Tutu, Osceola and many more. They were all assassinated, mysteriously died or died and we as a people are worst off now because whoever took your spirit still has it and that's evident from the way you act and live. We all should have the spirit of leadership in our quest to uplift fallen humanity. If the mental and spiritual focus of the people throughout the diaspora is on 1 accord for the same common goals, victory would be enviable. But it's not, why, because of the fact that there is not one in-_divide_-dual; an-divide-u-al leading a group of in**divid**ual minds. (Note: all vowels are inner-changeable) There is nothing good about being an individual except you individual personality which gives you distinction and separation from the masses as well as self-pride dignity and self-confidence. Outside of those attributes we should be operating as 1. All people need to operate on 1 accord and every individual mind needs to be in unison with the next *(Not divided)* in order to grow as a thriving human species. If we elevate our spiritual intelligence to the next level, no matter where we are on the planet the telepathic spiritual vibration will be felt across the land which will yield positive results. The hero's I just mentioned above weren't just fighting for political, human and civil rights; it was about equality as a people and the ability to live in harmony together. On a larger scale they were fighting for their right and our rights to live unabridged by bigotry and discrimination. "They were fighting for their lives." Their spirits cry truth, peace, justice, freedom and equality as we speak. The DNA of your ancestors is passed down generation upon generation. DNA of old bonds with DNA of new, as your spirit bonds back with the Creator simultaneously Satan and your flesh dies. "For Your Information, you are taught that Jesus scarified his life for us; what I find puzzling about the sacrifice is this, whenever we as humans have a chance to defeat the adversary, **by nature-God** you defeat it if you have the power to do so, right? Just a thought provoking question, the answer is in another chapter or your spirit already gave it to you. I need you to stay focus on this chapter and overstand this message before you move forward. Again why would God belittle him- self for the peons he created, "Peons; meaning us compared to the power of the Al-mighty and all things created that's greater than us" God bowed down to a mortal government for us to be saved "in-direct suicide" really? Wouldn't the lesson be exceedingly fruitful if Jesus showed that he defeated the government and people who wanted to tarnish his reputation and murder him, all fell to their feet? Imagine if Jesus did defeat the Roman Empire all by his self, he would be showing his followers strength and the unwavering desire to achieve, along with the concept that we must fight for what's right. I wonder where we would be if our mindsets were focused in that direction? Most people are taught to follow the footsteps of Jesus and it appears that you are doing just that. Due to the fact that Jesus took the low road and became subservient to Roman rule, the majority of the masses have the same convictions and predispositions. "Weak minds, weak spirits = weak people" Most of you don't take a stand for what's morally correct and when you do it's no support from the masses and we are back to square one because everybody accepted defeat. Talk about ignorance, shesh! Wake up!

By the same token, most organizations only take stances for politically correct issues when they are getting support for their goals and agendas. Politics are lower god-self driven; morals are higher god-self driven. What spirit are you driving? Most people in high places move toward a political based structure in life vs a morality based structure of life. "You never see most of the wealthy people fighting for the rights of humanity because they are blinded by financial freedom and they lost their spiritual identities and perception of who they perceive a higher power to be as well as the true purpose of life. On the other hand, yet another paradox, the rich that would like to fight are bound by their industry power elite and other indirect powers that be. This fact restricts them from totally supporting and up-lifting humanity for fear of losing their careers, family or their life. It was once said, "It's more than one way to skin a cat." Only the poor people who suffer a life of contention see reality for what it really is, outside of the poor, who cares. The paradox is those same rich people complain about the escalating crime rate, government subsidies that people use and abuse, high unemployment rates and the financial deficit. If "big brother"-government focused on building your spirit as a life-force that counts in life and showed you that your contributions to society matters, wouldn't that change the big picture, but that will never happen unless we become the gods that we are born to be. You have to change your-self to change the world. If we won't change morally and spiritually and deal with our personal issues of who we are and start to accept responsibility for our actions, no one else will either and we will never move forward as a people. Your higher god-self will never know victory, only defeat and we as a people will never gain the courage to win the unseen battle that's killing us off. Spirit is the life force that propels us in either direction and if someone sees a particular spirit in a person or group of people, they usually speak on it. I will give you an example regarding groups of people.

Certain groups of people are referred to as the, "Devil." The only reason why is because when you look at the attributes of the devil and the lessons you were taught about the devil's evil ways, the people that are relentless regarding the actions that mirror the devils ways are considered to be the devil. How can you see it any other way? By the same token, when the media says, a certain group's of people are calling certain groups of white power elite people Devils, the powers that be make the statement out to be offensive and unreasonable, "The proof is in the pudding," as they say, actions speak volumes "turn it down for what!" It doesn't appear to be deformation of character, slander or a lie when you have characteristics that are identical in nature to that of the devil. What's the problem? For example, what other groups of people treated melanated people so inhuman for as long as the colonial power elitist have? It's the actions of a people which give life to the name, "Devil" not the rumors of superiority groups and or one group of people. Keep in mind; I said for as long as colonial imperialism has, I know of no other people who enslaved other people for as long as they have, coincidently we all know of other nations that did enslave other people and oppress them but the oppression ceased to exist with all other people at one time or another and all those people have their "Independence Day" in their own country and even celebrate it in this country. **"So-called Black people do not have an independent independence day or the name of a higher power; they mostly borrow the name of the Christian and Mohammedian deity and adopt it as their own as they do the holiday of July 4th 1776."** Having independence brings about a certain pride spiritually in a people, a sense of freedom and achievement as a people along with a cohesive spirituality that flows through that culture of people at that time. These positive feelings subconsciously would empower us as a unified culture to achieve more in life. Without cohesive spirituality most individual's higher god-self can't grow at optimal levels that's why we are in the predicament we face now. Throughout the world our people are in desperate need of spiritual enlightenment, most people need this information, we need to spread this to the masses as if our lives depend on it and the reality is, our lives depend on it. Let's all work in unison to help spread the news and each 1 teach 1 to build 1 and bear witness to spiritual evolution and know you are a part of it!

On another note, I was taught as a child that a negative thought is a sin. A negative thought is not a sin. If you were taught that as I was understand that's a misnomer. As a child of **G**od you were given the supreme ability of top notch **intel**ligence over all other living creatures. Intelligence is also synonymous with spirit. It's the frame work that creates the DNA to a degree, the life-force, the essence of the unseen you. It's the force your body needs to animate it and survive. Comprehend this concept and you will grow mentally in 5,4,3,2,1, your spirit is your intuitive motivator, your body is the animator for your spirit, synergistically they work together as one mind. To think is natural, it's an innate ability. Not to think is unnatural. Even when someone asks you, what are you thinking about and you say, "nothing" nothing is something and in order to think of nothing, you would have had to think of nothing. The only other reasons to say you are thinking of nothing is so you don't reveal what you are really thinking or you can't consciously recall the thoughts you just had a second ago because you were in a self-induced trance and when you came out of the trance you lost all cognition of the thoughts you were thinking. It happens more than you think, laugh out loud. Most people don't realize they go into self-induced trances, you do it while you're driving, talking to people, walking down the street, at work, etc.; most people call it, "day dreaming." sounds familiar, right? It's actually a form of meditation and in meditation you focus is focusing on nothing negative or nothing to achieve something out of nothing; you would ultimately achieve bliss in the form of total medicinal relaxation along with the ability to heal ailments and dis-eases. It's so much to learn in life its mind boggling. I will share with you what I can within reason based on the intent and focus of this book. "Out of the darkness came the light" Know this, darkness is the initiator of knowledge, Knowledge is the pursuer of understanding, and understanding is liberation from the pursuit, liberation breeds wisdom, wisdom inherits discernment. A thought in regards to sin is the test of your spiritual strength or spiritual weakness and it's only a sin if you proceed to act on that negative thought. Understand this, If you pray outwardly to the heavens of God for forgiveness, you doubt and disrespect the power of **god** in you. If you're in a game **or** a fight for your life and you doubt yourself; you are willfully **willing** yourself to **loose**. Praying for most people implies you are waiting for a miracle or magic to fall from the sky and fix your weak self? Are you waiting to hear a voice to answer your prayer? Are you waiting for something to coincidentally happen that you can identify with and say, see God answered my prayers? Something you can relate to God answering your prayers; which in turn gives you false evidence of having something tangible to justify your delusion of hope and faith. Like Jesus is coming back?

Outside of that it's said that, "You feel your belief and faith are strong enough that your prayers will be answered." People can attest to that sometimes in their own uncanny way. Contrary to that, if the world-people as a whole prayed for things to get better and they all had unwavering faith and belief, wouldn't that mean that life as a whole should be better instead of worst prior to reading this book? From what I witnessed most of my life, people are reading and subjecting themselves to the same program/book but are on the wrong page and/or the wrong book. "Change your spiritual mindset-deprogram. Change your mind-set enhance your life reprogram. Some people say, "build & destroy" I say, "destroy and build" I am talking of Programming of the mind, don't get it twisted … I find you can't build and destroy with close minded people, chronic voluntary mind block won't allow it, you have to destroy 1st in order to build. I also find in his-story they did it the same way but it wasn't because of "CVMB" the focus was & is world domination as in a superior group of dominating people, not dominating the planet if you get the gist. I'm not making this up, other people spiritually feel the pain, and Lauryn Hill said it in her song.

Quote: "I stand in position, ELs known the mission since conception, let's free the people from deception" (Lauryn Hill aka El Bogie)

1. **Spirit:** I would say this is the celestial aspect of life expressed through in a physical form via physical animation. Hence the definition of spirit. Spirit from Latin (Spiritus which means breath) s**pirit:** has many different meanings and connotations, most of them relating to a non-corporeal substance contrasted with the material body. Thank you en.wikipedia.org
2. **Holy:** This would seem to me to be nothing more than a socially recognized status quo and purposely over rated by the abuse of authority through religious factions; **Holy:** specially recognized as or declared sacred by religious use or authority; having a spiritually pure quality; set apart (bibleinsong.com)

In all essence spirit means: breath, the life force that animates that jail cell our spirit lives in called a body. Without the body our spirits would be whole again. Hence, Holy Spirit Now to take it a step further, think of spirit as having mutable hats meaning your spirit can mutate into different spirits at any given time. Modern medicine would define spirit as multiple personalities. There's a lid for every pot, lol. Emotions and some actions are based on the feeling of your soul and are moved by your spirit. If you see a negative spirit in one person and see the same spirit in another person that would tell you how to react based on the inner actions and experience you had with the first person of the same spirit. Don't act as if it's something different about the same spirit you encounter with the new person because when you do, you set yourself up for failure. To ignore your god spirit that's showing you warning signs of danger you will pay a heavy price for rebellion. So don't blame the person you had a bad encounter with for your demise. Own up to it and grow as a child of the Most High. It's easy to identify spirits because all actions are a form of spirit; good, bad or indifferent. If you think it's more to it, it's not, it's really that easy. Procrastination, God, Satan, glutton, selfishness, giving, caring, honesty, loyalty, positivity, negativity etc.; all these spirit you can possess or have possessed you. When you have negative thoughts, those thoughts are spirits and at any given time they will occur but that doesn't mean you committed a sin. The only way a sin would be committed is if you act on the negative thought. Remember it's just a test of your stronger or weaker self. To say negative thoughts are sins inclines you in the direction to suppress your thoughts or try not to think of bad thoughts, almost the same, but not. It's impossible not to think. If it's a negative thought, fight it before it goes any further. That's why you have will power.

Flesh is the sin itself and it wants to indulge in selfish behavior. If you let your flesh run your life you will surely die. If the world did the same thing it would be mass extinction. You see how the word world and flesh are inner-related. Also do you see how living a **low** spiritual **life** will send us to damnation? Your lower god-self doesn't care about life; its soul desire is to satisfy flesh "the world" even if it means costing you your own life. That's why you have a balance in your life called your higher god-self. The Creator wants you to live for eternity and your spirit has the power to allow that to be possible as long as you abide by the rules of God-god which are conveniently stored in your spirit, your intelligence, your plasma, or life-force. You don't need a manual to tell you how to live. You can use one to help you along the way. Case in point, I know you experienced times when your spirit told you something and you either listened or you didn't. No one had to tell you or teach you that lesson, you learned from <u>experience</u>, that's where <u>wisdom</u> comes from; <u>Knowledge</u> comes from <u>understanding</u>. Understanding comes from a <u>willingness</u> to <u>learn</u>. Learning comes from a <u>spirit</u> that has the <u>desire to grow</u>. Growing comes from being <u>inquisitive and seeking information</u>. Please, people never use suppression in any of your life's experiences; it's a form of mental conditioning that stunts your spiritual growth. If you suppress anything, that means it never leaves, it's still lying dormant in you waiting for the opportune time to resurface. Overcome that adversity by embracing it; meet it head-on, face to face, it's nothing but trials and tribulations, tests to make you stronger as a person and in god. This allows you to pass down your experiences to your children so that they don't make the same mistakes. Your children should be a new and improved you. As you face your adversary you become stronger and life gets easier and you grow through what most people go through. What will also give you sustenance is the fact that you know you are 1 with the Creator, don't believe you are one, know you are 1 with God and god is 1 with you in the spiritual realm which makes you the god over negative spirits and the master of your own destiny.

If you are still a little fuzzy about understanding spirits, think of it like this. People who have multi-personality disorders are displaying multiple uncontrollable spirits. Like I said earlier, emotions and actions thereof are spirits. The difference with emotional spirits is the fact that you only see them once they are induced and their actions are consistent based on the current scenario. If you want to decrease the number of negative spirits in your life; tell yourself openly what your weaknesses are. Confess to the god in you. "Every knee shall bow and every tongue shall confess" Tell your-self, "I have the power of God in me, this power allows me to activate my godly powers which are stronger than my fleshly powers of my lower god-self and I can't allow the higher god in me to be defeated. How can I defeat myself knowing what I know now? Mission Impossible! Remember to internalize your confessions by meditating and focusing on the higher god in you. Your power begins within, the power of thought is from within, whatever you create in your mind came from within; Chi is internal power, again from within. I Chin, the science of internal power, power is created in darkness and is animated through light. "I am the truth and the Light" can only hold water through actions and deeds. So your words are the truth and your actions are the light that shines through your spiritual actions to personify who you are. Good, Bad or Indifferent.

Here's another way to understand spirit. Feeding your subconscious mind is like downloading information to your hard drive "subconscious." Whatever you see on your monitor "conscious" is what you just retrieved from your hard drive "subconscious" or another source. If its new information and you want to keep it, you simply download it to your hard drive to retrieve it later. Subconscious example of retrieving info; You hear a song you haven't heard in over ten years and the psych-kinetic energy-spirit of the song conjures a spirit from your hard drive "sub-conscious" mind and your physical body reacts to that spirit. The same psych-kinetic energy-spirit is in the food you eat, animals you come in contact with and anyone of these spirits can make you, happy, sad, crazy, mad, peaceful and loving. Bottom line is don't be fooled into thinking we are not 1. We are 1 with the Creator and the Creator is 1 with us. "Your god-spirit is the all-spark and the transformers came here to save us from us!"

Got cha, just kidding Lmbo, ha ha hee hee only funny if you've seen the movie

CHAPTER – 18

YOU HAVE THE POWER

If you don't have conviction for your higher godly self, you fall short of the glory. You can't see the glory but when you exercise your **god-self you will** feel it! If you have ever had a natural high, then you have felt the glory. If you want to be a user, choose to use your higher god-self because you might like getting high off of God and god might like getting high off of you, so you reciprocate the feeling to create balance with each other, that's how we are 1. Are you 1 with your creator? Are you 1 with your spouse? Don't have her walk behind you, have her walk beside you. She is good for more than the kitchen and the bed. She is the silent builder-creator of the universe and the foundation of life. Without her we can't exist. Without us she can't exist, so we come together as 1 to make 1 and the Almighty Creator lives in us to keep creation in balance through **god.**

For Your information, God doesn't create babies, we do. God never created a baby. It is written the Creator created Man in his image and likeness and with that, gave us the mortal power of creation. **FYI,** Creation; or who you call God doesn't have a physical image or gender. Children emulate the image that's being projected by their guardians, care givers or parents, that's the meaning of image in one sense. On the other hand, the only images that are physically created by a god are the ones you create when you have offspring. My children are created in my image. People see my image through my children and the likeness of me. You see my god-spirit in them when you acknowledge the fact of saying, "you act just like your father "good bad or indifferent," you are the splitting image of your father or mother. The explanation you just read should help you overstand the image concept and stop you from rejecting who you are. Creation gave us power to create in the physical realm. Most of you as socially driven people let society and religions dictate your mindset, beliefs and actions. You are blinded by your willingness to keep your eyes closed and choose not to eat the fruit. Eve had a lot of heart and I commend her in her quest for knowledge. She was a leader not a follower. Eat those apples! You go girl! You won't surely die. You might ask, why is there so much evil in the world. That's a Simple question to answer. Due to your physical fleshly form you are drawn towards worldly desires by your lower god-self. Most people unconsciously or consciously gravitate towards violence, sex, power; greed and dog eat dog, animalistic characteristics. Example: more people like to look at violence and sex as opposed to positive programs; Rap was positive in the initial stages of conception, until the media started purposely promoting negative rap over positive rap and now positive rap is called, "under-ground music." Even the news you watch on television, 90percent of all world news is about negativity. Some people are quick to criticize other people, but when the people who pointed the finger started doing the same things that they strongly opposed and criticized; now it becomes a positive influence through the eyes of the criticizers. I'm not making this up, you know who you are. "The spirit of jealousy and hate is devilish and you worship your God every Sunday, huh?"

"*Meet the double standard*" Selling alcohol was a crime until the government started regulating, selling and taxing it. Selling Marijuana was a crime until the government started regulating, selling and taxing it. Education was a crime. Reading the bible was a crime. So who allow you to do that? Reading any book was a crime. Who allowed you to do that? You can think of a lot more double standards if you look at the history in your own backyard. I can mention more but you get the gist. "This is the beast side of your lower-**god** spirit; your mark of the beast is the 666 so-called-curse that terrifies everybody for all the wrong reasons. Superficially it's your selfish fleshly satanic human nature. Bio-chemically it's the carbon "Atom-Adam" within your body which is comprised of; 6 protons, 6 electrons and 6 neutrons. Let's get back to the superficial aspects of 666 representing your lower god-self. You can evoke a balance called, your higher god-self. If people were taught to face adversity head on, face to face and realize that those are negative spirits needed to enhance spiritual and mental growth, negativity would not be so hard to defeat. Also understand negative spirits are counter-productive if they are not recognized by your higher-god-self. Your higher god-self must recognize the negatives actions of self in order to evoke the positive god in you to eradicate negative actions. What you want to do is to strengthen your spiritual core projecting inwardly, instead of praying outwardly into space up in heaven and waiting for something to happen. Life will be different if you are not projecting out, but projecting inward to the source of power afforded to you by the Creator. Only you have the innate ability to change your situation. You have the power. But if you give that power to an outside force, it's no longer yours, you lost it. People do this every day 24-7. If you think the Creator, the God outside of you will fix your problems, you are dead-sleep, Wake up!!! The power is vested in you from your Creator. Don't allowed society and religion to steal your strength, internalize your focus on the god you are, and take back what's rightfully yours!!

I have to get a little profound if it's to intricate for you to comprehend don't be A-typical and run away from the light. Embrace it and get off your lazy bones and research it as a child of God should. Prepare to do more knocking and the door shall be opened. Do more seeking and you shall find more. If you always ask to receive and never give, you are selfish and you will not retain much of anything. The creator created man on the 6th day that was a Friday. So we became 1 with the creator on Friday. On the 7th day God rested and said, "Remember the Sabbath day keep it holy. That was a Saturday. On **Sun**-day, Jesus rose from the dead who is the **Sun**-**Son** of God, which occurred in 3 days and fell on a Sunday. I will get into that later but we are talking about you having the power as god.

We represent the human side of creation; falling man, which in numerology and in KJV of the bible in the book of revelations 13:18, is represented by the numerical value of 666. It states. "**Here is wisdom. Let him that hath understanding count the number of the beast: for it is the number of a man; and his number is Six hundred threescore and six.**" The numbers breaks down to the same number no matter how you do the math "9." "6x6x6=216 2+1+6=9" "6x6=36x6=216" "6+6+6=18 8+1=9" "3scores=60 because a score is equal to 20." if I say 60x6=360x6=2,160 the answer is still 9 2+1=3+6=9+0=9, in numerology nine means completion and it also represents the highest number before starting back at one "meaning anew" "**John 2:16**" 2+1=3+6=9 "For everything in the world—the lust of the flesh, the lust of the eyes, and the pride of life—comes not from the Father but from the world." The world is your flesh, flesh is of the world and your spirit is of the Creator, when the Creator created the world which is of flesh the devil came to be the personification of that world through the spirit that animates it and that spirit is that of the Creator. The number 9 means completion and 666 is the overt (*in plain sight*) codified completion of man in the flesh. "*Mind=6 body=6 soul=6*" 666 is the breakdown of the 6's and makes the so-called Devil/Satan complete. 6+6+6=18★ 8+1=9: "9 in numerology means, change & completion" Coincidence or what? Read it over and over until you comprehend and internalize it, the truth will set you free. As I said in the previous chapter, in a nutshell, basically it equates to this little secret: hue-mankind is the sum of, 6 Protons 6 electrons 6 Neutrons which spawn the Atom/Adam that can only be animated by the spirit to bring light to the physical plane. Spirit is the ultra-light/energy borne in the darkness that cannot be seen in the physical form until a physical presence expresses physical animation for the hue-man mind to comprehend.

I want to show you another correlation regarding 2,160 which break down to 9 and it also means completion. This is about the precession of the equinoxes and how it's relevant to a new beginning.

"The age of Aquarius" is the age in which we are living in right now. We are in the acceptance of a spiritual epiphany that was prophesized before most of you were born. Is it possible that whoever wrote about 666 in its true essence knew about things in life that would uplift humanity but someone had excess to the same manuscript and decided to alter the true purpose and the masses were deprived of the knowledge too purposely hinder elevation of humanity so a few selfish power struck people can control the populous. Or is it possible that whoever wrote it, wanted someone to break the code as it says in the revelations to reveal the answer when the Age of Aquarius arrived knowing that people would only receive the truth in the new age? The correlation to 666 is the fact that in astrology, an astrological age is equal to about 2160 years per age based on the vernal equinox moving through the sidereal zodiac 2+1+6+0=9. In relation to the zodiac, the Bible makes mention about the zodiac and astrology; Pleiades, Orion, Mazzaroth, the Bear, the crooked serpent etc. The Quran speaks of astrology as well; Surah Al-Hijri; verse 16, 16th line of Surah Hizr, 61st line of Surah Furkan, Yusuf 12.4, Jonah 10.5 etc.

I guess I have wisdom and understanding; I counted the number of the beast. It's symbolic of us. It appears that religious and social propaganda, long drawn out interpretations and transliterations are intentional programming to keep your minds closed. If you are god, well maybe you still don't know you are. Do you realize you are denying the power of God vested in you via the Creator? That's insane and an abomination to you; the Creator and not to mention it relinquishes your power by rendering you spiritually dormant from your higher god self therefore allowing your "lower- **god** self" to reign supreme and take all your power. You can only be the god you were born to be through your actions and deeds that exemplify supreme god qualities. If you do not express those qualities there is no need to wonder why the world is in a chaotic mess, just look in the mirror. You live on a planet called Earth; you do not live in the world.

Understand what you are saying. Again, it's not the world it's the flesh you live in, your **lower god-self** that lives in chaos "Armageddon, Holy jihad" and when you go against nature; or God and the Creator you cause drama for yourself and everyone around you because by nature-God and Creation we are all connected. Knowing now we are all connected and the Creator who created everything that is and ever was, including you who represent one of Gods astonishing splendors and glory and all things seen and unseen, do you still dispute the god that you are? Overstand this; another form of 666 that's right before your very eye that's used for the sustainment of regulating time that we use every day. There are 24 hours in 1 day. 2+4=6. Each hour is divided into 60 minutes. 6+0=6. Each minute is broken down into seconds that equal 60. 6+0=6. This formula gives you the summation of 666 which completes a full day and once again completion is represented by 9. We as humans use time as a physical measurement to rationalize life, Creation, work, rest, play, religion, etc. But in actuality and in spirituality time doesn't exist. Time is only conducive for fleshly-worldly affairs of the hue-men species.

Moving forward, with the help of Martin Luther "not Dr. Martin Luther King" the printing press and the Catholic Church's fight over which side of Church would conduct government business and which side will represent God. Religion took the focus of the Creator away from self to gain control of the masses and put God in Heaven to take the power from the people. If you knew who you were god *"Greater is he that is in me than he that is of the World"* it would be hard to control and oppress you. The separation of Church and State is synonymous with **Church** the religion and **State** the business. That's one reason why religion is so powerful. The power is in heaven and not in its rightful place. You are taught that you have power over Satan but you are misguided as how to us it. You use your power by exercising your higher god-self through your actions and deeds, not by praying and wishing the Almighty will come to your aid in a dream or talk to you and give you an answer to fix your self-inflicted issues. You are the god that created the problem based on your actions and deeds. If you feel someone else created your hell, then remove yourself from the situation or have the patience and mental fortitude to endure until you can be victorious or simply retreat. I'm here to give you your foundation back and it's still up to the **god** in **you** to utilize it. Once more, "God helps those who help themselves." If you didn't catch on to the power of 666, in a nutshell the lesson for you to overstand is that government is not physically marking or stamping you with a number, 666. In regards to the beast it's still you as a human, monster and animal whatever science calls you, you are spiritually marked by Creation because God created man on the 6th day and due to the flesh you are falling man, a beast. Your spirit and flesh together makes you complete, that's why you have 9 holes on your body which symbolizes completion. The number 6 is divisible by 3 as is 2. Women have 12 holes because they are the givers of life. Life is manifested from triple stage darkness which translates to intrinsic intelligence which initiates the Creation. 12 is the sacred numeric value divisible by 3 because (12) 1+2=3. The true "Holy Trinity" Father, Mother and Child, Me, Myself and I are 3 in 1; Neutrons, Protons and Electrons form the Adam the (1); Spirit, **Seminal** vesicles, **Prostate** gland and **Cowper** glands form semen which in turn gives life to sperm; **Semen, Sperm** and the **Egg** become (1) for conception of 1-life. The number 3 combines, **birth, life** and **death; Past, present** and **future**, 3 Mary's, 3 crosses at Calvary, 3 days of death, Jesus rose on the 3rd day, The 3 Holy virgins, Al-Itab, Al-Uzza and Al-Manat. With that in mind, when referring to time as I mentioned earlier, my 24 inch gauge is also measured in 3's. I have 8 hours for work, 8 hours for God and 8 hours for rest. Coincidentally, 8 broken down in 3's equals 24 as I stated when I mentioned my 24 inch gauge 2+4=6 again, time is only for the purpose of gauging worldly fleshly affairs. God will come in a twinkling of and eye can never be measure in the physical realm. The coming of God is the god thoughts you manifest at god-speed in time of need because there is no real measurement of time except what we semis in relationship to measuring the speed of light verses the speed of thought. Only in total spiritual perfection of Gods' likeness can you comprehend the language of the Creator. When in doubt, check it out. Lastly when I spoke of Sunday being the 1st day of the week I wanted to peak your interest as to why some Church services are held on the 1st day of the week and not the 7th day. If I didn't peak your interest, you need to read this book from the beginning because the elevator doesn't go all the way up. Any who, due to the story of Jesus, and the **Son** rising at **East**er and the **Sun** rising in the **East**, which was on a **Sun**-day, the Church decided to have worship on Sun-day, even thou God said, remember the Sabbath, keep it Holy. It's much more to it, but that's not the focus. I'm just putting it out there to spark your interest. When in doubt check it out. I just want you all to reinstate your power as gods so the world-flesh we-*"spirits"* live in can be a better place to live. ***Throw the box away and throw away "chronic voluntary mind block"***

Proverbs 10:21 the lips of the righteous nourish many, but fools die for lack of sense. (KJV)

"Hosea 4:6" my people are destroyed for lack of knowledge: because thou hast rejected knowledge, I will also reject thee. (KJV) "Basically you are a blasphemer to yourself because God is in you and you are rejecting yourself when you reject knowledge/God, you are destroying yourself and the people you love."

Isaiah 5:13 (KJV) Therefore my people will go into exile *eyes closed-closed mind-sleep"* for lack of understanding; those of high rank will die of hunger "not able to be feed spiritually because their words fall on deaf ears" and the common people will be parched with thirst. "The ones who want to receive the knowledge cannot"

Quote: "It took me a little while to discover, that everyday people, they lie to God too, so what makes you think, that they won't lie to you?" Lauryn Hill's "Unplugged" Listen to the messages from one of the conscience Queens of light.

Chapter – 19

Superstitions & Dark Phobias

Before we move on to who is God, you people that are superstitious and people who are fearful of the dark, etcetera. Do you remember what religion said about superstition? Do you remember what it said about certain music "hip-hop for instance," astrology, astronomy and other religions? I think they discouraged all of it with a passion. Maybe I am wrong, you might remember what you were taught the very same thing and maybe your teachings were different. "So I'm I wrong for trying to show you a better way" ☺ Nico and Vince. Read this anyway because you might be able to shed light on people you love that's still in the dark; dumb, deaf and blind, and the "in the box thinkers," in the eyes of religious doctrine. Let me shed some light on the mis-teachings or the lack of teaching, whatever shoe fits. These definitions are straight out of the book, word for word. I'm not making this stuff up, it is what it is, Get out of the box if your head is still in it. You might want to baptize your mind, reprogram your hard-drive. Take your focus off of the body. Your body is fine. Instead of baptizing your body, it's your mind that needs up-lifting. To baptize your body although your head goes under water, the focus is still on the body being anew not the mind and that is one of the first mistakes because spiritually and mentally you are already on the wrong path. The baptism is should be about the mind but that's **not** what most people focus on. Anyway, back to the point.

Superstition: Most religious people are superstitious and don't even realize it. Remember it's a belief or practice resulting **from ignorance**, fear of the unknown, trust in magic or chance, or a false conception of causation; **irrational beliefs**: (Webster's Ninth New Collegiate Dictionary). It's a **system** of **irrational fear** especially in **connection** with **religion**. By the same token, it's an irrational dismal attitude of mind towards the supernatural or God Thank you (Webster's Ninth new Collegiate Dictionary) The sad phenomenon about human nature is after most of you read this definition you will still be a denial about who you are and continue to live a religious fantasy because of C.V.M.B. and relinquish your god power to another authority and that ignorance will be recycled generation after generation and life for you and your family will never grow past square one. This is the self-induced curse that's blamed on the God you believe in. Meaning; you learn through religious doctrine that if you are considered a bad person, religiously backslide or sin and you don't repent, you and your family may be punished and if you die before you are punished, the future generations and/or offspring of your family will be cursed by the God you believe in because you disrespected the Almighty. In reality you disrespected yourself and you are punishing yourself but the teachings won't allow you to comprehend the simplicity of your actions, cause and effect, so you believe the superstitious doctrine of the God curse.

When I decided to talk about superstition I had no idea that the definition was this involved and I wanted to make a point about using your Higher god-Self to combat your fear of the dark, because to be afraid of the dark and to know the Creator-Higher Power is contradictory to nature. Also why would you fear your father/God, you should respect your father/God and there would be no need to fear him. You can't have a relationship with someone you fear. Ok so far I can still get my point across. You were created in the dark. You will return to the dark but you will have eternal light and the light is spiritually and scientifically symbolic to the core of the sun in regards to what the eye can't see in the physical realm; gamma rays, celestial energy, other micro energy and the energy of the Creator. If Creation created it, then it's safe to say it's a part of God, and God is a part of Creation, so Creation is God as you believe. In quasi-similarity, it's sorta like the dominate gene in biology, whatever subordinate gene the dominate gene comes in contact with, all will succumb to the dominate gene, point being, whatever nature of the gene all others will submit to that dominate genes nature.

Your higher god-Self has the power of your will to make/will, make your phobia of the dark submit to your will. At will, at your command, "in the twinkling of an eye." You have always had the power in your possession but you never knew how to use it. It's that part of your brain they say you don't use, your pineal gland does more than control your other glands and regulate hormones and common sense does more than book knowledge. When you learn to combine them as one you will get closer to knowing your God-self. It's the spirit of the Creator, the power of the god in you. The only thing you need to do is start initiating your will to conquer F.E.A.R. "false Evidence Appearing Real." If something can only attack you in the dark, "*a demon, the devil, bad spirits, or whatever*" that would mean that the entity, person or thing is a coward. Who's afraid of cowards? We all sleep in the dark, if a coward was out to get you they would wait until you go to sleep. You wake up every single day without a scratch. Embrace the dark as if you own it, there is nothing to fear but fear itself. Now you know what fear really is, take a walk on the dark side to overcome those demonic cowards that's self-induced in your own mind.

For all intent and purpose, how can people who know the Creator have any form of superstition? Afraid of the dark, bad luck, hats on the bed, turn elephant ornaments to the east or west "whatever" to bring money into the home, don't walk under the ladder, the black cat syndrome, believing in magic, believing in Satan, doctrine coerced miracles, and the list goes on. Read the definition again. I'm not making this up. Question, is it superstitious to believe that your religion is the only true religion or is that a form of prejudice?

What about all of God's-Allah's children burning in the hell fire and your religion is the only sole survivor? As a Moslem/Muslim you believe that you will burn in the hell fire for having tattoos because you defiled your body. Depending on how many you have will depend on how much you burn, really? Are there different degrees heat in Hell? Your physical body doesn't return to the essence/Allah, only your spirit does. The life force/ the energy which transcends/ transforms and connects back with the original source of life which is Creation; this starts the process of life all over again. What you do to your physical body only affects you in the physical realm, not after you transcend. So the conflicts you have with your physical body are again, self-induced and as I said earlier, the spiritual realm does not mix with the physical realm. The implementation of tattoos,' is only judged negatively or positively by the cultures that approve or disapprove. In certain parts of what you might call Africa; aka Alkebulan, tattoos are a part of their culture and have been for centuries. So would God really condemn them to hell as a people because tattoos are a part of their cultural beliefs? Maybe they don't believe in God so they will be ok. The laws of nature are constant. Physical attributes remain in the physical and spiritual attributes remain in the spiritual realm. Your body will become fertilizer to enrich the soil around it and your spirit will return to the intelligent energy from which it came. Creation again is a constant it does not change. The question is, is burning in the hell fire because of tattoos ignorance or superstition or both? It could be that you were taught wrong about the meaning of superstition and now that you have a better understanding of its meaning I hope you use it to get a clear perception of your thought process and focus more on the Creator for spiritual enhancement instead of doctorial edification and/or mastering a foreign language for superficial acceptance by your peers as the head honcho. {HPIC} "Head person in charge"

Another superstition which is hard for most religious people to acknowledge is the indoctrinated image of the Creator that's embedded in your mind. This (1) concept alone is stunting the spiritual and mental growth of the masses throughout the diaspora.

It causes you to distort reality. The superstition that you will go to heaven or burn in hell is physically and spiritually impossible. Your soul doesn't have nerve endings; your body is buried six feet deep so we won't have a reemergence of deadly out breaks like the Bubonic plague and your spirit is returned back to the essence from which it came; Energy, Creation. Heaven & Hell are terms used in this physical state of mind as adjectives to describe a physical state of mind and when you believe that Jesus is God or you see a depiction of God, you associate it with a physical presence and that distorts your thinking. It creates a mental image of physical bodies in heaven and hell. It also allows you to believe you will see all of your family and friends again. Your body is made up of physical parts and the spirit is the life-force that animates those physical parts. The part of Creation that is given to us from the Creator is "spirit." Spirit will return to its energy source based on universal principles. Heaven and Hell are human ideologies, religious Godly principles, not intrinsic Intelligence as in Creation. There is no variant with the laws of Creation, Creation is a constant. The characteristics and actions of God as taught by the scholars of religion is that of a human nature. If you only read one specific doctrine, of course it will side with its self. But outside that box is a wealth of knowledge that might beg to differ. Superstition keeps you in the box and stunts your growth as a child of the Most High. Imagine this indoctrination as taught by your religious teachers. Ham saw his father naked and told his brothers what he saw. They walked backwards with a covering and covered their father and didn't see him naked so because of what Ham saw GOD cursed Ham the father of Canaan and all offspring after that was so-called black people. Do you realize what that statement is programming in the minds of all people? First off, a curse is associated with the devil/ Satan and on the contrary, throughout the Bible and Koran I never read where the Devil/Satan cursed anyone. Have you? Secondly it implies discrimination (male chauvinism) (Man over woman/Adam over Eve), favoritism (Jews), prejudice (Ham), and questions ethics (**don't tell what you see, hide it**). God discriminates obviously because God has a chosen people, God is a He, (Creation has no gender) God only burns his children for disobedience, People pray to God for favor. Must I go on? The point is this; these are all animalistic characteristics of hue-man nature and not what intrinsic intelligence would create. Creation does not have any prejudice, favoritism, jealousy or any other negative attribute. Did you ever think of the negative implementations Creation would have on our existence if it practiced mediocrity in the form of discrimination, and/or prejudice? We need to think for self and be arbitrary with god born innate common sense instead of letting doctrines and dogmas create **suggestive thought**. These indoctrinated beliefs and superstitions have created dark phobias and has altered the direction and path we should be plotting to resurrect the birth of our spiritual connection to the Creator and manifest a "**Borne Revolution**" for the upliftment of humanity.

CHAPTER – 20

WHO IS GOD

The last Revelation

Quote: "There's a hero if you look inside your heart you don't have to be afraid of what you are" Mariah Carey

Knowledge: It is clearly evident that knowledge is power and belief is weak but that's my perception. Your perception might be different based on your level of understanding. Knowledge has been defined as a **clear perception** of a **truth** or **fact**, **reality**; **to know**; to perceive with **certainty**; to **understand clearly**; (weegy.com)

Belief: implies assent on grounds other than direct proof. (Webster's Ninth New Collegiate Dictionary) I don't see anything wrong with formulating an opinion as long as that belief isn't manipulated to convey truth and/or used as a fact for argument or a justification to take the place of truth. Belief is just that, belief: **an opinion** or conviction; acknowledgement as fact by reason of the **authority**.

Know: I love the confidence in knowing, it brings about a feeling of assurance that personifies your spirit. Everyone can feel your energy and with that you attract positive energy and retract the negative. For me, it's a gift and a curse to know. If you are one who knows, then you understand what I mean. **Know:** Direct cognition of; exclusive knowledge of; perceive as fact or truth. Thank you kindly (Webster's Ninth new Collegiate Dictionary) it also means to apprehend clearly and **with certainty**.

God: Male deity, (*para-phrased*) a belief found in the monotheistic and polytheistic religions, the creator and ruler of the universe. I would like to know how God can or what you all think God is, be a male deity and still be accepted as the Creator of all things? To be male as a God based on your teachings is prejudice and it also restricts Gods ability as a God, it puts limitations on the multifaceted complexities of all of creation. It's a mono and polytheistic **belief system** and most people make it out to more than what it is based on indoctrination and social programming. In the definition of God there is no mention of **life** or **creation** and I find it odd when I was taught that God is the Creator. Thanks (Webster's new twentieth century dictionary second edition)

Creation: In this definition of creation there is no mention of God. Based on this definition, creation appears to be bigger than God because creation has no limitations. **Creation:** Creating or being created, the act of bringing into existence, the entire world the universe and everything in it. Secondly, Creation implies life, not the philosophy of belief. (Webster's new twentieth century dictionary second edition)

The reason the definitions are listed isn't just to give you the meanings of the words and this goes for all the definitions throughout this book. They are to disseminate the value and power of the words you associate with a sentence and to show how most of you take words and meanings for granted. In life when it comes to knowing God, that's one subject I want to be clear about. If I believe in God based on the definition of belief, I'm leaving room for doubt and I doubt if you or I want to do that. I know who **God** is and I know who **god** is. I'm breathing, so are you because God blew the breath of life, God-spirit into your limp body and it became animated "a living soul." You are reading this book, that's proof that you are here; you don't believe that because it's something you know. You understand that fact to be true, you are certain; it's established in your mind. Hopefully you get it and know it to be a fact from this point on.

Quote: "WHAT IS POPLUAR IS NOT ALWAYS RIGHT AND WHAT IS RIGHT IS NOT ALWAYS POPLUAR!" (Einstein)

Creation is the creative power of all things seen and unseen. Creation is 1 with everything and we are 1 with Creation. Most of us are taught, God is everything living, everything that ever was, is and will be. The Alpha & Omega as the Greeks put it. The Truth and the Life as the Kemetians put it and stolen by Greek philosophers; these are common statements that most people heard before. Some people believe it, some people don't. If you believe in yourself, believe in God or believe in anything, there's room for doubt in your mind as to the validity of the person place or thing you believe in; including yourself. If you lack confidence in yourself, you don't believe in you or you believe there could be fault somewhere somehow. In the same vein; if you have confidence in yourself, do you believe in yourself or do you know yourself? Accept the truth and the truth shall set you mentally free. The God spirit that resides in your body is the 18 breaths most of you breathe every minute if you are a healthy person. It's the higher vibrational processes of positive thought. It's the I Ching. It's the Chi; it's the 7 chakras or 12 for the spiritually advanced. It's the Life Force. It's the Electric energy that flows through your body. It's the intelligence that works with your body's chemistry and biology that formed you. It's the light that shines in the darkness. It's the inevitable creation of god from The Great Architect Allat, that Omni-presence you call the Creator. All people have their own interpretation of the Creator, so don't focus on the name and lose focus of the content. The content is the focal point throughout this book. The focus is you! God created you in his likeness and image. What's the rocket science behind that?

None! Obviously it must be in the teachings. Could it be possible that what you were taught was wrong? Think about this, most of you go to your religious organizations to learn, build knowledge of scripture, build religious strength in yourself through fellowship and some may do it to congregate with like minds. Overstanding why you go if in fact you have been going for many years and you feel as thou you have a pretty good understanding of your God is key. What else could you possibly be learning besides reinforcement of the same principles? If you are still learning and building strength at the same place of worship after years and years of worship, you are showing weakness in yourself, you show a lack of leadership, you show an unwillingness to be assertive and you represent the lost and unfound programmed masses of people across the globe who think they know the Creator, but do not have a clue. When it comes to knowledge, **no one thing begins and ends in one place, Knowledge is a constant continual**.

Its references in this book that states, perception and the power of thought can change your way of thinking and your actions. What you experience in life is your **reality**. What you perceive things to be is your **reality**. What you think, is also your **reality**. So what part of your **reality** is really **real?** Are you conscious as a spiritual being or unconscious as an indoctrinated person influenced by everyone else's ideas and philosophies? In life most people can recall a time when they were taught something wrong and that's ok as long as you corrected the era. If you believe a lie for too long it becomes **your** truth. **Your** perception is **your** reality, and you start to build **your** life around that falsehood **you** think to be truth and soon it will manifest into your **reality**. For instance, when people do things that don't make sense to you; you say, "Why did he or she do that?" "Who does that?" You ask these questions because, their reality and perception of life is different from yours. Whatever they might have done was real to them. Their perception of life was based on their teachings, thoughts and experiences which dictated their actions which caused an effect, good, bad or indifferent. By the same token, if I tell you, you are god. You deny that fact because of your teachings, perception and thoughts. So the true reality appears to be false and the false reality appears to be true. Most people can't handle the true, but they say they can. It's like being in a relationship and your partner says, "You can tell me the truth." If the person listening to the truth is not grounded and well-rounded as a positive person, you will regret telling them the truth for as long as that relationship lasts. OMG! "Oh My God," You know what I mean ☺ the point is you need to check out the facts, his-story. Do research, do what you have to do. Don't be the sheep slash follower of the shepherd. Be a Leader and lead people to victory who can't be leaders because they are weak-minded, lost and mis-guided. Virtually everybody can be a leader but some just don't have that fighting spirit or will to take responsibility. Here's something most of you believe to be true; simply, the sun is yellow in color and gives off a yellow light. But the sun is a star like the other stars in the sky and they all are white as is the sun. If you notice the light on the planet surface, it's white in color. The only reason the sun appears to be yellow is because the surface of the sun is cooler than the core and other variables. I just wanted to point that out. Back to the focus☺ here's a quote of some lyrics Michael Jackson wrote about us, he was on point when he said, **"We are the World."**

Quote: "there's a choice we're making, **we're saving our own lives"** Michael Jackson

Everything isn't always what it seems. "Greater is he that is in you, than he that is of the **world**." John 4:4 Remember the word world in this book is the representation of flesh. For all intent and purpose; when you reference the **world** as flesh and relate all issues about the **world** with flesh, it equates to you and your lower god-self. Look up the word, **delusion**; false beliefs that are persistent and organized. Now ask yourself, "Who or what organizations perpetuate delusion?" Do you know your position with your organization? Is your mind-set established through persistence and organization? Or do you know god through spirit and conviction? So who do you serve **Moor,** the organization or god? Of course 98.9 percent will say God, but looking at what actions, the actions you perform in the organization and or the actions outside the organization in relation to manifesting the spirit of the Creator through your actions? Did you just answer that question with doctrine orientated conviction or through the spirit of god?

Belief: an acceptance that a statement is true or that something exists; trust, faith, or confidence in someone or something. Example; You belief your wife or husband will be faithful, but you will never know for sure, you just have to trust them, have confidence in their word and have faith that they will be honest and true. **To belief is external**

Know: To perceive or understand as fact or truth; to apprehend clearly and with certainty. Example; I know I am god because the Creator breathed the breath-spirit of life into me and I create through the life force, source and energy of the Almighty universal power and I am created in the likeness and image of God, with the power to conger up and idea in my mental and bring that thought into fruition via my actions and power vested in me by the Creator to create. I know I am god. **To know is internal.**

Which word makes spiritual sense and which one makes physical sense? You be the judge.

Quote: "if we were made in His image then call us
by our names, most intellects do not believe in God
But they fear us just the same." "Erykah Badu"

Know this, when someone does something for you out of the kindness of their heart, that is a blessing from god. Don't turn your blessings down because of pride. You are blessed thru your actions and deeds. People witness of your works, deeds and actions reciprocate the action by giving back, which is the gift of the spirit of god. The karma of, "Give and you shall receive"

Question: who on the planet consciously acknowledges a higher power besides us? Think hard, who consciously acknowledges God besides us? Also who follows Gods laws in a general sense and who breaks them? Before I give you the answers I would really like for you to consider who does that. I don't want my answers to influence yours. Remember this book is about opening your mind to spiritual revelations and not programming it and or not to create a self-suggested thought or idea that you think I overtly or covertly place in the text to sway your decisions. So I hope your spirit will lead you in the right direction and give you the cognitive ability to answer some of the questions before I tell you. If you can't, it doesn't mean you don't have the cognitive ability, it's possible that you never been introduced to this kind of material before and it's all new to you. Or you could take the low road and be in denial, meaning; you can't see the forest for the trees. Anticipation is killing you right. Lol, ok people, nothing else on the planet consciously acknowledges what a higher power and or who God is but us. Reason being is that in order to consciously know God in a cognitive state someone has to teach you that God exists. I hope you can feel truth through the vibration of your spirit. WE either believe in a higher power, God, Life- Force, Almighty, or know it exists on a conscious level. Every other living creature is involuntarily and deliberately connected via spirit because spirit is breath and breath is life. Just as it's understood that, real recognize real, life recognizes life and spirit recognize spirit. Here's a bit of evidence to supports this philosophical truth. Animals can sense when you are afraid of them and they react to that spirit of fear with an instinctive response to defend themselves. You didn't tell them you were afraid but they are in tune with the spiritual vibrations around them as we should be. By the same token, animals can sense bad weather approaching through their spiritual channels, they can also sense death. These are vibrational triggers in the spiritual plane of life to help sustain life for the sole purpose of procreation and it's done through spirit regardless of the knowledge of who or what a High power is. Even the earth itself vibrates, and a fascinating fact is that we being connected to the planet by Maat, God, Allah, Allat, the Greater Power, vibrate at 6–8 mega-hertz and the planet also vibrates at 6–8 mega-hertz. Do the research and see for yourself. Let me ask you this, If God's laws are superior in the eyes of religious people and man's law is inferior to God's law, why is there a dispute over immoral issues that clearly go against the laws of Creation? Why is it a rebuttal? Is main-stream media and the Power Elite the new representation of God, or is a double standard that allows hue-man laws to override God's laws the new standard of life?

We are supposed to be the most intelligent creators on the planet but it appears we are the dumbest. Most of us acknowledge a higher power or Jehovah but we don't follow the laws of Creation via Mother Nature whom by the way could possibly be Al-Manāt and Al-Lāt, unless something else created nature. My understanding is that everything is from one source, right? I anticipate we all can agree on that. So why fight over which doctrine is the right doctrine; wage wars in the name of God; or print fiat notes to control the masses and inscribe "In God we Trust." God has nothing to do with the material aspects of currency, unless the people who printed the fiat money know something you don't. This negative energy is external energy being projected via your lower god-self; Satan is having its way through the flesh which is its only power. We as followers allow oppression to rule our lives by feeding separatism, prejudice and separation because of selfish motives which will get you nowhere in the grand scheme of things. We are slowly killing ourselves because of greed due to the fallacy of power, which will be our demise as a people. We will eventually wipe ourselves out if we stay on this path. This negative vibration is not in sync with the spirit of Creation and it has nothing to do with the higher-spirited god in you. Until you start to internalize your focus on the higher power vested in you by the Creator and employ it properly to overcome superficial rhetoric, you will continue to be consumed by religious doctrines and overt deception by the Power Elite. You will never be **liberated** from oppression. The first step to liberation is in the overstanding of knowing who you are. You are symbolic to, Neo! The one! The character Neo was in a movie called, The Matrix.

Animals, insects, reptiles and everything living follow the laws of God and animals are flesh just like us. "The wages of sin is death" Hum? They procreate at the right time. They only have sex when it's time to procreate. They don't commit adultery. In general, they don't drink other animal's milk. They don't kill for fun, they only kill to feed their family. They live in harmony with nature. The female still maintains the matriarchy structure. They don't have sex outside of their own kind or with the same gender *"generally speaking,"* hence: keeping the blood line strong and pedigree. "The comment is in no way shape or form to down play or belittle anyone's personal sex preference; I am only stating this from a moral perspective coupled with the natural laws of nature and the differences between man and animal on a spiritual level." They don't rape other animals intentionally to inflict harm to them or have voluntary sex with humans. They don't acknowledge a higher power consciously and oddly enough they all respect and follow Nature's law, the laws of the Most High, a Higher Power, and the Great Architect. We do the reciprocal and then some. But we are supposed to be the most intelligent beings on the planet. By the same token; the most intelligent people on the planet acknowledge a higher power and kill each other and everything else you can think of in the name of God or due to the sickness the power elite have called the, "Savage Territorial Imperative" which could be partly caused by the absence of the thymus gland medically speaking, because people who are missing that gland tend to be very evil and disorderly. With that being said you might also accept the fact that the most obvious thing of all is most of you act in opposition to nature and go about life justifying your dishonorable acts and punish other people for committing the same acts all in the same breath. (SMH): shaking my head. Most people justify everything contrary to God in the name of God and or use the name of God to justify their actions when it's convenient for them. By the way, if you were wondering, animals indeed have a spiritual connection with the Creator because of the intrinsic values that come with being born of this physical world. No matter what or who you are; all life breathes. Breath is a gift from Al-Lāt for all of us to acknowledge the spiritual divine power of life in the physical manifestation of mortality. You acknowledge the power every time you breathe, so stop and pay homage to the Creator for your gift of life. You need to stop being reckless as a people. We taught you how to be civilized and your lower god-self is sending you in regression and its affecting the existence of humanity. Here are some of the things you do as children of the Most high. You have sex with; fish, horses, ponies, chickens, sheep, sheep, sheep, cows, dogs, big cats, dolls, machines, and the list goes on. So let's go on; more of the things you do; kill animals for fun and I'm talking outside of a gaming license for food. You save animal parts as trophies, and at one time you saved human parts as well just to show off how easy it is to kill the Creators creation called, life for pleasure and then you bask in the materialistic façade of prestige to feel a quasi-sense of self-worth. You drink milk and blood from other animals. You eat certain animal parts for religious reasons. You beat live animals to death, cut open their heads while at the dinner table with your families and eat their brains. *"In your religiously sick minds, you think that will get closer to God, wow!" Eating defenseless animals will not get you closer to the Creator. Acting on the universal principles and laws of the Creator and learning yourself will reveal who god is.* The sickest part of all is that some of you perpetuate this same behavior generation after ignorant generation and then complain about the detriment that your world is in. "My people are destroyed by lack of knowledge" You teach what you think you know to be right and exact but what you know is not right and you may not realize what you don't know because you are accustomed to ignorance and classify it as intelligence. When some of you realize the truth, you refuse to accept it because you know you would be stripped of your wicked powers so you continue to live your selfish lie because ignorance is bliss. It's obvious you understand that once you know "The Word" knowledge and have the right overstanding of life and most of its complexities and responsibility, obligation follows that moral conviction for life. But you choose not to be accountable for your actions so you justify your life on the consensus of the masses to disguise your agenda. "smh." For example: and for all intent and purpose let's say big business is you and you want to mass produce genetically modified Organisms because it will bring you incalculable wealth for you and your family. So you start a campaign of propaganda to convince the people that the world is now too small for the masses of people and we as a people are consuming too much food. You convince them that you have a way to generate more food to alleviate the food shortage. Even thou the food is not natural and it does more harm than good you promote any way because it's all about money and power, not about the welfare and survival of the people. Imagine people start to die years later because your company massed produced toxic food and carcinogenic food that had adverse effects on the ignorant people who know nothing about "GMO's" I guess you would get away with murder because you were approved by the FDA and other federal regulatory organizations. The only thing that might happen is your company would get a fine and you would reconstruct your GMO's to meet a higher standard and start killing people all over again. And people say, "Where is God we need help to combat this evil." The answer is you and you possess the power of god but you are **too lazy to accept the responsibilities that come with the obligation**. Didn't I just say the same thing five minutes ago? I just wanted to touch on this because some of you might not be aware.

We consume genetically modified Organisms "GMO's" which are not natural. We eat cloned animals and consume GMO liquids and you pray over that food and thank God. What are you thanking God for? The food is un-natural going into a nature body. How can your body receive optimal nourishment? It can't! Your body will refuse inorganic processed food and shut down. Little do you know you are transforming your DNA through the food you eat? You are creating a weaker you; your bloodlines are being watered down and mutated. Why do you think more people are having problems trying to conceive? More dis-eases of the body. We have blood banks, ok normal. We have sperm banks, are you kidding me. After the consumption of these processed inorganic foods, you get sick and pray to God to help you through it. Pray to be fertile. Oh really? The power of god was there when you made the choice to defile your body and now you go to the source of life asking for help when you did it to your god-self. When the prayers don't get answered, you justify it with mediocre excuses. Do you realize how many women and men pray to God and seek medical help to conceive and wait for a miracle to happen as opposed to the scripture quoted, I think its Luke 11:9 states that "Seek and you shall find," Knock and the door shall be opened," "Ask and you shall receive" These are quotes powered from within you and you ask for help outside of your house. It's not and outwardly cry or plea for help from God externally, it's from the higher power that dwells in you. Change your mind and you change your life. Deprogram to reprogram because you are what you think and you are what you eat. *"Think right, Eat right, Live right"*

If **Alkebulan** aka Africa, **Kemet** aka Egypt is the mother, heart and cradle of all civilizations and we know it is. It is well documented that during the era of the Kemetian Empire, no other country before that had intellectual consciousness or values of spiritual religion and unparalleled educational resources on the level of Kemetic teachings. It is also a fact that Kemetic scholars went around the world to teach mathematics astrology, astronomy, religion, well basically; the seven liberal arts and medicinal healing. People of other countries found the knowledge astounding and because of this fact. Countries like Persia, Greece, Roman and many others came to Alkebulan and stole from the temples **"Pre-Neter's"** by which we were taught to call them by the Greek translation: "Pyramids." They stole history, manuscripts, teachings, gold, silver, artifacts, spices, women, men and religion. They burned down "The Royal Alexandrian Library" of Alexandria, Kemet, to hide where the original information came from. To add insult to injury they also burn, "The Royal Theban Library" as well and took all knowledge they stole and defiled the original teachings and distorted the **Kemetic** and **Ethiopian** schools of thought by changing original names, concepts, principles and philosophies. They started proclaiming all of the information to be their own and naming their predecessors and ancestors the founders of all academia; Democritus, Heraclitus, *Xenophanes*, Pythagoras, Socrates, Plato, Aristotle, the Rosicrucian order, the Masonic order, Neno, Hippocrates and many more. Whereby creating a new ideology of the original and imposing it on the same people they stole it from once they became a Roman Empire hundreds of years later and it still holds true to this very day. So knowing all this to be a relevant fact, wouldn't common sense tell you they did the same with the principles of God and who God really is for the sole purpose of world domination? The same perverted mind-set that taught you also enslaved you under the same fraudulent Godly principles you believe in to this very day. As I stated earlier, you should not believe in God, you should know God. This goes for all people of the world who believe his-story and abandoned their own native culture and history. Did your ancestors that fought and died for your freedom mean anything to you?

One fact that the Church doesn't want you to know is that the human nature of mankind regarding one deity or man saving the world is not in conjunction to the laws of Creation. What is written in the Bible referring to Jesus saving the world is a conflict of interest. In creation the balance of all things is always more than one. It takes more than one element to create life. Even if you see one thing happening when life is created, there is the presence of creative activity beyond the naked eye. There will never be **1** savior for humanity and there will never be **1** entity that creates existence. Based on multiple facets of universal laws, **1** cannot exist by itself. The false principles of one as you know it is part of the deception of life as told by biblical scholars. These are the same people who teach us that Jesus is coming back to save humanity from itself or should I say; the people that accepted the Lord Jesus Christ as their "Personal Savior" Why should God be personal if we are all God's children, shouldn't God be for everyone? Anyway, all of the people who have tried to save humanity in one way or another died of a mysterious death or were all assassinated including Jesus Christ. Superficial plutocracy would not allow the people-world to be saved by **one** significant person and the paradox is that global supremacy reinforces the Jesus concept that the world will only be saved by one supernatural force because the supernatural ideology would not take the power away from the Greco Roman Plutocratic Regime who reigns supreme. This physiological strong-hold is what allows super-powers around the globe to flourish and continue to wave the iron hand of oppression to weaken the higher god-spirit of the people. What are you all being saved from that you can't do it yourself? Huh? Did you ever ask yourself that question? Once you are saved, then what?

The **significant nature** of the **Creator** who governs **universal laws** wouldn't save the world by manifesting into a fleshly-being to save the same people of universal creation; it doesn't make sense when you look at the creative forces of universal law. "Let **us** make man in **our** image and likeness," no matter how you interpret it, it's **more than 1**. One organ doesn't create or sustain our lives. The science of the Creator created **us** with cells, muscles, blood, bones, ribs, heart, brain, legs, arms, lungs, eyes, kidneys, spirit, soul, intelligence, etc. and did you ever stop to think that almost everything that you have to make you a complete creation in the likeness and image of the creator came in two's? "Symbolic to the interpretation of the Ark which represented life" But the **1** thing that controls your entire body is your brain, with 7 holes in your head that is representation of the physical God that governs your body, without it you wouldn't exist. You have two eyes that work as 1, two ears that work as 1, two nostrils that work as 1 and 1 mouth, which equates to the number 7. With that in mind, your head is comprised of the **left** and **right** hemispheres that work as **1** to balance your mental and spiritual being. The same holds true about Creation as we know it; Wind, Fire, Water, Carbon, Protons, Electrons, and Neutrons. These are the principles based on our level of understanding creation, and without these principles in place, creation itself would not exist. My point is that, Creation has exclusive universal laws for exclusive creation and all creative powers unite under the universal laws of creation. Meaning, if you put Creation itself under one title of God and hold

JAHI ISSA JABRI ALI-BEY

true to your doctrines regarding what you were taught about God, you will always be confused because there are multiple aspects of creation that dwarf the concept of the way you were taught to perceive God. Again, universal laws based on balance and oneness is only represented by the unification of two or more "not as in the in-divide-dual" and if you overstand this your spirit should tell you that if you want to save yourself and have everlasting life, your spirit will submit to the universal laws of nature and the spirit that dwells in you will become **1** divine unit. "Not an entity in the sky" Meaning; unity with all life as a spiritual family united and unification as **1** body collective which will afford ourselves everlasting life. The power is within all of us **universally**, not **individually**. Overstand that changing laws, marching, occupying areas, protesting has never worked and never will. On occasion if it did work, it was for laws that were insignificant in the grand scheme of things because we are same fighting for the same things we been fighting for forever and the laws that did change makes little to no difference and they never really worked for the masses for an extended period of time anywhere on the planet anyway. If the oppressed across the globe execute an economic boycott it would render the Power Elite helpless and stop their cash flow, the power would be in the hands of the oppressed. Separate yourself from wanting acceptance by a people who will never accept you. One thrives on material wealth and one thrives on the progression of a people. Which one are you? Are you waiting for a savior or do you have the leadership ability to save yourself.

That was said to bring you to the harsh reality that **Jesus is not coming back** to save you as you were taught, **Jesus is coming back** in the form of wooly hair, bronze feet along with other cultures of people that will follow Jesus to be free from the Iron hand of Oppression place on us by the plutocratic values of Satan. Jesus is the representation of humanity uniting as 1 spiritual body taking action to save the world we live in called, flesh which we as spiritual beings need to survive in the physical realm until we return back to the essence. Satan is material in principle just like money. So when you say money is the root of all evil, remember it's not the money, it's the greed for power that we as people allow money to have and if you as a person are not grounded by the values of your higher god-self that allow you to see pass the superficial aspects of material. On the other hand, if you cannot see past material your lower god-self will be your demise. Having an economic boycott will result in a change for the better. Realize it or not, your demise is the **concept of hell** that you were miss-educated on just like everything else you were taught to believe that causes so much confusion in life to stop us from reaching our divinity.

A little note for the people who have "CVMB," chronic voluntary mind block, people who know everything have no more room to know anything else and people who know you think you know everything, know you know nothing at all. Furthermore: I pray that you destroy the wall that's stopping your mental and spiritual growth so you don't continue to spread involuntary ignorance to people in your life and perpetuate a delusional self-centered condescending state of mind that continues to plague the world causing insurmountable damage to our higher god-self.

A foot note for all the elders who refuse to change for the better. If living your life wasn't what your heart intended and you settled for less your whole life and never truly found god, this book is your answer to be content and grow spiritually before they throw the dirt over your face. You still have the opportunity to teach yourself and family the truth before going back to the essence. As long as you can still breath, that's the spirit of the Almighty in you god, you still have the power to instill in your family, your spirit of god and who you really are. In doing so, you will pass on your spirit to your successors' and attain everlasting life. Once you have done so you can finally "Rest in peace."

Think about this, if we are the only intelligent ones on the planet who consciously acknowledge a higher power and we all died off in the physical form but other life forms were still living and knowing nothing else acknowledges God but us, would God the higher power still exist? I have to answer this for some of you because most of you are still programmed to deny truth and believe falsehood. No!

God would not exist in the **conscience** due to the fact that nothing else is told a higher power exist on a **conscience level**. So in fact and theory God would not exist. But on the contrary, in the grand scheme of things, the Creators natural laws would still be carried out although nothing alive acknowledges the concept of God. Animals and insects would still procreate, the sun would still revolve around the universe, the planets would still revolve around the sun and life would continue to exist. The Higher power's only focus in life was creation itself, remember after the 6th day God rested, everything after that was given to us along with the mundane powers of creation. The Creator gave god the power to create. How many times must you see this to acknowledge truth? Are you looking at the big picture as to why you are this way? "You are god!" Are you getting the gist?

It's about you and what you were taught as a child or an adult as to why you are in denial, in bad health and programmed to think the way you do. Why do you think we are having so many health issues? It's because you have a choice. You choose to keep your eyes closed and become a zombie. Even Eve choose to open her eyes. Choices weren't an issue or topic of discussion in Sunday school when she ate the primordial apple. What happened to that part of the class? "Oh the focus was only about the deception, and boy did we get deceived!" In this day and age I still never heard anyone discuss her or Adam being created and formed of flesh from dirt. Flesh is sin and choices did or did not exist it that time. If you even start to fix your lips and start an argument over, they were formed from dirt, you are so lost. "For Your Information, dirt is irrelevant because flesh is the gift and the curse, not dirt" At least we create robots to have some form of intelligence. Zombies are dumb as hell-hell-o dummy. The sardonic thing is you created yourself ignorant because you are a follower and not a leader. Do you still need a Shepard little sheep people. You know what some classes of humans do to sheep besides pull the wool over their eyes and makes clothes; they force them to have sex with them. Are you worn-out from being violated yet? With that being said, people make the statement about if we didn't have a choice, we would be like robots. I never saw an insect, animal, or reptile act like a robot. Adam didn't act like a robot either, unless I missed that class to. Maybe you have witnessed robotize people in your lifetime, and if you did please tell me what creature or people acts that way, I know some that do and I will tell you about them in a sec. Other than that no one I know has stepped up to the plate and showed me a robot because the wool is probably still over their eyes. Looks like proof that if we didn't have a choice, we would not be robots. I have more proof, as I stated in another chapter, people on their death beds tell me they don't have a choice and I never ever seen them act like, look like, walk, talk like a robot. So if I'm human just like everybody else; why haven't you asked if God didn't give me a choice would I really have a robot mentality? From my experienced, most people who proclaim God give us a choice so we won't be robots, are the ones who are robots. These are the same people that are religious and do the same programs every single day. They are programmed to only read their prescribed religious doctrine. They follow deceptive propaganda schemes; they are susceptible to subliminal linguistic acrobatics by the media and local government. They are programmed to think and function in a unidirectional capacity. They follow social popular opinion without the thought of rebuttal.

Anyway let's get back to the subject of sex; too a degree we are as mundane as sheep to be the elite intellectual human family, we probably wouldn't have as much sex to procreate if we didn't have stimulating nerve endings and receptors to arouse our sexual desires. People would be more concerned with money and power than sex for procreation because if you are unbalanced mentality, power will greed selfishness and procreation is not selfish. We would probably be too I to have sex just for the sake of procreation. But on the other hand, animals and insects are smart enough to know that procreation ensures everlasting life for that particular species and they only breed with the strongest males. On the other hand, selfish human intervention could step in and deprive them of their life and they would become extinct. It's happened before and it will happen again. Humanity does it to self so animals are a drop in the bucket. But for us; again, the only way the **world-Flesh** would come to an end, if we do it. The planet will still be here. The planet is ruled by the universe, we are ruled by **god**. We have the power to build and destroy ourselves at the blink of an eye. The world governments do not want to have world war three. Don't you know they know that would be self-annihilation? They don't want to die no more than you. If they can reside on another planet, they wouldn't mind a third world war, they wouldn't be here to care. All the prayers in the **world** couldn't save you because you would be praying in vein. Anyway that's another chapter in life. The point of having the need for sex is to procreate and duplicate for everlasting life. We have the power as god to give life or take it away. The power resides in you. Here is undeniable proof, the Creator created everything natural and super natural; spirit, breath, air, wind, oxygen, stars, planets, water, snow, rain, natural law, etc.

We use the power of God's creation to simulate and create as well. Almost everything that the Creator created that's in our physical reaches as humans, we have learned how to take something from it and make our own creation. The sun taught us how to fuse protons and neutrons. We learned from the sun that uranium and plutonium are the elements that make an atom bomb. The dauphins that the Creator made taught us about the power of sonar. The animals and birds the Creator made taught us how to migrate for survival and give us the inspiration to fly, how to hunt, etc. Which leads us to the fact that, the Creator gives us the power to create on a physical level. Once we think of an idea, have a thought, think of an new invention, think of writing a book, think of building a city, house, medicine, sonar, car, plane, pipeline, bomb, telescope, satellite, etc. We process that thought and put it into action, bringing those thoughts into fruition-reality and those thoughts of creation become life. In the same vein, God never created babies; all books allude to the creation of man in the full adult stage. The teachings refer to man not children. With that being understood, the Creator gave us the power to duplicate ourselves via intercourse. The greatest gift we could ever have is the gift of duplication. The creator gave all species of life the gift of duplicating life. Also through the power of the Life Force we have the ability to be creative, we have ingenuity, the ability to think, reason, analyze, problem solve etc. We can't create the ability to reason, think, or create spirit that's all on an inconceivable spiritual level. We can only create on a physical level. The spiritual level of the Creator's image and likeness is manifested and projected through the creation of the physical being "us." Are you with me?

Quote: "When you feel like hope is gone, look inside you and be strong, and you'll finally see the truth, that a hero lies in you" Mariah Carey

Why do we separate, segregate and alienate ourselves because of our religious preferences? Do we all not come from the same universal Creator? "For all of you that wanna argue this point, stay on track, that's in another book, this is about god, stay focused" Our focus should be 1 in the same, "humanity" not the differences in our personal religious preferences. Religious preference is superficial, that's what's causing a spiritual disconnect and we will never be 1 mind if we keep our focus on religion and not god. The power will never be with the people, only the superficial governments you gave the power to by focusing your energy in the wrong direction. The government is a body of people who control the people for the people. If you had self-control of yourself and excised your higher power as god, would you still need a government? We are talking present government, not the original concept of government for the greater good of the people. "I know this question is argumentative," but I need you think outside the box" you shouldn't even have a box by now. You should have thrown it away after the first chapter. One more time, we have the innate ability to create, so with that gift we have god powers and if you deny that fact you will never develop your mind to reach a higher spiritual plane and at the same time, you are adamantly attending religious services, Friday, Saturday and Sunday. After that one day of worship, most of you are back to your daily routines living in a world-"flesh" of chaos and confusion.

Outside of going to a religious function and focusing on the doctrines of religion, we as a collective need to focus more on self-improvement spiritually, acknowledge our weaknesses, take responsibility for our own actions, internalize our thoughts and ambitions with a dedicated focus on god, instead of the external God you are taught to focus on, you will ultimately alter the course of your life for self and the progress of all mankind. Also by doing that, your eyes shall be open knowing good and evil and you will be like one of the Gods. Every person on the planet is a god from the God source that created them. If you denounce your god-ship-fellow-ship you are a hypocrite to your on existence. How can you say, "God dwells in you" and in the same breath deny who you are? Oh, as a man thinks so that he is. "There is one exception to the rule" Not in this case, the life-force is present regardless of what you think, because you wouldn't be here if it wasn't so. If you think a higher power doesn't exist in you, you give power to your lower power, which is still god. That's the exception to the rule. "Damned if you do, damned if you don't" Actually you won't be damned if you do, but it got the point across. That's an example of how people play tricks on you to play in their club. If you said huh, read it from the top. Remember everyone doesn't travel at the same speed and that's perfectly ok by me, I just want you to understand what you are read to the fullest extent of the passage, so I might throw in a fast ball to catch your attention. So you are what you think, and you think what you perceive to know and you know the spirit of the Creator is the gift of breath you received when came out of the womb because if it was not true, you would be here to read about it. That's the purpose of inducing the baby to cry so they can take their first breath that the creator gave them. Note: if they don't use the God given innate ability to breath as god, they return back to the essence. Meaning the Creator already gave you the gift of life at conception and once the baby is exiting the womb it's their responsibility to take that breath. God will not magically make you breathe, it's called intelligence. Everything living has it. "Internalize the power of god and stop giving it to the under-world, Satan.

Understand this and never forget it. Intrinsic intelligence the Creator of all life is universal and if you acknowledge universal laws and you have no choice but to. Universal laws never change and the god you are will never change for the worse only for the uplifting of humanity. On the other hand the only illusion to changing god's law is Satan, because some people serve Satan's universal laws as opposed to the Creator. Satan will die as flesh and god will live as spirit, you have the power to create your own destiny. "Surah 13:11" For all intent and purposes remember you are the little gee and the Creator is the big Gee. We have the limited power of creation and power to delegate our authority via the Creator as god on a small scale, and Allah, the Creator does it on a larger scale. We create concepts and bring them to fruition through actions and deeds. Cars, airplanes, streets, babies, rockets, gmo's, dis-eases, bombs, life, death, and every other physical manifestation seen and unseen in life through the naked eye, we did that. Magic and miracles played no part in the process. Again, The Creator played no part in the process. Get that crap out of your head. God didn't create disease, god did. God didn't kill your son or daughter to bring you closer to the Creator, god did. God didn't make you a drug user, god did. God can't help you with any of these issues, only god can, so when you pray externally for the Creator to help you and you don't get an answer, don't blame God, blame god. I agree that, "god helps those who help themselves." Hopefully before you die, you will have passed on your degrees to your family so that your spirit in them will shine in the darkness and give you everlasting life through all offspring that succeeded you.

Who are you? When your flesh dies, you will return to your Creator, your Universal and or life-force. Where are you returning?

When flesh dies so does Satan because the wages of sin is death and flesh is sin from conception to birth. Satan can't go to heaven with you so again, where are you going? Or does your spirit body split, half goes with Satan and the other half with the Creator? I'm just asking. Sounds like the devil give you; "Acts 17:11" Open your mind and you will see the light. "Don't be a sneak peeper, be an advent seeker, my sons and daughters of the east."

> **Quote:** "Stop looking on the outside, it's just the wind, you'll never find what you're looking for, until you to go deep within" (Terry Ellis)

At this stage in the book the true is even harder to shallow, so I hope you can handle the truth by now. I prepped you for this throughout the entire book. I told you to read each chapter in order to get a full understanding and that each chapter should help you overstand the next. This book is about, "Who is God" you should know now who god is. We are going back to "oneness" I hope you understood the concept of oneness. Remember we talked about, religious concepts regarding, the father, son and ghost, and how they are one and all the things that are two or three are one. Ok great. Yahweh, Yahweh Ben Yahweh, Allah, Jehovah, Elohim, Lucifer are all created by the Creator; the Almighty, the Life-force etc. They all have the same Godly spirit and purpose, "except Lucifer" they all have 1 common goal. That makes the names superficial because if they all have the same goal, then the name would separate the goal on the surface and looking at the surface is what put us in this predicament from the start. Now Lucifer, the Morning star, Satan, the devil, or whatever, was created by the Creator or man, depending on your religious belief. If you say, "man" to defend your religious doctrines and dogma, you just admitted we are god. On the other hand, if you say God the Creator didn't create Satan, you are seriously in denial and you are admitting there is more than one God and in the same breath in are saying no I'm not. Talk about being twisted, sheesh! Any whoo! If you worship cars, people, idols, money, and anything else, isn't that considered your God? Says who? Did your higher god-self tell you that or was it something you learned? I'm asking you to ask yourself. Also ask yourself what spirit is behind this type of worship? It's only two primary spirits outside of hundreds. Either your higher spirit has control or your lower spirit does but its only 1 you. Understand that both of those spirits reside in you like it or not. That brings me to the question of why would God say,

"I am a jealous God" First off it's an emotional reaction to be jealous and that's a human trait, not a trait of a Creator, higher power, or an intelligent supreme spirit. There is no spiritual or logical room for emotion in a God state of existence. In the same vein, it constitutes negativity, insecurity, and subordination to a higher power or a power just as equal. To be of the highest Intelligence known to man as the Creator why would the mighty and powerful creator say I'm jealous of other God's unless those God's are on the same level as the Creator and threaten the Creator's position? That statement would be a manmade statement coming from an animalistic state of mind. Also for God to say I'm a jealous God, would also depict a human attribute and it would mean that God is advocating jealousy to all of his followers? Remember we are not talking about religious dogma and what club you represent. This is common sense. Look up jealousy if you are having issues. Unless your religious teachers made a new translation for jealousy, it still means the same thing. To enlighten you a little, the only god that would have that type of and attribute would be Satan. Satan is the fleshly **worldly** lower god spirit that dwells in you. You are the only mortal source of Satan's existence and to be jealous is a negative attribute and your higher god-self would be secure because the Creator created Satan and Satan will die. So what's the Creator jealous of? "Please don't say, "Place no other gods before me" talk about redundant.

Remember the chapter that dealt with numbers and the power of 1, 2, 3 regarding the collation of 1 and how it's no duality, everything is 1 and that everything isn't always what it seems. With that in mind, man and woman come together to make one, animals do the same. Daytime starts at nighttime 12am and at 12pm they come together for 12 more hours to complete 1 day. Lightning and thunder are *"1 in the same"* one. It's just that the speed of light is so fast, that it breaks the sound barrier and you hear the delay in the form of thunder seconds after the flash. Point is everything is 1. I won't harp on it because we already discussed it. Hopefully you received the information properly. There is a balance in all life, seen and unseen. In the past I had a problem with the scripture that said "Vengeance is mine says the Lord" because what I was taught about the Creator was all **positive** and the devil was all **negative**. I would always ask myself, how can God be vengeful and still be God because that's a negative attribute and Satan is the negative force in life. As I developed my spirituality I understood the reality of the scripture. God created a balance in life because duality is oneness in this physical dimension. Satan is the balance; flesh in Satan's life force and within the flesh is the life force of the Creator. The flesh houses both spirits that are from the same Creator so that there will be law and order in respects to the principals of the, "Laws of Nature" and life can live together as one and depart as one. Meaning: the flesh-Satan dies and transforms to enrich and fertilize the soil and your spirit goes back to the essence and lives through your procreations with the power of the life force you call the Creator or another name. Again I state to you all, there is no duality in life, for life to exist it has to be oneness, two things come together as a union to create life and those two things stay together in life to create balance in life or one thing makes a sacrifice to die so the other can live.

Example: A seed is the essence of a tree but in order for that tree to be born, the seed must die and out of that seed the tree is born. The tree produces more seeds to ensure everlasting life for that species of tree. The process repeats itself over and over. Sperm and semen become one to fertilize the egg, the sperm and egg form a cell, that cell forms two cells and then four cells which transforms into a zygote, then an embryo and then a fetus, this is to illustrate how oneness brings forth life and death also brings forth life and we are one with life and death, we are one with the Creator, the Creator is one with us. Separation does not exist in the creation of life or the existence of life itself. The reality is; God and Satan are one in the same for the sole purpose of creating and maintaining a balance in the physical world, "flesh." The morning star is the sun. The sun is the hottest living energy closest to us. The devil is referred to as a living hell-fire. When we are upset, vengeful, fussing, cussing, stealing, cheating, fighting, mad, angry, jealous or depressed, by which these are all negative spiritual attributes, these emotions cause our temperature to rises. Ask yourself if that's a trait of God or Satan? If you deny Satan is in you, you are lost because of the teachings that were introduced to you. God and Satan are in us consciously, because we consciously put both of them there. They both reside in us and we have the power to evoke either one at **will**. What most of us lack is the spiritual well-roundedness to control both forces. "As above 360 so below 360 which equal 720 broken down in sacred geometry as $7+2+0=9$" the number **9** in numerology represents completeness. So temperature rises meaning you are hot about an issue or sick and tired, that's the lower self. Calm and peaceful, happy, drama free, that's the higher self. Remember, "Greater is he that is in you than he that is of the world" actually that phrase reveals that your higher god-self is stronger than the lower god-self. In the end the flesh will lose. It is said that, you fight fire with fire, never bring a knife to a gun fight, etc. If you were ever to encounter a negative situation that can't be defused by the higher power of god and there is no retreat. It's the fire in you that will save you. On this physical plan called earth you need Satan to help you survive. On a Spiritual plan all you need is the spirit of the Creator. Keep in mind that in this life you need 2 that are balanced as 1 to exist and that goes for everything on the planet, that's the laws of nature and that's why 2 is really 1 and theirs is no duality. This is a rule that can never be broken in natural law for life to exist as far as I know.

Quote: "What destroys us all, as I recall, envy, greed and jealousy, stop looking on the outside, it's just the wind, you'll never find what you're looking for, until you to go deep within" "Terry Ellis"

The same devil you deny in your heart will save you from a world of grief or death. Some people, who ignored Satan in times like that, paid the ultimate price and the price was death. This is the balance that the Creator gave you because of sin in regards to flesh. You can't fight a spiritual war in a totally physical world and you can't fight a physical war in a totally spiritual realm. The principals of physics and the laws of the Creator make that impossible. The proof is you. The spirit can only move through you, your body can't live without the spirit; the duality is oneness to complete life's cycle of everlasting life for both beings. If you are lost or rebellious to the point of no return as a person, you might tend to use false gods *"drugs-good, bad, or indifferent"* that would give you a euphoric feeling of what god can do, until you find your way back home. "Find your mind, because you lost it." Again, "My people are destroyed by the lack of knowledge" how about, 'They don't acknowledge god in them and are destroyed" In the grand scheme of things you need Satan to survive because this is his world "flesh" in without flesh the two spirits would cease to exist, and there would be no use for humans. All spirit would be 1 with the Creator as a whole. So to keep balance in the physical world the Creator gave you the spirit of Satan to be one with him to survive the physical world until your appointment is made to return to that from once you came.

Quote: Arm, leg, leg, arm, head, this is God body Knowledge, wisdom, freedom, understanding we just want our equality. Question religion, question it all, Question existence until them questions are solved. "Jay Z" FOR YOUR INFORMATION "throwback" Jay-Z beat out Elvis for the most number1 records sold in a time when duplication is ramped. Hats off to Jay-Z!

In this world you can't be 100percent Godly. People who try to mix physical properties and spiritual properties are going against the grain, that's like trying to mix oil and water, it won't work. To be all spirit, you would be perfect and perfection isn't physical, it's spiritual. When someone says, "We are not perfect." The statement only holds water in the physical realm. You need to have a common ground on both sides of the spectrum. When you go from one extreme to the next you are creating and imbalance in your life and death will soon follow. If you were all Godly, "for the sake of the people who think they are" conniving people would take advantage of you, constantly harm you and you would die from starvation in every aspect of the word. Based on the principles of God; God is all good all the time and your godly mentality would decay in this worldly plane. Unless you evoke that statement, "Vengeance is mine says the lord" whether that means karma or not the only way to put that statement into action is through Satan because vengeance is a negative attribute and you don't have time to wait for karma. So your luciferian complex which is the lower god-self could save your life. So you need to embrace Adonai as a whole for what it's worth. And know that god and Lucifer are one in the same which creates balance for the purpose of life in the physical realm. God made you flesh which is sinful. God gave you breathe through the spirit creating the gift of life in the physical form and the origin of Lucifer is with the Creator. The Creator created all life that ever existed and will continue to exist and if you say we created Satan, again I say, we are god and if you argue still, I say the Creator created us which created Satan and the origins are still one in the same, unless, you know of another Creator.

Don't wrap your-self around dogma and propaganda, that will only complicate matters, cause a lack of understanding, distrust will follow, separation will follow soon after and we will never have divine unification and regain the power we were born with. Seek and you shall find. You are 1 with God and god is 1 with you. I hope you have clarity as to who god is and use your god given power to be a better person and help your family have everlasting life. It's a long road and people have strayed away from reality so much that they can't accept constructive criticism from the people who love them dearly. Some people don't even know what constructive criticism is all they know is destructive criticism. Because everything they hear is negative to them. They refuse to be corrected as if it's a crime to be wrong. How can you learn if you are always right? They're so blinded by a false reality, they think, "Keeping it real" is real. We are allowing technology to detach the human bond and spiritual like we have as people and the godly principals of life. If we continue to move further and further away from self the contrast is, self-destruction. The other side of God is Satan. Know self, know god. Lose self, self-destruct.

> Quote: "what was once easy became confused and hard which brings us back, to the mystic question, who is God?" The God MC Rakim

> Quote: You may not interact with your mother as a son should, but the physical and spiritual ties she created with you **will** never be broken! "Your spiritual umbilical cord," so honor your mother until "death do you part." "Jahi" aka My Cable-Tow"

> Quote: Man's duty is to improve himself: to cultivate his mind; and when he finds himself going astray, to bring the moral law to bear upon himself. "Immanuel Kant"

He's speaking of humanity as a whole and responsibility of self to police self.

Some religious teachings, social ideologies and the so called status quo are the isms that keep you dumb founded to the realities of life. I could write books for eons or talk until you turn blue in the face and you are astatic, elated, over-joyed and ready to take the world by storm, and when you look at the big picture, it means nothing to most people because everything I say sounds relevant to you at that particular time and once you leave my presence you are back to your old self again. That's the same thing that happens when you hear prominent speakers. You are enthused about the content of the speech and after it's over you are back to the old you. Mostly because you are not grounded in knowing the power you possess and that's part of the downfall of man. If I force you to believe my ideology by, killing some of your family that reject me and do the same thing to every generation after that. Certain family members will want to live and go along with the plan whether they like it or not. After hundreds of years it won't be so hard for me to impose my philosophy on your family. Now I can give it to you in a passive way by placing it everywhere you look. You have no choice but to conform, especially when you think no other standards of living or philosophy exist, and if I have done this for thousands of years, it's too easy to convince the whole world of my doctrine and ideology. *"The world is flesh"* Along with absolute power comes ego and in position of power, too much ego makes a respectable well versed person exploit ignorance via propaganda, false doctrines and or unscrupulous concepts that will be detrimental to people that look up an organization or person for leadership. "Absolute Abbey said once, "Be a game changer because the world has enough followers."

I would like to express my thoughts on criticisms that might arise from the creation of this book. I know a lot of people will question me as to having a degree or make comments parallel to; who does he think he is to make such statements? "You should know who I am by now" He's not qualified lol. What you all say doesn't matter, if it's negative. My goal is to reconnect the spirit of god to its rightful owner. I do not, I repeat I do not need a degree to be accepted by your traditions and or philosophies' regarding what you might think qualifies my aptitude for expressing the powers and applications of god. I am god! The Almighty Creator gave me the power and overstanding to acknowledge who I am without the justifications of man. If you choose to overlook that for selfish and person gain, that's your choice. Aren't choices the gospel in most of your eyes? Don't be upset with me little man in the mirror, make that change. If you want change, start with yourself, take responsibility for your actions; good, bad or indifferent, be sincere in your quest, be thorough in your actions and deeds and have a profound sense of who you are and instill these priceless qualities in your families and the people you love. Consistency is the mother of purpose and if you persist on being consistent, changes are evitable. We fail if we believe in everlasting life. We will succeed when we know we have the power to perpetuate everlasting life through procreation and the propagation of truth and save a people and a nation. One of the problems we have as a people throughout the diaspora is, we only come together as 1 mind to accomplish 1 goal when 1 inclement catastrophic event happens or large gathering like the, "Million Man March" or on a small scale, a funeral and that's only if the family isn't dysfunctional. The sad thing is, after a day or two the hype is gone and nothing gets accomplished in the grand scheme of things. Believe it or not most of the problems are generated by your thought and your inability to let go of the falsehoods you were taught because of the sense of fear that was instilled in your ancestors DNA. The justification for your fear is, Hell. I will try and enlighten you in a different light in hopes to bring you to an appreciative understanding of God on a larger scale.

God as you understand the concept; is misrepresented by the perception of religion which affects the perception of God in science and the perception as an individual. The reason you can't comprehend the God concept or achieve an answer is because you think of God as a concept of your person ideologies. For instance, if you are a biologist your concept of God would sway in the direction of biology based theory. If you are a religious person your concept of God would be influenced by religious doctrine and philosophies. If you are a scientist your concept would be influenced by logical scientific data. My point is that all schools of thought have their own interpretation of what and who is God or if God exist at all. That's universal bigotry and a cause for confusion. Creation is not a bigot and Creation doesn't indulge in the affairs of man. Creation's job is to sustain life by any means necessary, anything else is excluded from the equation, that's keeps life constantly evolving and developing without falter. Back to man's selfish interpretation and theories;

The problem with all of these theories is that they are all prejudice in regards to their schools of thought. First and foremost God is a title and that in itself leads the quest of understanding in the wrong direction when trying to find the answer of, "Who is God" or what is God. The other problem is that humans only relate God to their personal existence as if God is exclusive to only creating the human family and the experiences thereof. That is the other flaw in perusing "Who and or what is God"

Creation would be a good term to use, not God. If you change the word, you change the perception and meaning and that changes the concept. That creates a different vision, giving you a different perceptive and a new avenue of approach when it comes to decision making and teaching. Throughout this book I pressed the issue of oneness and how to understand oneness in its true form. Oneness is not about and individual, it's about the unification of individual bodies forming as one to accomplish a single goal or task, and this is the universal laws of nature. The Creation of life is not about human existence alone, it's about the synchronization of individual constructs following a divine law consistently to produce life in multifaceted levels of creation throughout the universe to perpetuate its own existence, that's the purpose of life. Humankind only can hypothesize or speculate as far as the eyes can see. The paradox is, the more we see the more we incorporate these experiences with our own schools of thought looking for a purpose that already exist and this causes unacceptable reaction and or confusion among the masses and scholars of the world. If we as a whole would stop being selfish and accept the fact that we all have pieces of the puzzle that are relevant and if we come together as one mind we would accelerate the process for understanding creation. With that being said I want you to really understand what you are about to digest.

Everything I just told you about God and Satan was to prepare you for this. My definition of the Creator will give you an extremely vivid overstanding of creation and close the religious divide among all people by awakening the true identity of what you call God. When you look at creation in the way I define it, life will be lived by a universal perspective and you will have clarity in relation to creation. **Creator-Creation:** "A multi-faceted life-force manifestation of intrinsic intelligence and energy continuously transcending in and out of different states of matter seen and unseen to perpetuate life everlasting."

If you view God in the traditional way, conflict and a state of confusion will always haunt you and you will always have to defend that falsehood. The misguided understanding of who God really is ... inhibits your mental capacity to act because you are taught to give your burdens to God, pray and God will fix all things, etc. You will never be proactive, only reactive in protecting your family and your life along with all other aspects of life. Look at the world around you, people only react to things that they feel need attention. The sad issue here is that, they see negativity all the time but react when it hits home. "?" Viewing God in the traditional way also prohibits you from thinking on a higher level and it keeps you spirituality and mentality unconscious. Remember the traditional teaching only focus on religious doctrine and dogmas, not true spirituality and divinity. I will give you an abstract example of a built in God mechanism which is really "intrinsic intelligence." The **fever**, it's your own bodies' defense mechanism trying to burn out the viruses invading your body by forcing your body to sweat to eliminate the toxins caused by the virus. Intrinsic intelligence is a part of **Creation** that wants creation to live and the irony is it will kill you in order to try and keep you alive. By the same token, I will point out the power of **oneness in its true form** that **will** enable you to live. If you assist the fever based on understanding naturopathic remedies and the understanding of medicinal natural medicine you are more likely to overcome your illness. Reason being, you took initiative to unify with your higher god self as 1 mind for 1 common goal. "God helps those who help themselves." On the other hand, traditional religious practices will say pray for the sick and meek and they will get blessings from God, "sadly, you are waiting for magic" and it will never happen and when the people die you make justifications in the name of God. Huh? Then you repeat the rituals over and over and reap the same consequences hoping for new results. Don't we call that insanity? Understand that I wrote this book as a **blue print** for spiritual awakening and for the upliftment of humanity as well as a **blue print** for ending economic depression and colonial oppression. We have the Power to change the state of affairs that we are in, as long as we bond spirituality as 1 Global United Nation and remember as 1 spiritual body, "No weapon formed against us shall prosper." These two definitions should give you a true inner-standing of what "**Creation**" is and "**Who is God**."

Creation: The act of making or producing something that did not exist before: The act of creating something: The act of bringing the world into ordered existence: Thank you (Merriam-webster. com) keep in mind I gave you this definition again to remind you of in the truth in hopes you to really understand what this means the grand scheme of things as far as shaping your thoughts and perceptions.

God: The perfect and all-powerful spirit or being that is **worshipped** especially by Christians, Jews, and Muslims as the one who created and rules the universe. (learnersdictionary.com) these definitions are from different sources to illustrate the similarities to show the skeptics the truth is in the meaning. It's not me making this up.

A spirit or being that has great power, strength, knowledge, etc., and that can affect nature and the lives of people: One of various spirits or beings worshipped in some religions:

A person and especially a man who is greatly loved or admired

As always the original definition of a word defines the original premise for the usage of that word. As you can see the word **Creation** defines all things created and the word **God** is strictly a **Belief System** followed by religious sects especially the monotheistic and polytheistic belief systems (BS). When you make the distinction between the too, you will clearly see as to how the term God would relate to man and Creation is the everything of all things and God is only a part of Creation and not Creation itself. To say God is "the all" is a contradiction within itself because religion segregates and separates itself from the rest of creation by adamantly affirming that their specific doctrine and religious beliefs are the only true doctrines to follow. Creation created all life; Creation didn't single out you because of your religious beliefs. By the same token, these religions allude to creation being exclusive to human existence alone. Creation is the essence of all life seen and unseen. Animals, insects, fish, reptiles, and birds do not know God in any way shape or form and they won't burn in hell or be punished. The only rebuttal religion has for that statement is, "God didn't give them a choice" That's an ignorant answer. I already taught you about choices so now you know that answer holds no weight.

On another note, if you look at the big picture, all Countries have a dominate religion. That dominate religion is ran by the dictator of that country or masked as an indirect dictatorship. In the Western World the Pope and his doctrine is sought out to be the dominate religion. Japan's dominate religion is Atheist and in the so called Middle East the dominate religion would be Islam, etc. The world This only dictates the mindset of the masses and allows for easier control over the masses because as long as you cater to their beliefs and use the same doctrine that sets the standards they will follow because psychologically their do not think for themselves, they are led by the doctrine they follow. They are sleep walkers and don't even realize it. They think popular belief is truth and unpopular truth is ridiculous. Sadly enough, because of **belief** some people are reading this and are still in denial.

FOR YOUR INFORMATION- "If you don't know your opponent, you will lose the Battle, maybe your life and your purpose was-is all for naught" ... Jahi Ali-Bey

As a spokes-person for the underdogs of the planet, I would like for you to read the following chapters to understand the need for your higher god-self world-wide. Your higher life-force needs to be activated now, acknowledge your higher god-self. Our higher life source is an awesome gift of life we possess and I hope we, as a dying *"mind, body & soul"* people awaken our ability to assert the power of god in our everyday life before life is non-existent for all who live it. There are plenty of civilizations, cultures and nations in history that don't exist anymore, don't let yours be **one** of them.

The Nine Principles of Economic Depression and Plutocratic Supremacy

1. Corporations took the principles of morals and ethics from the business concept and replaced it with contracts while simultaneously taking assignment of transactions and the barter system from the common people and replacing it with fiat currency/paper verses gold and silver.

2. Religion took the focus of Spirituality, self-sustainment and Consciousness and replaced it with Theology, separation, duality and segregation.

3. The medical/pharmaceutical industries replaced self-sustainment, biochemistry and naturopathic sciences with allopathic pharmaceuticals and placebos

4. Technology took Innate Conceptual Intelligence and replaced it with Artificial Intelligence

5. The FDA allowed big conglomerates to reinvent farming, take the rights from farmers, demoralize self-sustainment of health by taking Natural Vitamins and Minerals out of our food and replacing it with artificial ingredients, laboratory processed resources and now Genetically Modified Organisms; "GMO'S"

6. "The Agricultural Society and FDA replaced natural occurring Magnesium in soil with Nitrogen producing manure. In laymen terms; the nitrogen molecules destroy natural occurring mineral formation and oxygen molecules in the soil. We live on oxygen not nitrogen." (You are what you eat, what are you eating?) (You are turning into zombies) "literally"

7. "The Judicial System replaced Ecclesiastical Law, Common Law and De jure Law with Admiralty Maritime Law; Color

of Law," We don't need a **legal** system, we need a **lawful** system. (The legal system is setup for business; we need to restore a lawful system setup for humanity.) "Business is controlling people, People need to control business"

8. "The Superpowers conspired to reform Gold and Silver by printing Fiat Currency to gain exclusive dominance over the masses." People can't produce gold and silver; only the Creator can. But people can control the printing of fiat currency and determine who will maintain wealthy and also use fiat to control oppression and the masses.

9. "Governmental Factions conspired and stole Our Birth Rights and The Rights of the Child for economic and political gain for a select few, whereby using the concept of a "Free Country" to overtly indoctrinate a Monotheistic and Polytheistic belief system as well as an westernized philosophical scholastic education system for total control of the masses."

Number 9 is probably over your head due to the fact that you have been programmed since conception; you can't see the forest for the trees. Just because the system works for you doesn't mean that it's right. It's set up to work for you ☺

Chapter – 21

Who we are

The purpose of this chapter called, "who we are" in lieu of "who is god" is a major concern of all people and cultures of the world who feel and know they are-were victimized at one point or another and it continues to plague the **world** over. With respects to the, "**Borne Revolution**" if we renewed our godly principals via our higher god-self and stood firm in our quest to make the **world** we live in a better place, harmony would be universal. We need to reestablish a strong spiritual constitution and pull the resources of unity together and establish justice, insure domestic tranquility, provide for the common defense of our people, promote the general welfare for our people, and secure the blessings of liberty for ourselves and for our posterity, by which is part of the preamble to the constitution, how crazy is that. As I said in a previous chapter most of us "live under the pretense of democracy and a falsehood of truth" that has existed for so long, we accept it as truth, live the lie and forget how far we came or where we could be today without the interruption of oppression and servitude. We start to ignore and forget the struggles our ancestors endured. Our lack of spiritual conviction and actions show we blatantly ignore what our ancestors died for. And if we continue to lay dormant and endure the continuing oppressive plight that we face on a daily basis, we are telling all who fought in the past, they fought for naught. From this point forward you should say, "I **will** be the voice and not the echo," by taking action as a child of "The Most High" and at the same time I hope this resonates throughout the diaspora and is that spark of low frequency that activates that electrical charge in the hearts and minds of all people which will prompt us to reunite as 1 spirit with our higher god-self to resurrect the birth of a spiritual strong-hold igniting a "**Borne Revolution**" for the upliftment of humanity. Everybody is going on about your daily lives allowing National and International mass corruption to run amuck; you are killing your future families by acting as if you don't care and/or are blind. Remember who we are, if you can't remember because of "Chronic Voluntary Mind Block," read the first two chapters and that **will** remind you. With the exceptions of deformities and other birth complications; we are all created equal and through the selfish views of society, personal prejudices, religions, bigotry, stolen identity, suppressed history and greed, certain groups of people have become the epitome of inequality throughout the globe. The burden of mis-education via the secondary school systems, higher level learning systems, religious teaching systems, have all taken a total on the mental mind-state of all people, good, bad or indifferent. We need to focus on being **self-sufficient**. We as a collective and our conscious minds need to recognize and accept our own teachings, cultures and principles to understand "**Who We Are**" We need to have the wisdom to implement change so that it doesn't cause massive global disruption that would cause the power elite to become forthright in displaying a direct goal of destruction to maintain power. Each culture of people on this planet are different by nature and that gives us distinction among each other, it doesn't warrant prejudice it only warrants understanding and respect for that specific distinction. We are all different species of the human family and the common detonator is our spirits. This is a revolution for humanity and the fight for everlasting life as a people united for life. (Wake up). Save your culture and your people by acknowledging differences in each other and at the same time respecting the differences with the fact that we all share the same planet and it's enough room for all of us if you disregard selfishness and greed.

One example of massive global disruption is when you statistically look at people and define them as a color and give them a negative social status. It has been well over **five-hundred years** and we are weary of being victimized, marginalized, manipulated, and abused by colonial powers and their successors. We have always looked inwards to maintain our identities and dignity. But for the past quarter century, we have also looked outward as well. It's time to take a stand to re-claim our rightful place in the world and we come in peace. We adamantly admit we are the descendants of; and are the existing bloodlines to autonomous aboriginal indigenous people throughout the global diaspora. DNA doesn't lie. The power elite has been and is still trying to break down our DNA and immune system permanently via; vaccines, viruses, food, water, his-story, images, medicine, physiologically warfare, psychological warfare, spiritual warfare, overt mental subversion, and oppression. We represent the balance in relation to the laws of the universe, if you kill us, the laws of the universe will kill you too. We are a part of the universal eco system and to have an imbalance would mean catastrophic destruction. For the power elite, your time is coming to an end, your arrogance breeds ignorance in the midst of all your embellished stolen knowledge and that will be your demise. For the record, everyone that's not melanated who thinks that Africa is the home of all melanated people, **it is not!** So- called people of color as most people refer to melanated people or the misnomer African-American, Black, Negro and Afro American all of which doesn't exist in the annals of nationality need to know this, **as Khalid Abdul Muhammad** stated, Alkebulan aka "Africa is not our home, Alkebulan aka Africa is our **Throne** and **the World is our home!"**

We are one of many autonomous aboriginal indigenous humanities of Kemet, Australia, Tasmania, Japan, Timbuktu, India, Alaska, Russia, China, Alkebulan, Alkebulan of the West, Turtle Island, North, Central and South America and the whole world over. We ruled North America 1000's of years before slavery so how can you all believe we only came here in the hulls of ships. Research Queen Khalifa and why California is named after her and in her honor. Research who built the Great Wall of China and the Black

Emporia's of China. While you are at it research the Black Queens of England. Back to the message, we are endeavoring for land, life, original languages, liberation and we also are the voice of aboriginal indigenous people throughout the globe that have our same mindset and who are ascertaining the same identical quest as we are. We acknowledge all who are oppressed by greedy criminal-minded bureaucratic plutocracy and we all want change. We embrace your struggles as our own and encourage you all around the world to unite with us as 1 mind 1 spirit 1 propose and 1 goal to manifest the power vested in us by the Creator to evoke the **"Borne Revolution"** that will give us the long awaited spiritual peace and new life of equality we all have internalized for over a millennia.

We are on a relentless struggle for survival as a people and social and economic independence regarding our culture and an unrestricted livelihood by judicial prejudice. We will secure our own way of life by means of dejure law and other ethical processes. We will initiate and continue an alliance of mutual support and coordinated actions from other aboriginal indigenous individuals, colleges, Human Rights organizations, dejure law and lawful ethics interrelated organizations and nations world-wide. Hey, we need to focus on being **self-sufficient.**

We are not here to undermine the rights of anyone, any organization or government official and or government office, nor do we mean to undermine the local, state or any federal system. The fact that we are "aboriginal indigenous" to the Americas and the entire Globe, does not give bureaucrats the authority to continue to keep us as a people throughout the world in a new-age colonial strong-hold, use psychological propaganda tactics, demoralize us, use illegal law practices and politically marginalized us at present and throughout history or try to weaken the structure of our DNA, use GMO's to assistance in altering our genetics just to maintain your status quo. Sadly enough, there will be people who reject and dispute this information because as I once read, most people don't want to hear the truth; they want reassurance that what they believe is truth.

I would love for you all to do the research in the areas regarding the subject matter below so that you will get a better overstanding what you are up against. The simplicity of it without doing research is in the meaning of Monotheism. It's so clear it could reach out and smack you. I could reach out and smack you. Some of you need to investigate further, so I encourage you to do so.

1. **Monotheism,** (the word belief is the operative word you need to consider.) The **Belief** in the existence of one God, it is distinguished from **Polytheism,** the **Belief** in the existence of many Gods, distinguished from **Atheism,** the **Belief** that there is no God. "Encyclopedia, Britannica" I drew the same conclusion based on my own research regarding these words.

2. **Catholicism** (from **Greek** katholikismos, "universal") and its **adjectival** form Catholic is used as a broad term for describing specific **traditions in the Christian Churches** in theology, doctrine, liturgy, ethics, and spirituality. I am trying to open your closed mind so that you will change your life for the better. Thank you "Wikipedia, Encyclopedia"

3. The **Concept** of **Original Sin** was **first alluded** to in the 2nd century by **Irenaeus, Bishop of Lyons,** *in his controversy with certain dualist Gnostics.* **The facts are evident** thank you "Wikipedia Encyclopedia" Check it out if you doubt.

4. **Judaism** is a **Monotheistic** *religion, with the* **Torah** *as its foundational text part of the larger text known as the* **Tanakh.** I'm revealing these definitions throughout the book just to enlighten you and give you information you might need to enhance your knowledge and help you along your path to enlightenment. I hope they will be helpful. Thank you "Wikipedia Encyclopedia"

Chapter – 22

Our Intentions

Our intentions are to engage directly in dialogue with national and international government officials and organizations to resolve and clarify the misconduct of the judicial system. Implement our own governmental infrastructure and educational systems that reflect our culture and spiritual principles. In the same vein, we will state our position on unalienable Rights, Human Rights and unethical-unlawful law practices of quasi, local, state and federal offices and officials who impede on and ignore our laws and Rights as a culture of people bound by the laws of the Creator of all liberated life ad infinitum needs to be addressed and ratified immediately. In the same light, if these concerns are not ratified by the said government immediately, to whom we reluctantly consider for approval, we will use the higher powers vested in us by the Supreme Being and the esoteric powers of our ancestors to restore spiritual law and order by way of Alkebulan and Kemetic "Instruction." We intend on having, maintaining and gaining essential long over-due acknowledgement as descendants of; and the existing bloodlines of indigenous people throughout the diaspora that's recorded in our DNA.

> **Quote:** "Most people do not see their beliefs; instead their beliefs tell them what to see. This is the simple difference between clarity and confusion." Matt Kahn

CHAPTER – 23

WHAT WE WANT

We demand to be recognized for who we are: distinguished as indigenous from sea to shining sea, from the Halls of Montezuma to the shores of Tripoli, to our Native Americas as well as other counties and places intrinsic to our unique nature and cultures. We want to enjoy and pass on to our children our histories, languages, traditions, modes of internal governance, spiritual practices, and all knowledge that shapes us as to who we are.

We want to be able to pray and meditate on ancestral lands without finding that those lands have been dug up for outside governmental purposes or to construct a commercial building or some land project for commercial use which does not benefit our culture or people.

We want secured ownership and protection of our property and land, water, and air that provides the basis for all life as well as recognition for our indigenous culture, indigenous education, spiritualties and governments which can be fully functional; for we know that these necessities are the foundation for our continuing survival as a people and a nation.

We want the governments of this country in which we live to respect our ability to determine for ourselves our own destinies. The right to freely determine our political status and freely pursue and capture our economic, social, and cultural development inside the country in which we live and aboard, to govern ourselves in matters relating to our internal, local, national and international affairs; to retain our distinct political, lawful, economic, social, and cultural foundations. Those rights are not only a Birth Right given to us by the Creator; they are also stated in the, Declaration of Independence, the Constitution and the Bill of Rights. To deny us of these rights is tyranny and an abomination in the eyes of God as well as a conflict of interest based on the laws of the Creator and all laws stated herein. Why would our Government call some of us social terrorist, radical groups and other derogatory names for upholding the laws of the land and acknowledging our unalienable Rights vested in us by the Almighty? A Government made for the people by the people. "Who are these people?" Hum?

We want to educate our children as well as the misinformed elders about our own cultures, languages and traditions, most of which were stolen and spread around the globe and claimed by other people. The most prolific and prominent history of ours was burned in the libraries of Alexandria and other places by Theodosius, Caesar and the Christians of that era in Kemet aka Egypt, some were tossed in the ocean during ship raids at that time, and or what was left is locked away in the Vatican City as well as various other places.

We want to establish media in our languages; to retain our traditional modes of resolving internal disputes; and to fully participate in any outside judicial decision-making that could have an impact on our lives. At the same time, recognizing your quasi interdependence you will have with us and with the country in which we live and with that being said be able to participate in the political and economic livelihood of our country for the benefit of the Nation as a whole. We need our own economic infrastructure to create our own education, health and judicial systems so we can start on the right path to being **self-sufficient** for the future survival of a people.

CHAPTER – 24

OUR STANCE

Children of the Light

I speak for all who can't speak for their self and pray you all will take this stance with me and be proactive ASAP. We bare witness that our stance is to strengthen indigenous self-determination and autonomous measures throughout the North, South, Central American diaspora's and the Globe to unify the power of oneness through the power of our Life Force by establishing true dominion and ever-lasting life as a people united in spirit for the purpose of everlasting life. With that in mind, we will be acquiring and establishing our own health professionals that overstand our physiological and psychological genome.

We want a re-empowering of our traditional governments and the establishment of lawful order. Defending and protecting our laws and our constitution, the natural environment and all living beings. Our Stance is for the Reclaiming our Birth Rights, renaming and reoccupying aboriginal Indigenous homelands, sacred spaces, places and restoring nation-to-nation relations for economic growth and a sustainable infrastructure for continued education. Our Stance also includes learning and teaching Indigenous languages, cultures-traditions, ceremonies and familiarity. Our Stance is to try an eradicate all forms of violence within our land and Indigenous communities by advocating and enforcing universal laws and principles of creation via the power vested in all humankind by Allah, God, Allat, Jehovah, The Great Architect, The All, or any other God title that will apply. Also discouraging violence based on gender, culture and sexual orientation. Eventually we would be working with local administrators to do the same. Taking responsibility to yield action by living according to our original teachings and natural laws is a must to ensure life everlasting for all of humankind.

Quote: *para-phased,* A song by, Nico & Vinz "Am I wrong for thinking out the box from where I stay? Am I wrong for saying that I'll choose another way?

Look at the turmoil in **New Zealand, India, Bangladesh, Nigeria, Liberia, Ghana, Sierra Leone, Cote De Voir** as a whole and the world over and then there is **Turtle Island.** As it is stated in law, "**Morals** have **No Place** in **Business**" Each state and country that conducts business is for the sole propose of just that, **business! Business excludes** the Principles of Creation and Morals. The Power Elite are Selfish, greedy and spirituality weak minded in-divid-uals who see business as a means of power and dominance. On the other hand humanity as a whole doesn't concern itself with big business. We need to stop being passive and take personal incentive to establish our rightful place on the globe and **stop** allowing a few greedy Power Elite organizations **to rule us** for personal gain and cultural supremacy. We should govern ourselves and have the governments we put in place to take their rightful place as **servants' for the people.** That's what we originally paid taxes for. Also for taxes to be lawful they are supposed to be apportioned, ratified by all States and there is no law stating you have to file taxes. Taxes are outta hand and so are the governments of the world. They tell you to live by God's laws and God said adhere to the laws of the land. That's a impractical paradox, My intellect tells me; if we live by God's laws, humankind should model their laws according to God's laws, dah! So why would you have to follow to different laws? The laws should be cohesive and parallel, dah! If you have cardinal rules set by God, how can humankind supersede universal Godly principals? In this world of double standards, to live strictly by the laws of nature is a conflict of interest in comparison to the laws of humankind's selfish, self-righteous, demoralizing, de-spiritualizing, self-centered, do as I please, go for self, type of philosophy. Sadly enough that philosophy is accepted by the masses that are probably religious, God fearing people. How can a person live and stand for God's laws become a criminal and law breaker in the eyes of the masses if they are following the laws of nature/God? When did a law of God/Nature translate to criminal? Also why do most of you religious people advocate, "God Fearing?" We should never have to live in fear just to abide by any law. We should learn and advocate respect. Respect is positive and fear is negative. How can most you so-called high degree having "holier than thou" point the finger, law abiding citizens fall for the semantic mind programming scandal of a life time and not realize or overstand the impact and damage its doing to humanity. Most of you do not have to wake up; you know what's going on. You need to take responsibility to ensure we as a people don't allow **greed** to extinguish us by replicating the annulation of our modern day civilizations as they did to prior civilizations. Where is the Creative Power in you? Where is your higher god spirit in you? **It's there!** It's in all of us! Activate what no man can take from you. You can be manipulated into thinking you don't posse the power but you do, use it! Fred Hampton said, "You can kill the revolutionist but you can't kill the revolution." Bring that statement to fruition and spirituality rise up to free your Nation from the "Iron hand oppressors." 1 mind 1 body 1 spirit 1 goal; unite and regain our right to live an oppressed free life.

Chapter – 25

Judicial & Political Stance

We plan on piloting lawful and academic research that will shed light on the problems in the judicial system and implement dejure law and propose concrete policy solutions for indigenous Rights that were bestowed upon us from birth by the Creator and inherited by the blood sweat and tears of our ancestors.

Advocate advancing our goals through our media and our communication networks, including public speaking engagements, media appearances, conferences and blog posts world-wide and other forms of social media which will show transparency so there is not spreading of false propaganda, speculation or accusations of terroristic acts or a government coop.

By actively engaging in legislative advocacy and policy efforts, also advocating federal and state policy. With this in mind, it would be imperative for us to start incorporating our own court administrators when reviewing legislation and judicial conduct rules.

Engaging in all aspects of appellate and trial litigation to promote our fair and impartial rulings in our court's systems that we intend to have in place "now," by the grace of the Creator as you read this book and not years from now, **right now!** As the blood of the beast moves through the veins of the power elite, your blood must be boiling with a vengeance, but **"Plutocracy"** disguised as democracy and democracy disguised as **Plutocratic** Capitalism must come to an abrupt end. The wages for plutocracy is mass extinction for all humanity, for humanities sake and consequently life as a whole; I rather witness your inevitable demise.

"I can't phantom Innate Intelligence/Creation allowing greed to extinguish the human race"

We will continue to defend laws and canons of judicial ethics designed to curb the influence of the banking system and special commercial interests on judges and judicial elections and challenging discriminatory practices while working closely with teams of lawyers, researchers, and communications professionals outside of our court system. Corporations such as, Well Fargo and Bank of America will not have the administrative judicial power to target certain groups of people again with discriminatory predatory lending practices that crippled upper middle, middle and lower class citizens of North America. Santander is also under scrutiny for discriminatory predatory lending and their racial profiling in regards to minorities. (smh)

We will formulate a judicial strategy and create an economic self-sufficient plan that will promote economic growth and simultaneously eradicate the "**Social Class System**" which will allow us to start taking a posture to stop nationwide plutocratic injustices that obstruct us to be protected from judicial abuse. By the same token, we want to stop certain classes of people from being the targets of misleading propaganda, subjective live stops that was administered by big insurance companies to be followed by State and Local authorities. By which is enforced by quasi State and local law enforcement officers. We want to stop forced relocation in the name of eminent domain and intentional legal loop-holes in the legal system which will give developers the ability to take property without just compensation to the land owners as well as forced adaptation by placing people in places that's not conducive to their mental and spiritual well-being or culture. Stop denying human-rights activist the ability to enjoy lawful rights to Freedom of Expression with in the limitations of the law. Stop the power elite from violating, Rights of Property and Social-Geopolitical Association by labeling certain groups; militant, radical, or terrorist for social acceptance to wage war and justify overt murders.

Somehow, someway amends must be made for the theft of our lands, birthrights, history and attempts to completely decimate certain cultures of people. As far as I know, all other cultures that went through similar quasi hardships and inhumaneness have been reciprocated and all respect and honor restored except one group of people. It's sad that in this day and age it's still a struggle to live and be respected and accepted. From the actions of the opposition hate runs so deep in your veins that you would rather die than allow us to be a truly free people from your iron hand of oppression. Is it really that serious?

A question for the people who despise certain groups of people so much whoever you are, Is it your lifetime quest to insure that the only peace some people will ever have is to rest in peace? I'm not asking for you to answer the question, I know the answer. I'm asking in hopes that you ask yourself the question and answer it while looking in the mirror, then ask yourself what kind of people (*Children of God would you say you are?*) would do this to people they don't know or people who befriend you and gave you anything you wanted when you asked for it? People, who never wronged you, people who never tried to take your land, women, children, your life, or freedom for no apparent reason. It appears to me that you are the God your ancestors wrote about in the KJV of your bible and other bibles with the same philosophies, the same book that you forced on the weak-minded, the spiritually strong and religious ignorant, people filled with love and gratitude and the physically defenseless. If I didn't know any better, I wouldn't have notice the resemblance. God did create you in his image and likeness and when I looked at the actions of God in the bible I see you. So I asked myself, "Who killed everybody in the bible, God or Satan? Who subjected Adam and Eve to a lifetime of shame and damnation because of curiosity? Who is the jealous one, God or Satan? Who killed the male 1st born babies God or Satan? Who generated all the plagues God or Satan? Who still punishes us for what Adam & Eve allegedly did eons ago; "*who are supposed to our ancestors,*" God or Satan? God made a bet with Satan and killed Job's 1st wife, Children, took his home, live-stock and made him walk in the wilderness for years to prove to Satan after taking everything he loved Job would still honor and worship him. "Really" Who made up the story of Adam and Eve to justify religious philosophies and authorized it as a truth? So I asked myself, who does all these things now? The only face I see is yours. If you do anything other than agree, I would assume you have "CVMB," "Chronic Voluntary Mind Block" Will you ever change your sinful ways God? It seems as thou everything you teach is really the opposite of the truth and you deceived the whole world, at least you think you did. The devil isn't one individual as you portray, Satan is a group of power elites that contend to rule the world, oops! Did I let out another secret? Sorry; **Gold, Oil & Diamonds**. God

By the same token, wouldn't all those acts of destruction equate to what the devil would do to humanity? I'm confused because all of the negative occurrences in the Bible were carried out by the ideology of your God and the doctrine you forced on my ancestors and other cultures. In the beginning, the lessons all pointed in the direction of love, truth, peace, freedom and justice. But, as I grow in the spirit of the Creator, Allah and life itself exposed to me the wickedness of a people who gave me a crooked smile and sadly enough some of those people look just like me but were taught by you, the power elite. Speaking of wicked, what did Satan actually do in your biblios that was so wicked or in any book that would equate to what God did or that was superior to God's wrath on his children throughout the book? If you say to me, Satan tempted Mary, Job or anybody else for that matter, you are as spiritually weak as the people who supposedly did the sinful acts and for the record; Adam and Eve officially did not sin. Satan never out-right did anything to anyone and you always make temptation look worse than the acts done by God. If Satan tempts anyone and they are weak enough to commit a sin, that's not on Satan, that's on the child of God who was too weak to **Will** him or her-higher god self to overcome that adversity and that's what's good about the Devil. Once you go through adversity and win the battle over Satan, Satan gets weaker and you get stronger. If Satan didn't tempt us, we would never have a true sense of direction because nothing would be there to compare or show differentiation. I speak truth and you; "The Power Elite" and "The Church" speak with a forked tongue. Why can't you teach instead of preach? William Shakespeare quoted that, "Hell is empty and all the Devils are here." I wonder why he would say such a thing."

Allah said in so many words that all children who disrespect him will burn forever in the Hell-fire. I know of people who have done similar things Jehovah has done in the Bible and yet they say they are God fearing people. Maybe Satan's name should be in the place of God's name when talking about negativity throughout the Bible. Your teachings are so conflicting to what I believed as a child, especially considering what I thought the Most High stood for, and too think God would be so destructive and vengeful with his prize creation. Satan didn't threaten to burn me forever, my Father did! I'm so hurt! "Shaking my head" it is, what it is, so I guess I'll move forward. Is it possible that the power elite are the collective mind of the devil we were taught about in the bible or Quran and wants us to believe that the one who does all the destruction to humanity is a Good God and the one that tempts humanity is bad or Satan-Devil? Are you tryna make me crazy? Metaphorically speaking, are you hoping that we be good ole-boys and get on our knees to pray to your God that will never come to save us when you put the gun to our head and try to shoot it off? When I was taught about the characteristics and actions of the Devil everything about Satan represented evil, destruction, confusion, malicious, criminal acts, burning, confined in the hell fire, torcher, rape, murder and violence. Consequently, when I look at the way certain groups of people behave, their actions and deeds are an exact replica regarding the actions and deeds of the devil. The only people that still do Satan's work are the power elite and their followers. When I was younger the educational system I believed in stated that, "All men are created equal" but the country I live in doesn't reflect equality in my spiritual eyes. FOR YOUR INFORMATION- if you are not branded with the **status** of what society calls black; oh, African American, same thing. You can't possibly phantom what I'm talking about because what happens to people that look like me, the same thing doesn't happen to people that look like you. The crazy thing is we as a people would think in 21th century those sorta things would be a thing of the past. Most of the people who are not melanated, highly-carbonated will say, "Why are you still crying over spilled milk?" Because certain people will not stop spilling the damn milk, and that's not acceptable to the mentally strong melanated man to whom you think sing the same ole song.

It appears to me that the Romans still rule the world under the disguise of the Vatican and the Queen of England is the Administrator. If the Vatican, the Queen of England, Council on Foreign Relations and the United Nations are for humanity, prove it and let melanated people have their history back. Let melanated people who are willing to elevate and uplift their culture while expanding their vision for autonomy, form their own government without obstruction. Let them educated their communities and children from a melanated perspective. Laugh out loud; I know you will never do it without confrontation. We have to do it ourselves; we have the unalienable right to do so. "The Rights are written in the Constitution and are intrinsic Rights by Birth." Oh I forgot about the, "N.W.O. agenda. As part of the, New World Order agenda you implement the Patriot Act so you can abolish the U.S., Constitutional Rights of the people and have a justification under the new commandment to call citizens of the United States who form their own Governments and educational systems for the greater good of humanity, Terrorists. But you have the nature of the Devil, you will find a way to **try** and stop positive progression by perpetuating propaganda campaigns and or instilling fear in the people so they might compromise their higher god-self or infiltrate a weak-minded hidden agenda, all about selfish gain of an in-**divide**-dual to sabotage the operation as Satan always does. What is it about melanated people the power elite hate so much? You people have 75percent of the people on the globe in the same negative mental condition regarding us as well as some of us. Because of this, a big percentage of people think negative about us and imitate the actions of the Devil, where is God in all of this. I'm talking about the higher god self in the people who act arbitrary to the actions of the Creator because of social engineering and weak minds that follow negative leadership and popular opinion. In spite of what plutocracy and the global bosses will say, I need you all to know what melanated people want before the dirt is thrown over my eyes. Keep in mind that this is the "Age of Aquarius" and the God you say you believe in and deny in the same breath is the one that's about to be resurrected. The spirit of the Creator give me the revelation of truth and stated, Jesus isn't the one that's coming back as you would like the world to believe; **Jesus is the collective spiritual mind of the Creator through god conscious people. That's what is coming back to save the world.** The god consciousness is about to be resurrected from the dead. The paradigm shift is about to emerge. "This is indeed the **Age of Aquarius**" This is also the **intrinsic intelligence** that neither science nor religion can explain. "**I can!**" You didn't deceive the whole world, just the spiritually and mentally weak-minded. The weak-minded will also be awakened. "The truth cannot die nor pass-away" Truth is the Alpha and Omega. The truth will set you free. The truth will be revealed and the people throughout the globe will be liberated from that which they didn't overstand or refused to accept. The one place where truth resides that you can't destroy is our; DNA and when you realized that fact you tried to breakdown it's structure by taking certain DNA patterns away and disguising it as, "Taylor-made Babies" "PGD" but it's too late. You, the Power Elite are trying to use **Henrietta Lacks'** cells to learn how to break-down our DNA and at the same time create stem-cells for your ultimate benefit. Some cell spilt and regenerate, others split and degenerate, it's not my design you couldn't be me, stop the hate and congratulate. Melanated people hold the history of thousands upon thousands of years in their DNA and the answers were always with them, Creation was always with them and they are always with Creation, **in essence all humanity is a part of**

Creation. Some of humanity is the lower-self and some the higher-self. Listen, all those books you burned in Alexandra, Alkebulan, land of Cush and the original Ethiopia and all the artifacts you still hide from us throughout the world, just slowed down the process of the inevitable. You will never stop it from happening! The Roman Empire will fall. Again, Fred Hampton told you, "You can kill a revolutionist, but you can't stop the revolution." Not This Time!

We want U.S. Government officials, the **International Courts** and the United Nations to recognize that our people as a whole and as individuals have indigenous autonomy as God's children "as you put it," with relations to Human Rights, Dejure law, Rights Of The Child, Declaration on The Rights of Indigenous People, International Human Rights and that these Rights are **Innately endowed** and are **unalienable Rights bestowed** to us by **the Creator of all life** and **shall be secured ad infinitum** by your **courts and governments** as well as **us as a people** and via our **Ancient Guardian Angles of Kemet and the laws written in antiquity by our ancestors.** *"The truth cannot die nor pass-away" Amon Ra!*

Also our purpose is to enforce equally with respect to opportunities for education, health care, employment, and other basic needs The right to give our "free prior and informed consent" regarding International development, State policies and or practices that affect us and ensure that those policies are compatible with our culture and are in no way contrary to our goals.

To recognize that the full body of international human rights standards applies to us Just as States must yield a degree of sovereignty in order to live under a global system that requires respect for human rights, so too must indigenous people, we have no problem with that. We emphasize the fact that what we seek is to be officially recognized within any local and global regime, and to have our rights explicitly stated and to be part of the decision-making process when it comes to the procedures of our education, health care, economic development, Judicial decisions and other areas of cultural and governmental development until we establish our own governmental infrastructures.

The legal, educational and health systems must be reevaluated. These systems stunt our growth as a melanated people and it imposes ignorance amongst our people while perpetuating violence, oppression and stagnation. Defining, securing and protecting our Birth Rights, Human Rights, freedom of speech, non- impedance of our governmental structure and functions, Rights to travel, inspiring cultural awareness and all that encompass aboriginal indigenous Rights, land and property of autonomous aboriginal indigenous people throughout the North, South and Central American diasporas are the most important goals in the initial stages of development.

The movement for improvement should start now. We do not have time to develop a think tank of people to co-operate with the governmental officials we employ as "We the people." **We have tried** that **before** and or **during** the imposition on our land, medicine, schools of thought and culture by Greece in Kemet, during the fall of our Chinese melanated Emperors, **we have tried before** the Turks and Arabs in Timbuktu, the Arabians in Alkebulan, before the slaughter of our people on the island of Tasmania, before Spain conquered the Moors, during the British enslavement in Guyana and the Caribbean, during the Catholic/Christian Inquisitions, before Christopher Columbus invaded the Americas, before International kidnapping and murder of melanated people around the globe, during the deployment of the so-called Negros, Colored, Black, nigger and so-called Indians to support Britain in fighting the U.S, cavalry because of the impressment of British Settlers in North America and the main fact that they didn't want to pay taxes and interest to their homeland/Britain no longer. Britain gave Negros and Indians the false hope of getting our land back from the British brutish settlers who colonized our land and established government here and never reconciled with the people they stole it from. I could write a book on this topic along. Maybe another time, if you lost focus the gist was; (we can no longer co-operate with the governmental officials we employ as "We the people.") Based on the minute portions of information you just read, it would be foolish to continue to co-mingle with Satan. We need to employ self-sufficiency as a people and implement that mindset throughout the national and international diaspora if we truly want to survive as a culture and elevate to the next level. People understand this; if you believe you are a "victim of circumstance," know that you are not. Everything really happens for a reason. If you make a decision to do something, or make a decision not to do something, whatever you decided there will be an outcome, good bad or indifferent. "For every action there is an equal and opposite reaction." For the most part we are the creators of our experiences if there are no outside influences and most of the time there are no outside influences. But we blame everyone else for the decisions we make just to run from the truth. If we as a people do not take heed to this information in this book and change your ways and mind-state. We will be on the brink of extinction. We will rapidly move from "The age of Aquarius" to "The age of Extinction" We the People" possess the power to change our situations. The focus is on making our lives everlasting via the power that's vested in us by the Creator. I keep telling you this because I want it to resonate in your subconscious and conscious minds. I hope you all can feel my pain, heartache and mental anguish for all people who are suffering in this thing called life. Bring the spirit that you were born with back to life via action and deeds.

Quote: I came to win, to fight, to conquer, to thrive; I came to win, to survive, to prosper, to rise. "Nicki Minaj"

Side bar, why do we not know about **Henrietta Lacks,** who died at the tender age of 31 from cervical cancer in **1951** and her DNA/cells are still alive as you read this book (**2015**). Her family has never been compensated for the research they are doing to date.

What group of people's DNA/Cells has the integrity to withstand the process of stem cell regeneration? Its only one group of people, so who is it? Henrietta Lacks is the biggest hint of all. Do you people understand the implications and magnitude of this scientific discovery and why you are so despised and needed at the same time?

CHAPTER – 26

NATURAL LAWS OF CREATION

Animalistic Nature in all beings

Abstract concept, animals all have a natural environments that they claimed by birth. Loins don't invade bears territory, alligators don't invade hippo's territory, and bears don't invade gorilla's territory, you get the idea. The beauty of territory with animals is that it's a nature law to protect your territory, The Laws of Creation that they naturally acknowledge, not so much of the theory that Charles Darwin coined; "Natural Section" in relation to "Survival of the Fittest." Survival of the fittest from my view point, infers living by the laws of nature, the strongest and the weakest actual survive. By the same token, people took it out of context, because the weaker species do not die off, they still manage to have enough of their species left that survived to replicate themselves. They are here by "Natural Selection" to do a specific job. Even if that job is to be the food supply for a stronger more aggressive species. It's the eco system of life and the Laws of Nature. On the other hand, "survival of the fittest" in terms of how selfish people should use it, would infer one species will be destroyed because it's weaker and one survives because it's stronger. Totally not the case, the correct usage would relate to a catastrophic event, whereas, the weaker of a species would die based on the, "weaker-stronger" factor. That would be a relevant response in regards to Darwin's theory in my book. Back to territorial organisms interacting in their own environment. The only time there is dis-harmony is when one of the animals invades another's territory. After the difference is settled or the stomach is full, everything is back to normal and all animals reclaim what's rightfully theirs.

Everything has its rightful place in the eyes of the Creator. Or should I remind you of the multi-faceted life-force manifestation of intrinsic intelligence and energy continuously transcending in and out of different states of matter seen and unseen to perpetuate life everlasting, for the sole purpose of creation, which is the purpose of life. Period!

Humans on the other hand who are God conscious steal and claim territory that's not theirs, unlike animals who have no concept of who the Creator is, but animals follow the Laws of Creation without falter. Animals also maintain a balance in life by following nature's law unlike us who break Nature's Laws all the time and create and imbalance in Nature and then try to fix it before all hell breaks loose. How backwards is that, but we are the most intelligent of all creation. Which brings me to the purpose I introduced you to the animalistic principles of the Laws of Nature and the Humanistic principles of what supposed to be intelligence. Just to enlighten you in the next paragraph.

Territory: Of regions defended **by animals** from 1774; derivation from terrere "to frighten" **terrible**; thus territorium *would mean* "a place from which people are **warned off**." Thank you "Etymology Dictionary" You need to understand the ramifications of the definitions and how they are used in contracts throughout history and in-law as misleading and purposely is-used.

Territory: Under the jurisdiction of governmental authority "Webster Merriam"

Note: **territory** can be used in a **connotative** or **denotative** expression. For all intent and purpose I will show you that the definition is in the denotative form, contrary to that of certain groups of people who mis-used the word for personal gain and transformed territory to a connotative state by which it takes on a negative meaning.

Example; for an original group of people who are indigenous to their land, "**Domicile**" would have a positive meaning, thus personifying the denotative aspects of the word, territory.

On the other hand, as a settler, colonizer, or self-proclaimed land owner, the word territory transforms to a connotative meaning for people but it would hold true if we were animals, obviously certain people feel that way, why else would they use the word out of context?

The land that was naturally owned by the natives-indigenous people *"owned without a dispute"* without question was taken by hostile means; murder, rape, deceit, disease, and other unmentionable hostile acts to claim the **domicile** of these natural land owners by calling it a **territory.**

Domicile: A country a person treats as their permanent home or lives in and has a substantial connect with. All of these words are useful in law so a good practice would be to use them in every day conversation. Thank you kindly (Oxford Dictionary)

To **colonize** land means; to send **illegal** or **irregularly qualified** voters into colonizing doubtful districts, to <u>infiltrate</u> <u>with usually subversive militants for propaganda and strategy</u> reasons colonize industries, parasitic, to create a colony in or on "a place" : to take control of "an area" and send people to live there. What did you learn in grade school about the people who colonized North America? Did you ever consider the meaning of the word?

With that in mind, a couple of questions from the author of this book to all people that were taught his-story. When the people who settled in North America colonized it by murder, rape, deceit, the spreading of disease, treat duress and coercion, are these the same self-proclaimed God fearing people who were fugitives running from persecution in their native lands aboard? Also how could someone named, Christopher Columbus discover land that was already occupied by the aboriginal people who lived there before Columbus's so-called discovery, The government placed the aboriginal people of North America on reservations in their own land and said that the so called colored, negro, Afro-American, black, African-American people who were there as well all came via ship by God fearing slave masters to America which would deny them any ownership to the land that they are indigenous too as well and the general populous or should I say most people of North America and beyond should know by now that most of the history written was intentional fraud and deceit for personal gain by the wealthy for perpetual power over a people to establish and keep their evil agenda with a veil of a "God fearing people" which enables them to keep up a façade for social acceptance and indirect programming to regulate the mind state of the people and maintain subconscious submission. So if, "We the People" in order to form a more perfect union know this to be self-evident, why are we dormant in our efforts to write "Right" the wrong? Where is the Creator in you? Where is the **Adonai** in you? What do you as a child of God, at least that's what you say you are, or positive person in life, or you who claim to be one with nature and or one with the Creator, God fearing, Green Party, Libertarian Party, or you who say you are a lover of humanity, or a cultural activist, freedom fighter, or a pro-life activist: what do you really stand for? Are you using the power the Creator gave you or the superficial powers of and organization that's claims to wanna help the world but is restricted by the government they received their license from to operate under a big superficial name? After reading this book, by now you should understand the power is in you so use what you were born with and stop being programmed to think the organization you are with can really help as a whole, you have to go the extra mile and show the **world** that you have the power. The world is you and you are the world, we can unite the worlds and become 1 universe that will empower the people in it and force the non-compliant universe to submit to the will of god via social and economic segregation.

Unswerving action will allow us to live free from strife, oppression, economic bias, social & political degradation. Do not believe this is possible, KNOW this is possible and employ your will via your higher self to start a insurrection for change that will unequivocally revert evolution on the path of true salvation and up-root a Borne Revolution for the greater good of hue-mankind.

I have a question for whoever can answer it. If history can be told and was told from the time of Kemet, Adam and Eve, Noah and Shim, Mohammed, the Ming Dynasty, Sumerians, Aztecs, Berbers, Vikings, 45,000 years ago era, the Dinosaur era, the Ice age era, Neanderthal era, Big Bang theory and the beginnings of religions, and at least maybe 20 percent of is true, why the hell is all the **true** history about the so-called Moor, Black, Negro, African-American, Afro-American, Colored people and the Kemetians of Kemet suppressed? Why was it burned? Why was it stolen? Why is some of it inaccessible and stored in vaults in the Vatican City? There are pictures of Hannibal still depicted as being pale-skinned, but all his coins show his face and features as being brown-olive toned? Why would certain researchers throw acid on the walls of the tombs of (Kemet)-Egypt to change the brown complexion of the kemetian deities, Pharaohs and people to a lighter brighter whiter color? FYI; Kemet is the original name of the Greek word Egypt. Why are there no record showing olive complexed, brown-skinned, melanated people in North America before the slave trade? Did you burn them too? Why is it that the majority of people across the globe know their own history and the history of all other cultures? No other cultural history has been suppressed and/or destroyed purposely except the true history of the olive complexed brown-skinned melanated cultures throughout the global diaspora before the establishment of, The Roman Empire, before the 13 colonies adopted the constitution from the Iroquois Indians, before the First Continental Congress? Why hide, lie, and deceive the world and the brown-skinned melanated people of their history and allow everyone else to have access to their own history? Why haven't people heard of the Black Presidents that held office before the Continental Congress and during the Continental Congress? Why do you not know two of the original names of Africa are Alkebulan and Cush? KRS1 told everybody about Alkebulan years ago in the song called, "You Must Learn." He also mentioned what not to eat in a song called, "Beef" Maybe if the so-called black, colored, Negro, Afro-American, African-American people learned of their greatness and ancestral legacies they would strive to be better people, crime would decrease in the areas they live in. If they as a whole had those teachings and understandings Maybe they would uphold the "well-being" of, "I am some body!" because maybe leaning about their history might give them a sense of self-worth, dignity, cultural pride, responsibility, respect for life and each other, etc. Because of a lack of cultural education and a lack of jobs I see why most of them act the way they do. It's as if life in their eyes appears to be like a perpetual downward spiral to damnation, so they feel they have nothing to live for. Living a mortal life of strife and oppression throughout the diaspora is all they see through the eyes of the media, social media, traditional popular rhetoric, overt propaganda campaigns and reinforced in the neighborhoods they live in via the Public Servants who perpetuate it. So how can you people on the outside looking in expect change when no one is doing anything of substance to change it. We don't prisons, we need real education. Everybody knows what really going on, you all play dumb like a foreigner acting as if they can't speak English, and when one of the ignorant youth put a gun to your head, now you understand but in the same breath you ignore the root cause and blame the superficial status quo. "Smh" Shaking my head

We don't need more police, we need more jobs. All the jobs are being out sourced overseas because of cheap labor. It's about the money, not the people and you all see what's going on and do nothing but complain and pray things get better. "You killing me" If I think about how greedy the **power elite** is when it comes to just-us, their justice system wouldn't make much money advocating cultural education and educational practices outside the scope of their programmed agenda, huh? I have more whys but what's the point, we know why. As they say, "Why ask why" What the hell, I must to do it again. One more why, why would you, whoever you are as a whole, go through so much trouble to deceive the world and you will inevitably die with nothing? Personally I wrote the answer in this book but I wrote the question to see if the people reading this book get it. All life is precious and no one person is better than the next and you will not live forever. As long as we carry the dominate gene we will never be extinct, get over it. For all who love life, exercise the higher god in you and all of your whys will be answered, because the Creator is the truth and the light. Try it for life; learn who you are! You will see how great you truly are as god. I will end this chapter with the beginning.

Genesis: Here's outside the box, just to intrigue you for a second, take it or leave it, don't take it personal. ☺ In the beginning God created the heaven "man" and the earth "woman" the earth was without form, and void; "the egg that came from woman" and darkness was upon the face of the deep. "The womb protected by amniotic fluid" And the Spirit of God moved upon the face of the waters. "Seminal fluid-semen" And God said, Let there be light: "sperm & semen" and there was light. "Intelligence & conception" I might as well make some kind of substance of the myth, it makes more sense than trying to convince me that the mythological story is true.

By the way, did you ever stop to think if the word Atom-Adam was thought of or created before modern religion? What about the word Atum?

Analogy by "Travis Simons," you tube this "Defeating discouragement" 4 minute video

My perception of the video is multiple but the one I want to share is, when someone falls unite and support that person because the walk is different for everyone, the climb is harder for some and easy for others. If we all show love and not just one person showing love but all who witness the fall, we give optimism and power to the fallen. We give them their life back and their spirit is rekindled and now they can get up on their own because we as "1 unit" gave them strength in the form of patience, love and love is you, me, us, Adonai, El Roi, Allah, Yahweh, God, Great Architect, Nature, Mother Nature, The Creator, The Almighty, Jehovah, Elohim, the point is, no matter what the name you use, the action and spiritual essence is from the same source, so burry the superficial name game and live in 1 mind to accomplish 1 goal for the sake of all humanity. With that being said, it was stated by Cardinal George Pell that the Adam and Eve story was mythological and used to depict the aspects of good, evil and the origins of life by the Catholic Church. Catholic Priest, Fr. Dwight Longenecker also made similar statements alluding to the mythological concept.

Throughout this book I have focused on universal oneness to show you the correlation with the Creator, the creation, us and everything else in creation. We are 1 in the same outside of the magnitude of what Allah creates. Focus on building a relationship with yourself and the universe will reveal god in time and you will live life with the equilibrium and the power to look Satan in the face, smile and walk away with your head held high. You will be able to detect B.S. belief systems and walk away. You will feel the power of your higher god in you. I personally, **aspire** all of humanity happiness.

Think about this, If who you call God made the fish, trees, air, gas, sun, moon, stars, reptiles, birds, insects, clouds, galaxies, universes, gamma rays, plasma, magnesium, gold, silver, vitamins, food, rock, lava, iron, magnetic fields, animals, oceans, Satan, angels and anything else you can think of. Why would you think, the Creator only looks like you? You were the last to be created as far as you were taught. It's selfish and foolish to think that the Creator looks like you and only you. You think the Creator is a he. Wow! You need to start thinking for yourself.

I need you to know about the tricks the power elite play on another level so that there is no doubt in your mind as to whom and what you are dealing with. The devil is a smooth dude and his name is the reciprocal of what you were taught and if you paid close attention to every little detail in this book, you would have picked up on that. Everything in life is not what it seems as I said before. We all have been played by the best, but not the best that ever did it. It was once said, "I taught you everything you know, but not everything I know" ☺ It is said that, the greatest trick the Devil ever pulled was convincing the **world** he didn't exist." I hear most religions harping on statements like, "The Devil is a liar," the "Devil is alive and doing his work on earth," the Devil this and the Devil that. So who is being convinced that Satan doesn't exist? You better know who Satan is after reading this book. "Kept it simple stupid" (K.I.S.S.) To easy, right? Again if the Devil is doing anything, its' through weak spirited and weak minded people that blame a mystical Satan for the evil that man do and use their religious doctrines to justify the lie. This insanity needs to stop. Let's move on to the next topic so I can enlighten you on another aspect of game. I say game because I'm an average person and I know what I know on this level, and the majority of the power elite, Bishops, Pastors, Theologians, PhD's, honorary PhD's and the Ay Bee Cee's and one, two, three's, know what they know on their vast academic levels with unprecedented scholarship. I want to teach the unequivocal truth, unbiased morals, and be able to direct humankind on a positive path that promotes progression for mankind not commercial business. The people I just mentioned that are in the position to really help humanity but choose to serve Satan. The content in the next chapter is what these powerful people already know and as a matter of fact they know everything that's in this book and refuse to tell the masses. It's a sad state of affairs.

Chapter – 27

The Correlation

THE NEXUS BETWEEN GOD, SCIENCE and MAN

What I am about to reveal has relevance in relation to the correlation of God, science and man. As I stated throughout this book everything comes from one, therefore everything is one and one is a part of everything. All creation is related in some form or fashion, either; spiritually, chemically, biologically or all three. Before we go directly into the particulars, I feel the need to start from an abstract approach and build you up to ensure you comprehend the total concept of the evitable connection in relation to God, mankind, science and the principles of one. As I always say, bear with me because everyone doesn't travel at the same speed. I want you all to understand who god is with irrefutable conviction. First of all, how can religious scholars allow the power elite to say overtly that Church and State is separate? This division causes discord with Godly principles as well as spiritual unrest. No matter what capacity you work in or who you work with, operating as one union brings about harmony. I remember when the Catholic and Christian Church was 1 in the same and the Catholics separated from the Christians because of political and catholicismatic differences. They split in half to justify dual agendas. In the same vein the Catholic Church is still the authority over the Christian Church at the end of the day. That's why they both have Bishops and the highest Bishop of the land is the,

Pope. It's like the democratic and republican parties. The Republican Party is really the only true party. **"I pledge allegiance to the flag of the United States of America and to the Republic for which it stands one nation under God indivisible."** I wonder if that's why the Pope conducts commercial business for the Church which includes religious agenda as a front to justify deceptive practices because it can't truly be separated anyway. "Allah is one," right? Romans 13: 1-7 implies the oneness of Church and State in the passage. I will show you as you read on. But the sad thing in life is that the laws of the Creator and the laws of man will differ in so many ways that life lives in opposition to its self. In other words, to follow the laws of local, state and federal government officials alongside the laws of the Creator creates a conflict of interest. That's why people are mentally and spiritual lost, and, to this day they never understood why. They have been under a spell for so long, that the spell becomes an inconceivable reality. This is one of the reasons why most of us ask ourselves, "What is the purpose of life?" To live in confusion is a living hell and it's also spiritual and mental bondage. But remember to understand something is to be liberated from it. It is noted in **Romans 13:1-7** let every person be subjected to the governing authorities. For **there is no authority except from God, and those that exist have been instituted by God.** Therefore **whoever resists the authorities resists what God has appointed**, and those who resist will incur judgment. I would like to know what rules do we follow that are written in a governmental structure and employ the work of the Creator on a daily, weekly, monthly or yearly basis? Because some of the laws the government enforces are quasi moral obligations to uphold the status quo and not to uplift humanity. Romans 13:1-7 is written under the assumption that man would follow the laws of nature and creation whereby affording the people to do the same by incorporating the laws of the Creator with the laws of man. If this was not the author's intention to make that assumption, these statements would not exist in that text **"and those that exist have been instituted by God."** The second half of that scripture says, **"Whoever resists the authorities**

resists what God has appointed." After all, Yahweh Ben Yahweh said; I created you in my likeness and image. Why aren't our laws written in the image of the Creator in the context of the law? Better yet, why didn't man "as a human family" give unequivocal respect to the Creator and parallel the laws of Allah if they are so-called "**God fearing**" as the people they claim to be? With all this confusion how can you achieve spiritual wisdom and physical fulfilment before your appointment with the Creator? It seems as if the confusion is intentional if you ask me, confusion causes disharmony and division. The point of this section is to show the deeply rooted duplicity is in certain doctrines, dogmas and education. Scriptures, Hadiths, Sura's and all other religious doctrines will teach you all you need to know about that specific religion but all the information on the planet will not get you closer to knowing the Creator because knowing the Creator isn't rooted in the words or scriptures, hadiths, sura's or other religious material, it's rooted in the your spirit of the higher-self through actions, deeds and a conviction of "I Self Law Am Master" of self via the Almighty Universal Laws of Creation. With that being said, your focus in life should be a mental and spiritual quest to obtain and maintain a relationship with the Creator as 1 mind and body united in divine spiritual matrimony.

Ok now that you have and I pray you have understood that it should not be a separation between Church and State due to the fact that it creates confusion and a conflict of interest in the hearts, spirits and minds of the people to achieve oneness with the Creator. I also hope you learned the fact that everything needs to operate in unison with the other to create a **balance** called **harmony**. If this makes common sense, we can move on.

Yahweh created the Sun, moon, firmament, plants, all life, planets and everything that ever was, is, and ever will be. When we study the science of the sun we find out that the sun has some of the same properties to sustain it as we do and or other properties that mirror other life that Jehovah has created. Some of the properties of the Sun include: Hydrogen, Helium, Oxygen, Carbon, Nitrogen, Silicon, Magnesium, Neon, Iron and Sulfur. The process of nuclear fusion changes hydrogen *into other elements* that are curial to the sustainment of the sun and life on the planet. The sun produces gamma radiation, ultra-violet radiation, "uv" electromagnetic radiation and inferred light. FOR YOUR INFORMATION; learn about, Atum-Ra-Re-Atum, learn the etymology of Ra-di-ation, learn about, Auset not Isis; Heru not Horus, learn about, Sekhem and Nunology, research this and you will overstand at least ¼ the higher spiritual power the Kemetians who are our ancestors and the power they had in their possession as a people. Outside of their spiritual power that doesn't even equate to the scientific knowledge they are so tremendously legendary for. The beauty of it is, they incorporated the complexities of their spiritual likeness of the Creator with the scientific aspects of the universe and reached phenomenal achievements as a people. Culture is a language and if we never learn our languages we will never restore our power.

With that being said, we also would not exist if it wasn't for the elements of the **sun** and how those elements work on a scientific scale to produce the light that we need for warmth on the planet. One element is Ultra-violet light and one form known as uvb radiation initiates the production of D3 which transpires through a chemical process called transdermal application. The process starts when the rays penetrate your eyes and also hits your skin and your skin converts a prohormone on the surface of the skin forming cholesterol and that travels to the liver where some of it is stored because of its oil based properties and the rest starts to metabolize into vitamin D and in the final stages of conversion the vitamin D converts into a hormone which is in the steroid family. On the flip side of that, when you use sun-block and wear sunglasses to block the uv rays, you stunt the process of uv absorption which in turn initiates a process called chronic dis-eases. "My people are destroyed by lack of knowledge." Malcolm X made a profound statement when he said, "No religion is greater than truth; no faith is greater than fact."

Plants absorb and manipulate light through a process called photosynthesis by which they covert light into food-Chlorophyll to create energy to grow, live and reproduce. Chlorophyll is to plants, what hemoglobin-blood is to us. Chlorophyll is what gives plants that green color and the ocean its illusion of aqua blue which you learned in the beginning of the book regarding the nucleus of a cell in plankton which is the vegetation that predominantly floats on the surface of the ocean. By the same token, hemoglobin is what gives blood its deep rich burgundy color and when exposed to oxygen it instantly turns red. Unbeknown to the average person all plants regulate the concentration of gases in the air which in turn allows us to breath clear air. This is why it's so much smog in the inner city. There not enough plants to combat the over powering pollutants which is another reason for the initiation of chronic dis-eases. You can experience the differences in the freshness of the air when you go out in the woods or the country-side; the air is totally different there. All life ultimately depends on plants for sustainment, in the water and on land. Plants give us a vital element to live that they release in the atmosphere called oxygen which is a byproduct of photosynthesis. We in turn exhale CO_2 which is "1 part carbon" "2 parts oxygen, hence the term; carbon dioxide" by which the plants use synergistically via the same photosynthetic process. So we need plants and plants need us and we both need the sun to survive.

Without science we would have never acquired the understandings of elements and chemical compounds which is essential information for the overall quality of life as well as life itself. The Creator who created the universe and everything in it, also created in us the intellect to explore, question and conquest. If we didn't use these blessing that the creator give us, we would not exist as we are today and maybe not at all when you look at it from a medical prospective. "My people are destroyed by lack of knowledge. By the same token, knowledge is a gift and a curse when in the wrong mindset of a people who thrive on a lower god-spirit called Satan and willfully commit acts of degradation in nature and oppress a people in the name of their God and greed. There is more than enough space on the planet for all of us to live comfortable and yet the power elite betrays the masses-programmed people into thinking we are running out of space and people are producing more children faster than we did in the 30's,40's and 50. Research how much land is not occupied by humans. Do you even realize how much land on the planet is not occupied by human existent? If we did, we as a whole wouldn't fall for the B.S. and I know most of you fall for the BS, because you believe that the system you follow is doing what it should do for, "We the People." That same B.S. "belief system" is why we are in a "State of Emergency" as a people and as a planet.

Let's look at the ocean water for a comparison as to the chemical makeup of it. I think the ocean has about six major elements in it which are essential for the inhabitation that lives in it as well as the planet we live on. There are 72 trace minerals that we use to help sustain our lives and other elements as well, but the main six is the focus. Two of which are, magnesium and potassium, it also has calcium, chlorine, sodium and sulfur. By the way potassium is the mineral form of vitamin K and as logic would have it, vitamin K is the vitamin form of potassium, but only the vitamin K form comes from the sun that the Creator created. The Chlorine, magnesium and sulfur is what helps purify the water and air for ocean life to live. Did you ever think of what happens to the urine and feces that is discharged by all the animals in the ocean? Maybe you swallow it at the beach when you inhale water instead of air. "LMBO" Laughing my butt off, seriously the ocean is extremely self–sufficient and it too was created by the Creator eons before the creation of humankind and it produces chemical and biological reactions that are necessary for the sustainment of life and is a vital part of the earth's eco system of life.

The human body is made up of six major elements and as you know the ocean is made up of six major elements as well. The elements are: oxygen, carbon, hydrogen, nitrogen, calcium, and phosphorus. There are trace minerals and other elements in our bodies as well, but the main six is the focus, along with the first six are, potassium, sulfur, sodium, chlorine, and magnesium. These chemical compounds, cell structures, molecules, atoms and minerals are all incorporated in some form of life, whether it's one element or one hundred elements they are all created by the Creator to perform a job or multi-task in order to sustain life. Every chemical reactions, chemistry, physics, protons, electrons, carbon, krypton, gold, silver, oxygen, gas and any other atomic structure you can think of are all created by, Allah, the Universe, a Higher Power, the Omni Present, again whatever name fits. The main idea is science, spirit and Nature all have a place in this game called life and they all work in harmony to sustain life. From the Alpha to the Omega this same process has been in existence and nothing has changed. The truth cannot die or pass-away. The truth is the light, light is the knowledge, the way is the action directed by the truth manifested through knowledge. "I am the Way, the Truth and the Light"

The correlation is evident and extremely obvious, the Universe only operates on universal laws as does the sun, the moon, the oceans, rain, hail, snow, atoms, plants, everything seen and unseen plays it's part and obeys the laws of creation, expect man. Everything that is created by Nature does not change, it stays constant, expect man. Atoms just like carbon are a part of all living things and the atom operates by the laws of creation. The mitochondria, elements and minerals all adhere to the laws of the universe, expect man. I had to reiterate the scientific portion of this commentary because you need to understand science, man and everything in creation is a concept of 1.

When I talked about the Catholic and Christian Church and how there were one, years before Martian Luther came up with his concepts of who God is or the Church deciding to separate Church and State creating division and superficial duality. My point was to show you through science, the Creator and in man there must be order in order to be in harmony as 1. There is no choice. There is no duality. You either do or you don't, you will or you won't.

There is no choice in the principles and laws of Nature. Because of this fact, when you look at the universal laws of life, choice within itself would prove all religious teachings that teach the principles of having a choice are flawed. If all life chose to do as it pleases. It wouldn't be much to life. I will now tell you, "Who is God" outside of what I taught you in that titled chapter. I saved this because most people would probably want to go straight to the, "Who is God" chapter when I expressed in the beginning of the book that I need you all to read everything chapter by chapter in order to get the full overstanding of the next. If you found yourself lost with some of the material maybe you skipped chapters as well. I urge you to please read each chapter in it's entirely and take notes if need be. With that being said, I would like to make a statement in the name of science to shed a little light on the subject of "nothing." Science will never have the power to create; honesty, thought, human intelligence and intellect or common sense. I mentioned this as to answer the question of nothing in an abstract way to compliment science. Thought is formed from nothing to produce something. Meditation is the process of ultimately thinking of nothing producing another mind-state of something. In darkness there is something undefined by human intelligence that only appears to be nothing but based on the end result, there is something due to the fact, the end result proves that out of non-existence it begat existence.

The Great Architect is not just spirit alone; it is energy, light, atoms, plants, planets, stars, snow, rain, the good, bad and the ugly, water, oxygen, your mind, body, soul, Satan-devil, thoughts, air, gases and the coming to know self in the highest degree. To know self is to know who you refer to as God. God is the universal brain manifested in everything and everything yet to be. To deny the Creator is anything less than Satan-devil, you are denying oneness because there is no duality. Worse than that, you are declaring that there is a higher power that created Satan, other than the Creator,

I mean if you think so its ok with me, you are entitled to think what you please. But all things that operate on the principles of the universe all come together as 1. All that is created GOOD BAD or INDIFFERENT is all created by one source. Your programming needs deletion if you can't grasp oneness because you have, "Chronic Voluntary Mind Block."

1. Negative and Positive come together to create lightening, two energies that become 1.
2. The speed of lightening breaks the sound barrier expanding air creating a sonic boom.
3. The electric cord as a negative and positive prong merged by 1 wire to create electricity.
4. Natural man and woman come together as 1 to procreate.
5. The spirit can only be animated by the physical body, so they become 1 and life is born.
6. Daytime and night-time come together to form 1 day.
7. Protons and electrons work together to form 1 cell with 1 purpose.
8. Two gases come together as 1 to create water; hydrogen and oxygen.
9. Plants give us oxygen & we give plants carbon dioxide, synergistically we sustain each other's life as 1. These are some of what I call the eco systems of ever-lasting life.

I will show you oneness that we all witness in another sense of the eco system that will overtly occur until death do you part. This is also irrefutable prove we are one with all of creation and all of creation is one with us.

The "Beauty of Death" is the sacrifice of death to create life. Yes natural so-called death is the human sacrifice for life. There is a warped concept of death for life by weak-minded mis-guided people who kill people as human sacrifices to gain eternal life, but we are relating to the positive aspects of life today. I will show you the unwavering fact about death and I hope you will come to a better overstanding and accept natural death as a gift of life. Who wants to be in this place forever? ☹ The paradox is that, death still hurts like there's no tomorrow but I intend on easing the pain by explaining what it really is. A small example would be the butterfly. These are the transitions the butterfly goes through; the Egg, eggs dies and turn into larva, larva dies and turn into a Caterpillar, the caterpillar dies and turns into Pupa, the pupa transforms into a beautiful Butterfly. Speaking of death I want to shed some light on the words "dies and death" with respect to what's really going on. The fact that the egg, larva, caterpillar never actually dies. I hold most religious teachings accountable for this mis-understanding. Reason being, most all religious people think of death as a negative connotation, you only see negative aspects of death, even when you here the Bishop preaching the home-coming eulogy. Even at a Janazah you can't feel the concept of paradise for the deceased. Your mind is trained on the aspects of the death. Reason being is because the focus isn't on the transition of returning to the Creator to perpetuate life in respect to the universal eco system that creates life on a continual, the focus is on the death. With that in mind, one of the reasons a lot of you don't cry at a Janazah outside of the unspoken rule, is for the sake of embarrassment and sometimes that leads to breakdowns at home after the Janazah. That's why funerals are so hard for a lot of families and friends. Some people never recover from the loss of a loved one. But, if you were taught the proper perspective in relation to death, your families and friends would not fall apart like they do. Each metamorphosis is a transition into another stage of life. What I am telling you is, what you were taught about death and what's being conveyed at the ceremonies lead you to believe it's a dreadful event. Clearly looking at it from the universal laws of the Creator it's not what you thought. Understand this, we as humans go through a continuous progression of life just like any other living creation on the planet because, again, we all are one with God's creations and

God's creations are one with us. With this overstanding, you should look at death in a different light.

The procedure of life for a tree is not much different. The seed transforms into a plant, the plant transforms into a tree, the male tree pollinates the female tree creating fertilization, the female bares the seeds and they fall in the dirt and convert the Sun's rays, minerals, sugars and water synergistically to fuel the process of photosynthesis and this starts the process of life all over again. This is the science of the Creator in the form of universal law and universal law is constant, it will never change under normal conditions.

We as humans go through a metamorphic state of change just like plants, insects and animals do to live and accentuate life. I would like to take you through the 12 stages of life and death and show you how they co-exist simultaneously through the science of God. Just as I did in the previous paragraphs you will see it from a scientific perspective. This will prove once more that the Creator and the science God created are 1 in the same.

Darkness is the beginning of life for everything living and through one aspect of darkness thoughts are born and reborn by human-kind; unconscious, subconscious or conscious. For all intent and purpose of this lesson, thoughts are manifested through the procreation process and expressed through sperm and that intelligence is embedded in the sperm and carried to the egg whereas they transform and become 1. The egg transforms turns into a zygote. The zygote transforms into an embryo. The embryo transforms into a fetus. The fetus transforms and turns into an infant. The mother gives birth through the birth canal which is her birthday and the baby's born day and the baby transforms into a child. We are not KIDS only goats have KIDS. Humans have babies. The child transforms into an adolescent. The adolescent transforms into an adult. Adults transcend back to the Creator from which we came. The transformation back to original creation will create life because we were granted salvation by the master of creation through the gift of procreation. We are born to live and we live to die and the beauty of death is life! We die in order to live forever via the eco-system of the Creator as 1 human species and all of creation follows the same pattern. When people in your life transcend back to the essence, celebrate their greatest contributions to you by perfecting their actions and deeds that you witnessed while they were alive. The spirit that you project will reflect theirs and they will live through you. What I am saying is this; as you grow in life and display your spiritual and mental attributes to your children and the people you love, your spirit has already manifested in them replicating multiple spiritual attributes and enhancing DNA from your ancestors, your great-great grandparents, grandparents, and immediate parents so on and so forth until you are called back to the essence of creation. How beautiful and honorable is that? To live is to die but to understand life gives life everlasting meaning to all that embrace the comprehension of the thought. Tupac said, "Death is not the greatest loss in life, the greatest loss in life is what dies inside you while you are still alive!" This is dedicated to, Barbara and Wanda Scott and all people who lost someone close to them who were never shown the, "Beauty of Death."

Life is about balance and the laws of creation are in perfect balance. In nature's law 2 will always equal 1. Two is needed in universal law for balance and harmony and when you separate 2 from 1 you create imbalance. Again you have a higher god-self and a lower god-self and those two should always be in balance as one, If not there will be chaos. It cannot be one extreme or two extremes, either extreme means there is an imbalance and that leads to illness, disease, high blood pressure, bad moods, temper tantrums, etc. and once balance is restored all the abnormities dissipate. I am really trying my best to breakdown the overstanding of self and the correlation to the All. Know and comprehend this. Do you know who god is? If you do, exercise gods will to make the world a better place and pass on the knowledge.

Nature is not one life form but all life forms. Allah is not a material substance, Allah is nothing and everything simultaneously, Yahweh is not a feeling or thought, logic doesn't have emotions. Emotions are a human characteristic, Allat is neither time nor space, but time and space is Allat because Allat created it. Jehovah cannot be defined by the words of humankind. The Creator has many names given by us but the names only give a distinction for humankind to relate their difference ideologies based on cultural perception and the Creator has no distinction because everything that is and will be has its own distinction, except the Creator. Hence, how can the Creator be a he or a she? That's universally impossible!

I used different names throughout the book to express the variations in the names of the Creator just to show you the end result. No matter what name you use the Creation doesn't change with the name. Why get offended over the name. The name is superficial when looking at the big picture. Your focus is to learn self and discover the Creator and exercise the universal principles set forth in this book for the greater good of self and humanity for obtaining everlasting life. Do you know who god is? I do! ☺

Because of your inability to take responsibility for yourself, you gave the responsibility to the government that was formed by "The people" "For the People" who are the voice for "We the people" and we represent the masses that have issues with the same government we employ and complain about. Year after year all the issues that have been concerns are still not resolved by our government offices and or the power elite that we entrust our lives with. Big Brother has always seen the weakness in us to exercise our higher god-self. This is why the power elite-Satan continues the wrath of demise because Satan knows as long as we are dumb, deaf, blind and ignorant the **worldly** powers that Satan unleashes will never be relinquished or exhausted. We must change our minds to change our lives, we must become leaders and we must accept responsibility as leaders now, right now! Delete that old program and get rid of that robot mentality.

Remember God is a title and not a name and the masses have used the word, "God" in a connotative sense, it's out of context in lieu of what is being conveyed. Example; Men are men and woman are woman and what gives us distinction and outside of gender is our personal names. The Creator is on a magnitude incomprehensible to our thought processes so we can't name the Creator, that would imply distinction and individualism, that doesn't make sense. The only distinct creation is us, the animals, plants, planets, the sun, the moon, clouds, etc. Are you starting to overstand now? Even Satan has a distinction because Satan was created by the same Creator as we were. The exchange for life is death in the form of life and when Satan-flesh-world dies our spirit will return back to the 1 and that reciprocates balance. The best way to explain the Omnipresence is like this; the Creator is the manifestation of energy transcending in different states of matter seen and unseen to perpetuate life everlasting. We are one of many by-products of that life-force. Understanding who we are as gods, we need to mentally access our spiritual will to manifest the adequate higher energy to motivate and exercise our higher god-selves throughout the national and international diasporas of the globe as 1 mind and 1 body to create a balance bringing forth a harmony which will not be denied by the Creator or laws of the universe. When we take action on a consistent basis, all will be in sync, Satan will submit to the Creator and the prophecy will be fulfilled. Peace, love and victory to all the gods! "Greatness is what we on the brink of!" "Nicki Minaj" By the way, "resurrect the birth of spiritual revolution and the upliftment humanity"

CHAPTER – 28

MASS ACTION MATTERS

I want to start this chapter off by talking a little about **human Nature** because this is one of the most important subjects you must overstand throughout this book in order to overstand what you are mentality and spiritually up against. Once you overstand this, everything you have read in the prior chapters will be totally clear and you **will** realize the strategy of how to manage and overcome psychological and sociological warfare that has oppressed the world for far too long. This will enable you to invoke the changes in you that need to take place to reverse the suffering of the masses by showing you how the Power Elite started the process of programming us to submit to the will of man instead of the will of our higher God-self which was given to us directly by the Creator and the seven creative powers. **NOTE:** this is outside of the fact that the Power Elite breaded people to be submissive just like they did free-range animals so that they could be manageable and work for their master without aggression or rebellion.

1. **Colonize:** as I recall is to send a group of settlers to different areas and have them **take control** of that area and **spread their control** throughout the new area until they have total control and domination. **Civilizations**; For the sake of knowing, are organized in densely populated settlements "throughout the globe" **divided** into hierarchical **social**

classes with a **ruling elite** and **subordinate urban** and **rural** populations. Did you notice how the word civilization is semi-positive compared to the word colonize, which is totally negative in aspects of the meaning. Thank you Wikipedia. Dictionary.com defines, **hierarchical**; People who have to work together in a hierarchical structure end up deceiving and manipulating each other. "Etymonline.com; from Greek, hierarkhia" ... Another fact I learned is that, hierarchical means; to be governed by a high Priest. I wonder if this is why the Pope ... Hum?

2. **Philosophy** in **classical Greece** is the **ultimate origin of the western conception** of the nature of a thing. According to **Aristotle**, the philosophical study of human nature itself **originated with Socrates**, who turned philosophy from **study of the heavens** to **study of the human things**. **"Wikipedia"** "ARE YOU SERIOUS?" This justifies the past and present mind state of the masses as well as the Power Elite. By the way, Aristotle and Socrates and their counterparts are thieves to the highest degree. They stole all of the exoteric knowledge from the High Priest of Kemet rewrote the concepts to fit their philosophies, twisted it and fed it to the world as their own philosophy and coined it original and the people of the world still accept it as truth to this very day.

3. **Monotheism** is the belief that there is just one God, "Mono meaning 1 and Theos meaning a God" monotheism is a **Greek belief** and it's nothing wrong with believing that philosophy if your Greek. The word Theos is Greek and so is Mono, so is your God Jewish, Hebrew, Greek or all three? If God is all three why is there a difference in all three philosophies and interpretations? On another note, the key factor in the meaning is the fact that it's a belief not a reality and they have the majority hung up on a belief, amazing. So did Islamic philosophy originate Araba, Greece or Rome to? It really doesn't matter. I just wanted to pose the question. I won't get into that because it's another 500 pages. Our focus

is for humanity to unite using the higher creative powers vested in us by the Creator. Recognizing this misconception regarding the triad/trinity will help you rise to a new level. Could it be the, (Sun, Moon and Stars?) The (Morning Star, Mid-day Star and the Falling fade to the west Star?) Or could it be the (Father, Sun/Son and Holy Ghost/Spirt?) Or could it be the (Father, Mother and Child?) Which Trinity would be the one to sustain and create life on a continual?

4. In monotheism the concept is that God is one. The shield of the Trinity represents three entities that are separate but are one. The problem with the Triad Symbol, ☺ Laugh out loud" the three as they show/teach two of the three is one in the same form and they are side by side in heaven and side by side at all times The Father is the Son, The son is the Holy Spirit, The Holy Spirit is the Father but they are all the same with no distinction. Huh? What? Purposely confusing? A true trinity is three different entities coming together as **1** for the progression of life and perpetual existence. Mother, Father which in turn creates child who duplicates the process, over and over again. (Simplicity) **For instance**; Sugar, Carbon Dioxide and Water; Mother Nature, Universal laws and Creation; Senior Warden, Junior Warden and Worshipful Master; Mind, Body and Spirit; Father, Mother and Child; the three aspects of the mind; Me, Myself and I; Head, Upper body and Lower body, Cause, Effect and Reaction; $E=mc^2$ Energy, Mass and the Speed of light. I stated all of these different scenarios to show you how none of the three are the same. However, they all work in conjunction with each other and become 1 to do 1 specific job. Also I want to point out; universal laws of Creation will never be different from each other and the same at the same time to produce the same effect. It's like science says, "the same mass can't occupy the same space at the same time. Science didn't make that up; they simply uncovered a universal truth. Even when you read that explanation it makes you say, huh? Religion is written in that

same way and the masses accept it. That's against universal law and universal laws are controlled by Creation. So when you believe in that crap you are disrespecting creation and for every cause there will be an effect followed by a chain reaction. Again monotheism is only a belief, NOT THE LAWS OF CREATION or GOD as you was lead to believe. It's just the Greek philosophy.

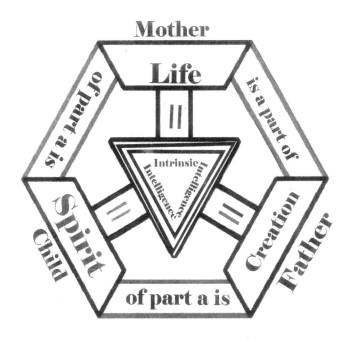

Shield of The Trinity

Before I continue, it's clear that most people don't respect Wikipedia and I understand, by the same token, cream rises to the top so I exacted the cream for the nay-sayers. Truth be told; the three passages above are unequivocally true based on historical facts in history regarding the worldwide spread of an infectious distorted philosophical programming manifested by western culture and adopted by all the super powers of the world. People who followed these philosophies of **Plato, Socrates, Aristotle,** and **Xenophon** as well as many others practiced the same ideologies and all have the same inhumane programming. Their concepts of human nature appears to be; divide and conquer, cultural supremacy, human domination, social classes, weak vs strong and superficial color status; yellow, brown, light skin, dark skin, fair skin, black, white, Olive, red skin, etc. This is animalistic behavior as in the beast; lower god-self Induced behavior, tendencies of the beast as stated in the second paragraph; Socrates, turned philosophy from study of the heavens to study of the human things. Western philosophy is Greek philosophy not mine or yours and if you do not have a Greek heritage why are you following that doctrine and conforming to their dogmas? Genealogy of Greek philosophy in a nut shell; I might be a little out of order with the sequence but all of these Nations had their hands in Original Kemetic teaching before it was contaminated, Greece relinquished power to Roman, Roman conceded to Persia, Persia receded to Mohamed at the Strait-Rock of Gibraltar. "Study this history and you will come to know who the original JEWS are."

As "Children of the Sun," Children of the Most High, People created by the Creator, creatures created by Universal Laws that work in uniformity with Mother Nature's laws are a people who aspire to reach divinity and who seek spirituality in its highest form to be 1 with our higher god-self for the upliftment of humanity and nature itself. We do not seek to destroy life, oppress people or divide and conquer any one. We need to redirect the focus of hierarchical ideology to a mandatory spiritual awakening. We must and I say we must bring forth a higher level of consciousness that must rise to a level resonating equal vibration around the world. If we as a people want justice, equality, freedom, truth and peace, we need to resurrect the original concepts of our ancestors and bring heaven and spirituality back to the conscious state of mind, and the time is NOW! Remember, **Socrates**, turned philosophy from the divine **study of the heavens** away from the people and thousands of years later a devolved catholic named, Martin Luther "not Dr. King" psychologically took your God-spirit of the Creator from within you and psychologically placed your God-spirit manifested by the Creator in the sky and then Martin formed the "Lutheran Church"

In the same vein, another individual perpetuated the concept even future, he was another devolved Catholic who did not want to follow the Cardinal Rules of Catholicism and started his own religious philosophy by creating the "Protestant Church" and he was, King James. Coincidentally, if you did the etymology on Protestant, the root word would be protest and he definitely protested against Catholicism.

The power is in all of us to defeat Satan. I wrote this book and made it available for all of you to use as a guide to help you enhance your mental and spiritual states of consciousness and I have showed your mind and spirit undisputed facts, concepts and principles to use so that we as a people can **finally win** the, "Battle of Armageddon." You **will** be a new person after reading this book and the light that emanates from your aura will be the shield that protects you from your adversary. Every adversity that follows after reading this book **will** be easily dealt with and you **will** notice your spiritual growth and mental strength. You **will** also notice more like minded people who become attracted to your aura. It would behoove you to enlighten people with like minds to read this book so that we can initiate the return of the higher god-self. With that being say, we can finally have true law and order and not legalese, color of law, statutes, codes and disorder.

People of all nationalities need to overstand that we as a union united as one, have the power to be the sovereign people that we truly are and the "mighty Wizard-government" in the movie, "Wizard of Oz" is just 1 big hoax in all countries portraying to be something they're not, just to maintain power over the people. Most governments and or the power elitist are the exact replica of the movie mentioned above, but in real time. We cannot wait for 1 savior to save us, we have to save us. Don't you see by now that; that concept is a smoke screen for all of us the stay mute and idol in our actions so the "Power Elite" will continue to reign over the weak-minded and the thought-provoking programmed traditional mindset of a trustworthy populous who are unknowingly being led to slaughter? I really don't know what it will take for you all wake up, I surely hope this book has ignited a spark which will set the fire burning in your solar plexus awakening the god you are born to be before it's too late, because to late is around the corner. Let's unite ASAP.

We as a people united need the world to know that deception is in the reality that you perceive as truth. The biggest trick the Devil played **is not** convincing the world he doesn't exist. How can people believe that statement? Satan is all you see and hear about; scary movies, television shows, every Halloween, the bogie man, haunted houses, ghost, exorcisms and evil spirits. It's in all the teachings that tell you Jesus is coming back to save you so you wait and do nothing. Years and years go by and people believe the same his-story and faithfully wait to die. The next generation is taught to do the same and the next, and the next and history repeats itself. WE as a people believe these things and never advance spiritual in life and 6000 years have passed and we are still waiting. When are we as a people going to realize we need to take a stand as individuals and unite as 1 mind to accomplish 1 goal and that is to regain our freedom by taking action as a human family and will our freedom back in the hands of the Creator's children? Marcus Garvey once said, "We are going to emancipate ourselves from mental slavery because while others might free the body, none but ourselves can free the mind." If he spoke of mental slavery in the 1930's and other people before him spoke of it and more spoke of it years after his passing, don't you see they all have relevant points they addressed. Sadly enough, this is 2014 and no one has successfully eradicated the issues that keep us clinched in the "Iron hand of Oppression" as a people know matter what nationality we are or where we live.

Greed has no color or racial preference, just a wicked kind of prejudice that's only bread by greed and power via the Power Elite. A plutocratic regime formed to reinforce everlasting life and total domination for a select few as well as try to convince the super powers throughout the globe to become Plutocratic. The origin of plutocratic is from the Greek word ploutokratia. By the same token, the highlight of the meaning is synonymous and a vail for democracy. Because of our inability to act as a people united using the powers vested in us by the Creator is greatly contributed to the democratic philosophy. With that being said, it reminds me of what Tupac said, "Death is not the greatest loss in life. The greatest loss in life is what dies inside you while you are still alive!" Never surrender your soul and mind by being a weak-minded person, think for yourself and be a leader not a follower. Don't let the doctrines of man dictate your destiny, create your own destiny and think for yourself. They say, "Pain Changes People" why wait for pain to change you. Be different; think different so that your children will be different. "Pain is weakness leaving the body" but you do not always have to experience pain for the sake of mental and spiritual growth. Aren't you tired of the same old struggles in life? If you have nothing to live for, live for the future of your family and the children in your life, so that the work you have done or will do will make a difference. With that being said, the work of your ancestors will not die in vain and you can transition back to the essence knowing you helped change the mind-set of your people to overcome oppression, that's called, being a part of the solution, because if you are not doing anything for the cause you are part of the problem. Everyone needs to understand the power of a leader. Would you rather have 1 leader to lead 30,000 people and risk your leader being assassinated as history would have it. Or would you rather have 30,000 leaders with 1 mind 1 focus 1 spirit all supporting 1 common goal leading humanity to victory. If people all over the globe had that kind of mental and spiritual driving force how can we as children of the Most High fail? If we all focus on the same goals and have moral obligations, set principles and standards we honor and follow, we wouldn't have to physically be in the same place at the same time to bring that mind-state into fruition. All we would need to do is be on 1 accord spiritually and mentally to get the job done. **Self-sustainment, loyalty, relentless focus and determination** are the keys. To unite as 1 and become leaders would lead us to the unequivocal truth in this statement "UNITED WE STAND, DIVIDED WE FALL." In the same vain, the "Power Elite" is using that same principle against us. Once we unite we will never fall again because we will appreciate the glory of Creation and all it has offered us. Imagine, the struggle and hardship we endured over thousands of years would be at a minimum and we can finally live in harmony as 1 human family as we once did. If we lived that way before, we can "**Will**" it to happen again. We have the power to control our destiny. We should commit to a quest (NOW). Take the control back and stop letting greed and the Power Elite control our destiny. The Presidents' of the world are not the puppets; the masses are the true puppets. The presidents' of the world are doing what they are elected to do. Their oath is to the Nation and Power Elite they serve, not the people. Our unspoken oath is to Creation and the upliftment of humanity, so why blame one person for your personal inadequacy? We have been doing that for far too long. We as a whole must change our ways to make a difference. Consider this and open your mind for a second and understand what I'm trying to convey. To call your-self **Black** is worse than being called a **nigger.** To call your-self **African-American, Colored, Afro-American** is worse than being called **nigger. Black, African-American and Colored** are supposed to be your nationality/cultural heritage but there is no origin or culture associated with those terms or phrases, no origin or native tongue or Country exist that is associated with those terms or phrases and if you continue to call yourself or refer to yourself as such and let other nationalities refer to you as **Black, African-American and Colored;** you are saying you don't exist. The word, "**Nigger**" is like any other propane word that is used to connote negative feelings. On the other hand, in order for so called black people to accept the word "Nigger" in their own mind, they decided to flip the meaning of the word nigger and make it inner-changeable or synonymous with the word, "Brother" to inspire a positive mental reinforcement for acceptance. **R**eferring to your friend as, "**My Nigger**" is far less offensive in the grand scheme of things considering the negative actions of the Power Elite and the impact they have on the psyche of a people that have been oppressed for so long that most of the people that are oppressed accept it and retaliate against their own people which gives them a false sense of power because they can't phantom defeating "The Wizard Of Oz"

"The Oppressor." The racist one still treats you in the same manner they perceive a nigger to be and you accept it because they can't directly use the term, Nigger, because of the simple fact that they would be considered racist. Psychological warfare is their ultimate weapon and the masses are like Adam and Eve, dumb, deaf and blind. You all are losing your lives and freedoms as we speak. Soon <u>you will allow yourselves to become extinct</u>. It is far worse for a person or group of people to abstain from using the word "Nigger" and at the same time treat you like one through their actions and deeds. So now they have a justification that implies, I can't call you a "nigger" so you can't call me racist. But I can treat you like a "nigger." Most melanated people feel defeated so they rebel against the laws of the land and as a result of that, their unconscious and or conscious acceptance is an **expression of permanent defeat** that radiates self-hate and social misunderstanding for other cultures to interpret as criminal and animalistic. Melanated people of North America and abroad reciprocate the negative aspects of oppression generation after generation. We as oppressed indigenous people across the National and International diaspora need to look within and summons our higher god-spirit. The Strong-hold can only be broken by a determined unified self-sustaining spiritual people who start their own governmental infrastructure and educational programming. Again, the powers that be and the media put so much emphasis on the word "nigger." You are still considered a nigger, you are still treated like a nigger, you will always be a nigger in the eyes and minds of the Power Elite and that truth is evident in their actions that are represented on a daily basis. My point is this, whether the word is verbally mentioned or not, you are still treated and considered a nigger. It's not the word nigger that is the problem; it's the mind-set and actions of the people who will always consider you three-fifths human. I feel for the people of Bikini Island, we are one. United we stand divided we fall. The problem is that we unite with a culture that doesn't want to unite with us and we continue to want acceptance when there's no need for the want. To want acceptance shows weakness in a people. We need to take charge of our future and destiny by separating ourselves from the culture that doesn't accept us. We threaten the future of our very existence as a people if we continue to want acceptance. Intelligence can't exist in the same cell of ignorance unless you blatantly ignore logic. No matter where you are on this planet, if you are the oppressed, you would be better as a people if you all band together as the majority by separating yourself from the minority. Can you, "for the sake of common sense" see how the slave masters and the "Power Elite" of today **separated** and **oppressed** all people of color across the globe as well as other people and not just from our **families** but our **culture**, our **religion**, our **customs**, our **nativity**, the **human family** and you also were separated from your **own minds** and they rebuilt your minds to adapt to **their ideologies, cultures** and **customs** and we accept those same doctrines as if they are our own. All people need to overstand that we are all created as 1 creation by the same creator but we as people differ in our physiological anatomy and cultures. With that being said, we can't possibly have the same exact health education, cultural needs and philosophical understandings as other cultures of people around the globe. So why is it that in western culture, people are overtly taught 1 universal way of implementing life? We can live as 1 universal spirit and mind because that's on a different plane, meaning; universal laws of the Creator remain constant so spirituality and mentality would also remain universal if its taught in it's true essence, regardless of what physiological and philosophical differences we may have as a people. One thing that we all have that is universal for the sustainment of life is spirit.

With that in mind, a psychological and pseudo criminal judicial strong-hold has been implemented throughout the world and mostly in the countries with the most natural resources and weakest armies. It's time to change the world we live in; "the skin you're in." If we want to live free of oppression, degradation and a government based on plutocracy and or oppression, it can be accomplished as long as we exercise the will of god as a people united with a relentless focus on the cause.

Most importantly we need to face the challenge as a collective spiritual body that knows the power of god and recognizes the power of self. By consistently displaying actions of god you will produce confidence in the human family to be by your side, seen and unseen. We have the greatest tool to unite common ideas and strategies via, social media. I'm calling all people around the globe to end this war on humanity and resurrect the god in you for everlasting life. Commit to a leader driven mentality find people with like-minded spirit who are willing to do more than talk about god consciousness but are willing to act. Learn about the summits and meetings throughout the year around the world regarding spiritual enlightenment for the upliftment of humanity. Make it a priority to have all people you know and love to read, "**Borne Revolution, Fight for Humanity**" so that they will have a complete overstanding of who they are and how to awaken the god in them. We will be the positive life force for humanity and we will maintain to sustain everlasting life.

We as a new **mentally and spiritually strong resilient people** will begin with two philosophies;

1. **We will make the future better than the present.**
2. **We possess the power to free ourselves from the "Iron hand of Oppression"**

"LET'S UNITE'
1globalunion@gmail.com

CHAPTER – 29

CONTEMPLATIONS OF WISDOM

I have a poem I wrote to answer the question of "Who is God" on a larger scale in hopes that it will give you an overstanding of the true magnitude of the **Creator** which is unconceivable by a layman and understood by the astute.

Awaken Creation

Creation is exclusive to whatever creation **creates.** Creation
follows a construct of rules it never **breaks.** If creation breaks
the rules regarding what it created, whatever was created will
cease to **exist.** Referring to the original form of thought creation
dismissed. Each organism is alive based on divine **laws.** A
perfect union without **flaws** which follows all **protocols.** The
annals of **antiquity** are a **mystery** for **history,** they burnt
Theban and Alexandra, it's no way we can't **list them, they
live in infamy.** We summons the inherent genius of deific
intrinsic creative **wisdom.** The answers of creation are not
in a mathematical **algorithm;** concurrently religion took
conscious spirituality out of perpetual **rhythm.** This is true for
everything in existence, seen and unseen to the depths of my
soul. Thinking of creation, you think of conceptual individual
laws that come together as a **whole.** Creation isn't only about
the human family or the God you **believe.** Selfish Schools of
thought gave birth to, "Oh what a tingled web we **weave."** It's

about multiple aspects of creation coming together as **one**. Sadly the individual (in-divide-dual) will always be divided and never overstand the <u>uni</u>fication of **one**. <u>Uni</u>versal laws oversee divine **communication**; the laws sustain life for the existence of all **creation**. **Translation:** The eco systems of life exist to maintain the **situation**. "**Celebration**, for all our ancestors I pour water in **libation**." The Fight for Humanity is my **presentation**. Creation recognizes inseparability as **sacred,** how can humanity be selfish and be **latent** with **hatred**. The Spiritual conviction of our god-self must **overtake it**. Now is the time, "**Borne Revolution**" Awaken! Now is the time, "**Borne Revolution**" **Awaken!** Now is the time "**Borne Revolution**" **Awaken!** **Written by**: Jahi Issa Jabri Ali

Weak minds + weak spirits = weak people "Jahi Ali"
Religion is not the foundation of
god. YOU ARE! "Jahi Ali"
Darkness: "my subconscious thoughts and the manifestation of knowledge" **Light**: "knowledge manifested" **Creation:** "**the application of manifested knowledge**" "Jahi Ali"
PHD "Practice Helping Dummies" Jahi Ali-Bey
"Be a voice, not an echo" "Abundance Child"
"CVMB," "**Chronic Voluntary Mind Block**" "Jahi Ali-Bey"
"BIBLE," "**Basic Instruction before Life**
Everlasting" "Jahi Ali-Bey"

I never lose, either I win or I Learn "Unknown"

"People never remember what you did for them;
they only remember what you do now."
Jahi Ali-Bey

"To live is to die but to understand life gives
life everlasting meaning to all that embrace the
comprehension of the thought." Jahi Ali-Bey

"**Darkness** is the initiator of knowledge, **Knowledge**
is the pursuer of understanding, **Understanding**
is liberation from the pursuit, **Liberation** breeds
wisdom, **Wisdom** inherits discernment, **Discernment**
produces universal harmony" Jahi Ali-Bey

"**Think right, Eat right, Live right**" Jahi Ali-Bey

"**You Change your mind, You change your life**" Jahi Ali-Bey

Jogging "**Run For Your Life**" Jahi Ali-Bey

"**Will** yourself to **embrace** what you **don't
understand** and you **will gain understanding**"
Jahi Ali-Bey

Creator-Creation: "A multi-faceted life-force manifestation
of intrinsic intelligence and energy continuously transcending
in and out of different states of matter seen and unseen
to perpetuate life everlasting." Jahi Issa Jabri Ali-Bey

"If you want change, start with yourself, take responsibility
for your actions; good, bad or indifferent, be sincere in your
quest, be thorough in your actions and deeds and have a
profound sense of who you are. Instill these priceless qualities
in your families and the people you love. Remember,
consistency is the mother of purpose and if you persist on
being consistent a change is definitely evitable." Jahi Ali-Bey

Know this; "it's enough natural resources in the world
for everybody's need but not enough for everybody's
greed." Mahatma Gandhi … I'm aware he didn't like
people of color; I like the quote because it makes sense and
it's relevant to my book, so I exacted the cream. ☺

The Womb; "Before Christmas there was Eve, before New Year's there was Eve, before Allah there was Allat "Eve," before you existed there was Eve (Mother), a lot of religious buildings are dome shaded with a button-top symbolically symbolizing the belly and naval- the eve of birth, the Mother. Considering there are many conclusions I can come up with, these are for this book. Every time I see the word Eve my spirit tells me the name represents birth, nativity, nature, nurture, mother, savoir and salvation." Jahi Ali-Bey

SPIRIT: "In most religious doctrines it is believed you can't live without a spirit and the hypothesis is every living thing has spirit in some form, shape or fashion. By the same token every living thing has carbon. The most abundant mineral in the pineal glands is carbon. The pineal gland is said to be the link to the third eye in connection to the spirit. This can only mean that carbon and spirit have an intrinsic relationship with each other. Ops did I give away a secret? The paradox is that **spirit** doesn't seem to have a place in religion only with Creation." Jahi Ali-Bey

Quote: "Alkebulan must unite as ancestors of mankind with ordained leadership responsibilities to repair, restore and renew our troubled earth. **Naiwu Osahon**

Know this: "Just because you can't see it doesn't mean it doesn't exist. By the same token, some things you see don't mean they exist either. Electro-magnetic fields and right brain activity allow you to see passed the physical dimensions of your eyes and at the same time the fields of electromagnetism or brain waves reflect a physical image in your eyes which sometimes will give you a false illusion of reality. How many times have you seen something and when you try to focus on what you saw, it really wasn't there or it seems to have disappeared? Different dimensions create different experiences." Jahi Ali-Bey

T.E.A.R.S by Robyn Hawkins "ISBN: 9781484935033"

This is a book written by my sister. It expresses the trials and adversities that she faced in her life that opened her eyes to new beginnings. Her experiences are written in detail to give the reader a vivid understanding of her hardship and triumph and what it took for her to endure when she hit rock bottom. "Inspirational read" Love & Respect your brother, "Jahi Issa Jabri Ali-Bey" **Quote:** "Unite, and regain our right to live an oppressed free life." Jahi Ali-Bey

"Let's Unite"

1globalunion@gmail.com

It is to be noted, The Surah's are extracted from "The Holy Qur'an. The Scriptures and or quotations are from the New Living Translations, The King James Version of the Bible and BibleHub.com. The picture of the Shield of the Trinity and number line was provided by, Wikipedia, it's deemed public domain. But as a point I need to make, I recreated the Shield of the Trinity.

The Chaos and serenity hand drawn interior image is accredited to A. Roldán Jr. and the exclusive work of A. Roldán Jr. Any reproduction of his work is strictly prohibited without his expressed written consent. Copyright and Trademark laws apply and will be enforced.

The picture, "Breaking the mold of tradition" is a multipurpose picture owned by the author and co-created by A. Roldán Jr. Any reproduction of this work is strictly prohibited without the authors expressed written consent. Copyright and Trademark laws apply and will be enforced.

Acknowledgements are given to "Encyclopedia, Britannica" for some of the definitions in this book as well.

Acknowledgements are given to, Merriam-Webster.com pertaining to the meanings of, Creation and God

Respect and acknowledgement to Reinhold Niebuhr who wrote the Serenity prayer

Some of the song lyrics are accredited to rapgenius.com and some are committed to my memory.

Printed in the United States
By Bookmasters